Dark Skies

Select Readings in Therapeutic Astrology

Brad Kochunas

THE WESSEX ASTROLOGER

Published in 2024 by The Wessex Astrologer Ltd
PO Box 9307
Swanage
BH19 9BF
England

For a full list of our titles go to www.wessexastrologer.com

© Brad Kochunas 2024
Brad Kochunas asserts his moral right to be recognised as
the author of this work

ISBN 9781916625150

Back cover photo courtesy of Debbie Grant
"On Turning Ten" from The Art of Drowning by Billy Collins, © 1995. Reprinted by
permission of the University of Pittsburgh Press.

Cover design by Fiona Bowring at Bowring Creative
Typeset by Kevin Moore

A catalogue record for this book is available at The British Library

No part of this book may be reproduced or used in any form or by any means without the
written permission of the publisher.
A reviewer may quote brief passages.

"When we try to pick out anything by itself,
we find it hitched to everything else in the universe."
JOHN MUIR

"Some people are more certain of everything
than I am of anything."
ROBERT RUBIN

"Happiness is the absence of striving for happiness."
ZHUANG ZI

For Marjorie,
Abigail,
Brendan,
Kathryn,
Norman,
and Zora

Brad Kochunas is an absolute gem in the field of astrology. Engaging with his material invites one to calm their focus and rest in the shade of the embodied experience. In this work, as he did with his first book, Brad helps one foster a deeper, more soulful connection with the subject, ultimately moving the reader to appreciate the felt experience of astrology, and by extension a more integrated sense of their own beingness.

Crystal Eves, M.A. Toronto Astrologer

In *Dark Skies*, Kochunas hasn't simply thought deeply about astrology, although that is already a great deal; he has also thought *through* it. The result is a vibrant testament to the wisdom of this ancient tradition when freshly considered, and a renewal of the tradition. As part of this process, his book reclaims the vital importance of darkness as well as light, of shadow as well as substance, of appreciating melancholy as well as seeking happiness. What's at stake is a life, in mutual dialogue with the stars, lived more fully and deeply.

Patrick Curry Ph.D., co-author of *Astrology, Science and Culture*.

In his book, *Dark Skies*, Brad Kochunas offers us a pathway to a more embodied astrology. Along the way he challenges us to question assumptions that may have gelled into dogma, and reimagine what astrology could be if we root it in our actual experience and our shared humanity, rather than our preconceived ideas about what ought to be true. This is an incalculable gift, and a potential cleaning of the lens for anyone brave enough to take it in.

Joe Landwehr, author of *Astrology in the Era of Uncertainty*

I've always loved reading Brad Kochonas. His voice comes from a place few of us have experience of. He has journeyed deeply into human nature from his many years as a therapist with those in the "dark monastery". I can't think of a better antidote to the glibness of social media astrology. *Dark Skies* is moving, deeply soulful and full of excellent astrology.

Lynn Bell, author of *Planetary Threads* and
Cycles of Light: Exploring the Mysteries of Solar Returns

Brad Kochunas's astrology is infused with teachings of depth psychology, tender imagery of poetry and literature, and the wisdom accrued through his decades of work as a professional counselor. Building on the views of writers such as Rilke and James Hillman, he challenges astrologers to shed flighty illusions and to evolve an astrological practice that is grounded, attentive to the soul's emotional valleys and existential realities, and focused on fulfillment in embodied life, in this present world. His book celebrates the power of astrology to heal, guide, and inspire, to reveal the light of meaning during times of suffering and adversity, and to evoke new vision of vibrant possibilities.

Greg Bogart, PhD, author of *Astrology as a Therapeutic Art: Healing Human Relationships*

Brad's work tells us we are caught in a progress-oriented fixation. He attends to the movement of soul, which is a process of descent, and of dreaming and imagination. Astrology has mirrored our culture's discomfort with descent by its bias of overvaluing the upward ascent of the fire and air elements, and undervaluing of the water and earth elements. He brings a fresh perspective to our art that will speak to your soul.

Andrea Conlon LICSW, psychotherapist/astrologer

Brad Kochunas has captured my attention since hearing him speak in 2009 on his career in prison mental health. I remain very much impressed by his humanistic approach to the incarcerated and his sincere efforts to be helpful through his use of astrology. His shared experiences inspired me to start research on serial killers and their psychology. His earlier book, *The Astrological Imagination*, demonstrated his elegance in creative writing and familiarity with philosophers and belletrists through history. In this new book, he is wandering shadowy corridors of the psyche and continuing to enlighten our "Dark Skies." This one is a must read book not only for astrologers but anyone who wishes to develop a deeper understanding of themselves and others. Strongly recommended.

Sirin Mitrani, Certified Astrology Professional

Brad Kochunas's *Dark Skies: Select Readings in Therapeutic Astrology* is a beautifully written collection of 18 previously published and unpublished pieces that are all different yet equally insightful and reflect his unique understanding of astrology, psychology, mythology, and philosophy. Brad's lifelong career as an astrologer and professional counselor has allowed him, especially through his work with prisoners, to delve deeply into the hearts and souls of all types of people. His compassion, desire to understand how the psyche works, and acute knowledge of universal symbols make this collection a rare jewel, a must-read that will hold your interest from start to finish and will quench your thirst for a deeper understanding of human nature.

Ronnie Gale Dreyer MA, Author, astrologer, and teacher

Brad Kochunas deserves recognition as a modern astrologer whose practice is informed by his vocation as a psychotherapist. His work synthesises the thought of luminaries such as James Hillman and Rollo May, together with voices from many other disciplines including philosophy, religious studies and poetry. Perhaps the most important quality of his work is his refusal to settle for easy or comforting half-truths. This shows, for instance, in the way he questions what astrology truly is, how it works. It also animates his determined engagement with aspects of the psyche often suppressed and ignored as dark, threatening or somehow irrelevant to spirituality and fulfilment. The chapter 'The Dark Monastery' in this new book, which describes some of his work with long-term prisoners, epitomises this quality but it is present throughout his work. There is a determination here to engage with the visceral realities of living – from despair to realisation – and to not shy away from difficult questions or emotions. This marks his work out as thoughtful and deep, and I really hope that 'Dark Skies' will find a wide audience.

Garry Phillipson, Ph. D., author of *Astrology in the Year Zero*

An illuminating and insightful book which is beautifully written.

Wendy Stacey, B.A, M.A, DipLSA, Chair Astrological Association, Principal of the Mayo School, author of *Consulting with Astrology*

Brad Kochunas compiled *Dark Skies* as an invitation to look at his deep and thoughtful ways of practicing therapeutic Astrology. Each essay pays homage to darkness (my old friend) in a way that might inspire your own use and celebration of those "hard times." Brad's writing is sensitive, broadly referenced, and applied to life in search of treasures hidden in the darkness. Some essays could well expand into a volume; some are cut and compressed into polished gems; but altogether this collection is a gift for those ready for another way to see and use Astrology.

Victoria Smoot, MS. Ed, teacher, editor, astrology consultant

There are astrology books that aim to help us "become our best selves," and realize our fuller potentials. But sometimes that first requires understanding those parts of our selves that may be uncomfortable to face, or are shrouded in the darkness of pain or denial. A fully holistic astrology requires that we be grounded in the emotional and earthy realities of the present, of ordinary life. As Kochunas writes, "When our spirituality no longer promises paradise but plants us firmly in the present...then our lives, in tune now with the rhythms of soil and sea, may truly blossom." This insightful book helps us to do that, and does so brilliantly.

Ray Grasse, author *So What Am I Doing Here, Anyway?*, *The Waking Dream*

Table of Contents

	Introduction	vii
1	Confessions of a Therapeutic Astrologer	1
2	Imagination, Astrology, and Deepening Your Practice	10
3	The Dark Monastery	37
4	In Praise of Melancholy	51
5	Empowering People, Not Planets	61
6	Astrology and Grief	74
7	Parenting and Astrology	86
8	Chiron: Learning to Fall	103
9	Born Under a Bad Sign?	121
10	Astrology as Spiritual Path	151
11	Without Shadow, There is No Substance	159
12	Astrology and the Unseen Side of Relationship	183
13	Belonging to Nature: As Below, So Above	195
14	Watering Our Field: Imagination in Astrology	211
15	Emerson and the Transcendentalist Legacy	224
16	Moving Astrology Toward the Sciences	241
17	Elemental Spirituality	246
18	Letter to a Young Astrologer	260
	Acknowledgments	270
	About the Author	272

Introduction

The title, *Dark Skies*, is a blessing that I occasionally use when parting or signing off on social media or email. It is the idea that during the day we are often blinded by the light, a metaphor for self or ego consciousness in which everything is distinct and it's easier navigating a path through the day. Dark skies, however, grace us with the capacity to leave the detritus of the day behind and observe the gods at work in our lives; we see Luna, Mercury, Venus, Mars, Jupiter, Saturn and with some optical assistance are able to view Uranus, Neptune, Pluto, and other intriguing celestial bodies. Dark skies provide astrologers moments for contemplation for discovering what claims the gods may have upon us so that we may (paraphrasing Ficino's Book 3) bring our lives in accord with the heavens or to put it differently, learn to gladly accommodate the Great Flowing of the Turning World.

It's my understanding that one of the ways by which soul (psyche) was imagined during the medieval and Renaissance periods was as the entire night sky. This is a lovely image for our interiority. It lets us hold a cosmos within and is echoed by Origen, one of the early church fathers when he wrote, "Thou art a second world in miniature, the sun and the moon are within thee, and also the stars." And as a therapeutic astrologer who deals with mythological deities like Venus, goddess of love, Mars, god of war, and Pluto, lord of the Underworld, the vast blackness of the night sky allows me to see these imaginal gods at play in my life and in the lives of others when working with their astrology charts. Without the endless darkness of space, the magnificent turning of the cosmos could never be experienced. The great lights both wandering and constant shine brightly and help instill humility within me knowing that I am but a small expression of a larger natural process.

All too often we focus on the starry light in the foreground and ignore the backdrop of cosmic blackness, failing to realize that without this darkness there would be no light. Though in several creation stories darkness often precedes the light into being, I think it more likely that light and dark arise mutually into awareness.

So, as I wish dark skies to readers, it is my fondest hope that all will experience an opening into the inner heavens and receive the deep blessing therein.

I first heard the phrase "therapeutic astrology" in 1996 from my friend, Greg Bogart, Ph.D., a psychotherapist, astrologer, educator, and prolific author with numerous books on spirituality and integrating astrology with psychology. Other astrologers with backgrounds in psychology had also been creatively engaging astrology's therapeutic potential such as Stephen Arroyo, Richard Idemon, Glenn Perry, Michael Mayer, Maritha Pottenger, Liz Greene, Howard Sasportas, Roy Alexander, and Christina Rose to name a few.

Therapeutic astrology may be considered the application of counseling principles to the practice of natal astrology. It is a budding and vibrant branch within humanistic astrology. I once gave a lecture to a graduate counseling class on the topic and published a review of Greg's early book, *Therapeutic Astrology*, in the University of Cincinnati Graduate School of Counseling Education publication in 1996. Both appeared well-received. Greg has been in the forefront of promoting therapeutic astrology in the United States and beyond for several decades.

At numerous conferences and lectures, people have approached me regarding where they might obtain my writings as they were scattered throughout a variety of journals and magazines. In addition to my first book, *The Astrological Imagination,* I was fortunate enough to have discovered that Margaret Cahill of The Wessex Astrologer found my articles and essays of value and offered to publish them as a compilation of select pieces previously published and unpublished. This will settle much of my work in one easily available book and reach a wider audience of interested and curious readers seeking something deeper from astrology as a wisdom tradition.

Since a number of chapters have appeared at different times and in different publications some of the thrust of my thinking has been reiterated throughout but hopefully in differing contexts. I have also revised several of the pieces to reflect the maturing of my thought. I have opted not to use extensive citations but have offered sufficient sources for those readers wanting to track down where quotations can be located. Interested readers may contact me via email noted in the brief biography at the end of the book. Charts of public figures can be found on the internet or at www.astro.com in their freely available Astrodatabank. All charts have been generated by Solar Fire v.9. Though I don't use the nodes in my work, they have been included in the chart due to their widespread usage.

1

Confessions of a Therapeutic Astrologer

I tend to make a distinction between psychological and therapeutic astrology. I think psychological astrology is more heroic and ego driven with a focus coming out of humanistic and positive psychology. Therapeutic astrology comes out of a branch nurtured by James Hillman and Thomas Moore that is more oriented around what life wants out of us, what claims the gods have upon us, how our goal shifts from winning at life and more toward coming into accord with how we can fully accept the Way we've been gifted.

Much of psychological astrology is concerned with striving for personal growth, self-improvement, actualization of potential, and/or making our lives better. The focus has been upon what we want out of life, whereas very little has been devoted to what life wants of us. How do we honor the claims that the gods have upon us? Though there is no clear answer to this question, perhaps we should at least address it in our approach to astrology.

By disposition and practice, I am a minimalist. I use ten planets, twelve signs, twelve houses, six aspects, current transits, secondary progressions, and an occasional Sabian symbol. I practice therapeutic astrology using a dialoging process. I don't do readings telling clients about themselves in a one-way performance. I don't do readings in the sense of giving advice. I don't help clients regain balance in their lives (to which I will return later), and I don't make predictions. I suspect many psychological astrologers eschew the predictive aspect of astrology recognizing that it moves the client away from their life in the moment, which is after all, where each of us really live with its attendant anxieties, worries, and joys.

I don't believe the stars and planets have any literal influence in our lives, I don't believe in karma, past lives, or future lives. I don't believe astrology is hard science nor is it simply empirical.

I don't use nodes, Chiron, midpoints, harmonics, eclipses, parts, asteroids, decanates, fixed stars, or other such categories. Is there anything wrong with these? Of course not, but for me they simply tend to clutter up the scene like having too many actors on the theater stage. There is such an abundance of astrological methods, numerous techniques, and objects for consideration for use in the chart that it leads me to believe that most of what has been written in astrology over the last two decades has given greater breadth to astrology with precious little having been published that deepens this grand wisdom tradition. I find it sufficient to keep a narrowed approach.

I truly believe that therapeutic astrology is foremost about imagination and language, providing a framework for imagining a profound intimacy between ourselves and our world. The chart reflects how we envision ourselves being in the world, mirroring various beliefs and attitudes that we hold about life that guide us through changing circumstances. By shifting the way in which we understand ourselves, we can alter how we move through life. For instance, I can visualize myself as hopelessly stuck or free to respond to life in a more satisfying fashion. I can picture myself as disabled or as differently abled, as a victim of forces beyond my control or as an agent of change. What are the limits of my ability to modify my root beliefs and everyday assumptions about life? Can I recognize that it is not whether the glass is half full or half empty but that both perspectives are equally and simultaneously valid?

As for language, it allows us to differentiate and deepen our experience of the world. It is a powerful factor in the way we experience ourselves. When transiting Saturn is on my natal Moon, perhaps it reflects a period in which I am experiencing a depressed mood. I can simply say I'm depressed or I can fine tune my experience and say that I'm feeling melancholy or malaise, downcast, blue, overwhelmed, trampled, dejected, worthless, put down, empty, barren, dry, dense, weighted, heavy, leaden, stuck, heavy hearted, despondent, sorrowful, captive, gloomy, woeful, glum, dismal, disconsolate, unhappy, or mournful. Each of these words carry subtle nuances that deepen and enrich my experience of Saturn as depression, allowing me to invite Saturn into my life, befriending him, and possibly learning something of value from him.

Additionally with language, when astrologers use words and phrases that exhibit ideas like cause, force, fate, or that planets are doing something to us, or that there are bad signs, bad planets, or bad configurations, we victimize our clients and ourselves. When I hear myself say that I am experiencing some personal difficulty and follow that up with the statement that such or such a planet is transiting such or such a house or squaring or opposing this or that planet, I cringe inside. My language is not simply correlation; it betrays both a cause and explanation for my distress that can be disempowering. Admittedly, it is at times comforting to not have to take responsibility for every darn thing that happens to me but beneath that, I believe there is little difference between my responsibility for what I do and what happens to me. These are like two sides of the same coin, separable only in the abstract, not in reality. As the chart so visually suggests, I am a particular and specific expression of the whole universe so what I am doing is at the same time what is being done to me. These ideas reflect two distinct conditions that in reality, are not separable from one another.

From my perspective, my chart is not something different from who I am, it is a reflection of who I am and the movements in the sky mirror, reflect, echo, parallel, image, and symbolize that which is manifesting as me. I believe that the chart is an image of psyche, the archaic Greek word for soul. Consequently, I don't believe the chart is something to be mastered, overcome, or transcended as if it were something different from my true nature, nor do I believe it can be actualized, fulfilled, or realized as if it were in my command to do so. The chart as a fixed moment in time is, like my life, a small whirlpool in the river of life, swirling into being for a brief moment then dissolving form without trace into this great flow. My sense is that the chart is to be imagined, plumbed, fathomed, and sounded into its depths, of which as Heraclitus noted, there is no end. This process leads me ever deeper into meditations, contemplations, reveries, conundrums, struggles, mysteries, and further queries into my life.

Astrology regarded as a discipline of the imaginal is aesthetic, poetic, mythic, and psychological. This stance shapes how I approach the chart. I don't believe that it is best used for alleviating uncertainties by providing answers to the problems of life but rather, for generating more questions, thus sinking the client firmly into life.

My focus then is somewhat different from the humanistic approach that emphasizes personal growth, self-improvement, individual effort, overcoming problems, and actualizing potential. That style is a little too muscular for me, too heroic and Virgoan. I prefer a softer, transpersonal approach, more contemplative, more Piscean, a perspective holding great faith in the organic process of change and unfolding according to our own inner rhythms. The beginning question is not what do I want but rather what does my life want of me? How do I honor the imaginal figures that clamor for my attention and yearn for expression and acknowledgement?

I like to think that I have a homeopathic approach rather than the typical allopathic approach that we find in medicine. An allopathic approach is exemplified by the antidote perspective. In medicine, this means that infection calls for antibiotic, inflammation, an anti-inflammatory, excessive stomach acid, take an antacid, muscle spasms require an antispasmodic, depression, an antidepressant, too much histamine, as in an allergic reaction, try an antihistamine, too much fire, as in fever, how about an antipyretic? This entire approach circles around the notion of compensation and going against the flow. The focus is upon a return to equilibrium or center, to homeostasis, where the person feels balanced and better. This allopathic approach is played out in astrology in a variety of ways. If the client is heavy in one element, the astrologer may prescribe working on developing the one that is weak or lacking. If there is too much Venus expressed in the life, the astrologer could encourage a martial assertiveness program. If the client has problematic squares, ask them to practice using their trines, developing their talents. These prescriptions may or may not be helpful for the client but there is another way.

Astrology for my purposes is a fiction, something to be taken seriously but not literally. I am not concerned with questions of astrology's truth or falsity, the client and I bracket disbelief and proceed "as if" it were true. Together we will imagine a lot about his or her life and explore various fantasies contained therein. What are the stories the client is living out? Who is the author of his narrative, which god is speaking? In line with Hillman in *Re-Visioning Psychology*, I use the word 'god' not in a theological sense but in a psychological one. In other words, these gods are not to be believed in but rather, to be imagined, configured, and elaborated. We will explore the chart and the life together recognizing that emotional difficulties and problematic circumstances are inherent in beliefs i.e., the stories we tell ourselves, not horoscopes, (as noted by Glenn Perry in *An Introduction to Astro-Psychology*).

My overall purpose in working with clients is the cultivation of imagination. Cultivating imagination means exploring the imaginative possibilities within our natures. It is the differentiating of a middle ground or psychic space within us, thus turning and deepening an event into an experience, as Hillman further noted. It is the creation of psychological space for reflection, a reshaping of our inner landscape. Sometimes a walk by the river is simply an event, at other times with an engaged imagination, it becomes an experience of the numinous as in Wordsworth's "Tinturn Abbey."

A homeopathic approach recognizes that like cures like, that the very god that visited the calamity upon us is the self-same divinity who can alleviate it. In some ways, I might prescribe the symptom, asking the client to do more of the same, to follow the god into their temple as will be seen in the depression example below.

I characterize my work in terms of cultivation and constellation. Cultivation in terms of the chart has to do with working with the planetary function that is either excessively or poorly expressed or acknowledged in the client's life. In either case, the god needs attention either through myth, poetry, art, praxis, or psychology. I will work with the client helping them cultivate the experience of the troubling divinity.

Constellation is the recognition that all the planetary gods have a rightful claim upon us and we may sanctify ourselves by attending to those claims. For those readers familiar with the

Greek story of Paris and the apple of discord, when we are asked to choose amongst the gods, it is best, if possible, to choose them all. Astrology and psychology especially require a polycentric perspective, an ending to the one central self-notion (an echo of a monotonous, monocentric, monotheistic world view), and an affirmation of our many selves.

To serve the diversity of powers and principles within and without, we need to be flexible, adaptable, comfortable with uncertainty, and able to shift allegiances in line with the context in which we are embedded. We need to allow ourselves to be off center, unbalanced and eccentric if we are to discover our true natures. Embracing all of our inner figures leads us to novel and unusual psychic spaces. Author C. S. Lewis, a close friend of Tolkien, is said to have remarked, "You can't enter a strange land and come back unchanged." Indeed, exploring our own depths in an imaginative manner with the help of the chart may lead us into dark labyrinths where familiar markers fail and we feel cast adrift but this may be precisely what we need in order to arrive at a new shore of being.

These are the places and situations that push us, drive us, and force us deeper into our lives, to the abode of the gods. If we are to discover who we are then we would benefit from acknowledging and affirming our shortcomings, flaws, quirks, failures, disappointments, and sufferings, following them into their own textured richness. Clients wishing to rid themselves of problems and annoyances in quick order, seeing no value in their presence, suffer from a simple failure of imagination. They do not recognize the sacred work going on within.

Let me use depression as an example. As a therapeutic astrologer, I don't want, like some thief in the night, to rob my client of the experience of Saturn. The client's depression may have great undiscovered value for them. Metaphorically speaking, what is it that Saturn wants that he has visited this depression upon the client? Has the client been living too much in the fast lane or on the surface of things? Have they been living in the future, distracting themselves from matters requiring attention in the present? Can the client appreciate slowing down, adding substance to their life, experiencing the gravity of their situation rather than avoiding or escaping from it? Either directly or indirectly I will ask the client to engage with the slow dance of Saturn. Perhaps they can read some of Saturn's mythology, or depending on what would be contextually relevant, read about time or architecture, maybe see a movie about aging, or volunteer with the elderly, study the bones of the body, or immerse themselves in loneliness. Additionally, I will want them to explore the various nuanced shades of their feeling life.

Our focus would be upon acknowledging and honoring Saturn, giving him his due. I don't want the client settling upon an answer such as Saturn transiting their Moon, or blaming their childhood, or assigning depressed mood to a chemical imbalance. When we fixate on answers, imagination curdles, and we can remain stuck. This reasoning cuts off the flow of fantasy and short circuits imaginal process. Ralph Waldo Emerson believed that the nature of imagination is to flow and not to freeze. I would want to alternately heat matters up and cool them down. Soul making, as an alchemical process characterized by simmering, mulling, fermenting, and cooling brings a ripening and depth to life. The client's original problems may remain unsolved or only slightly changed yet they report a difference that matters in their life. In his essay on "The Stages of Life," Jung wrote, "The serious problems in life are never fully solved. If ever they appear to be so it is a sure sign that something has been lost. The meaning and purpose of a problem seem to lie not in its solution but in our working at it incessantly."

In the end, therapeutic astrology for me has little to do with strengthening the ego, seeking happiness, or satisfying desires for personal growth. Psychological astrology in its transpersonal aspect is beyond the person and I argue that its proper field of application is to psyche or soul and how we can learn to cultivate and discover what soul wants. It's not always a long, healthy life filled with happiness, or a lasting marriage, or a successful career. Sometimes it is a life interrupted by trauma, disaster, failure, or illness. Read the late Christopher Reeve's book, *Still Me* on his life after being thrown from a horse and breaking his neck or Michael J. Fox's, *Lucky Man* about his struggle with Parkinson's disease in which these men express a life worth living after it has gone terribly awry. They speak of a life fertile with creative challenge, meaning, and worth, yet few of us would choose that life. To call their situations mishaps is to view it only from the perspective of what the ego wants. These two men arrived at an understanding that in an odd way brought great blessing to their lives despite what the public deemed tragic situations.

Therapeutic astrology, dedicated to exploring and discovering what psyche or soul desires, rather than ego, brings us to a different understanding of what it means to be human. Astrology has been literalized to so many fields of human interest as to be almost limitless in its applications. For psychological astrology, however, I believe that it is its metaphorical power, its capacity to cultivate imagination, to link us to the cosmos, to move us deeply into our own suffering, into reverie and fantasy, that can be of great usefulness in how we go about our daily business and in how we imagine our particular weave in this vast cosmic tapestry.

2

Imagination, Astrology, and Deepening Your Practice

"Mythology is a psychology of antiquity. Psychology is a mythology of modernity."
JAMES HILLMAN

"To think of myth as a false tale is to confuse literal truth and symbolic truth. Taking myths seriously does not mean taking them literally."
TROY W. ORGAN

"Astrology is a myth and requires the language of myth."
ROLLO MAY

"All activity of the psyche is an image and an imagining;"
JUNG

"Our reality is created through our fictions, to be conscious of these fictions is to gain creative access to, and participation in, the poetics or making of our psyche or soul-life,..."
GEORGE QUASHA

"What then is truth? A mobile army of metaphors,...truths are illusions of which one has forgotten that they are illusions;..."
NIETZSCHE

The above are powerful and radical statements.

As you can see, there is some very interesting juxtapositioning and fusing going on between cherished concepts of what we think of as real, factual, true, and valuable with that which is typically regarded as metaphorical, figurative, false, and of little status in Western culture.

Part of what these writers are doing is turning everything topsy-turvy. What we take for granted in our common understanding of reality is generally at odds with what these thinkers are attempting. They give new value to astrology, myth, psyche, imagination, fiction, and truth. Imagination can be regarded as so much more fundamental to our lives than Reason and that having that realization will transform the way we see astrology.

When Hillman writes that psychology is a mythology of modernity he means that our culture has adopted the tenets of contemporary psychology to perform the mythic function of providing a guiding narrative for understanding human experience in relation to self, other, society, and cosmos. Do we as a culture turn any longer to philosophers, theologians, priests, shamans, poets, story tellers for answers to modern problems? No, we turn to mental health professionals of all sorts: psychiatrists, psychoanalysts, clinical counselors, psychologists, social workers, and marital therapists. They seem to be present and available in large numbers on social media, cable news, podcasts, and in the justice system to explain to the public why someone did what they did or why a group of citizens behaved as an unruly mob or did nothing to help.

I'm imagining that astrologers give astrology this mythic function and often explain matters in terms of planetary activity, eclipses, ingresses, etc. Look at all the astrological commentary that we have had on the topics of serial murderers and mass shootings. In any case, competing explanations or narratives, whether Divine will, economic trends, biological anomalies, natural forces, psychopathology, or planetary activity, determine how we make sense of the world and provide us with the comfort of knowing.

My own thinking relies on the work of Patrick Harpur, Roberts Avens, Thomas Moore, and James Hillman. Much of their work grew out of the contributions by Jung, the NE Transcendentalists, the English and Germanic Romantic traditions which include Goethe, Novalis, Wordsworth, Coleridge, Blake, and Keats, then reaching back through Paracelsus, to the Renaissance and Marsilio Ficino, and rooted in ancient Greece with Plotinus and Heraclitus.

My objective is to look at astrology less from the direction of a scientific astrology that wishes to legitimize itself through methodical research and prove its value in accordance with the demands of the dominant culture and instead, view astrology more from the direction of those who consider it an imaginal discipline more closely attuned to the arts and humanities.

Because of astrology's pliancy and almost universal applicability, there is, of course, room for both the scientific and mythic approaches to it and many more. The focus here is primarily about natal astrology and more specifically about psychological astrology within that.

With broad brushstrokes let me highlight the dichotomy between Reason and Imagination that holds the back story for our astrology.

Oddly, two embodied contraries in the historical controversy between Reason and Imagination are Isaac Newton, representing Reason and William Blake representing Imagination. Newton's chart (available www.astro.com in their database) has Sun/Capricorn/3rd sextile Jupiter conjunct Saturn in 5th suggesting a Saturnian bend to his thinking and self-expression and evokes an involvement with mathematics and formal logic. His Uranus in the 1st trining both Jupiter and Saturn place him far ahead of his era in

Imagination, Astrology, and Deepening Your Practice

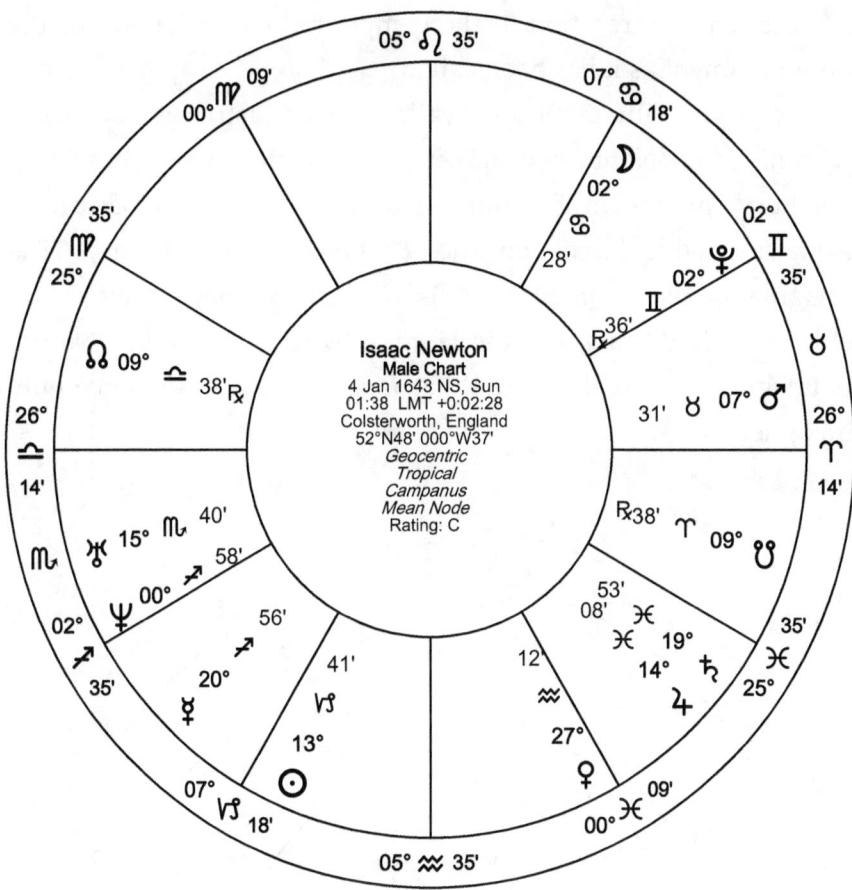

his pursuits. Despite being both an alchemist and astrologer, he is best known perhaps as the greatest and most influential scientist who ever lived. His book, *Principia Mathematica* is considered one of the most important scientific books ever written and laid the foundation for classical mechanics in Physics, fundamentally giving us a clockwork vision of the universe and a way of understanding it for 300 years.

Reason gained ascendancy in Western culture during the 17th and 18th centuries while Imagination was in cultural decline. Imagination enjoyed a resurgence in the late 18th through the

19th centuries in reaction to the competing age of Reason or the Enlightenment as it has been called.

We have William Blake (available www.astro.com database) with his Mars/Neptune conjunct in Leo in the 1st, widely trining his Sun/ Jupiter in Sagittarius, and opposing his Saturn in Aquarius, with Pisces on the 9th house cusp, stating, "The Imagination is not a State, it is human existence itself." And elsewhere, "All things exist in Human Imagination." and "Nature is Imagination itself!" and "What is now proved was once only imagined."

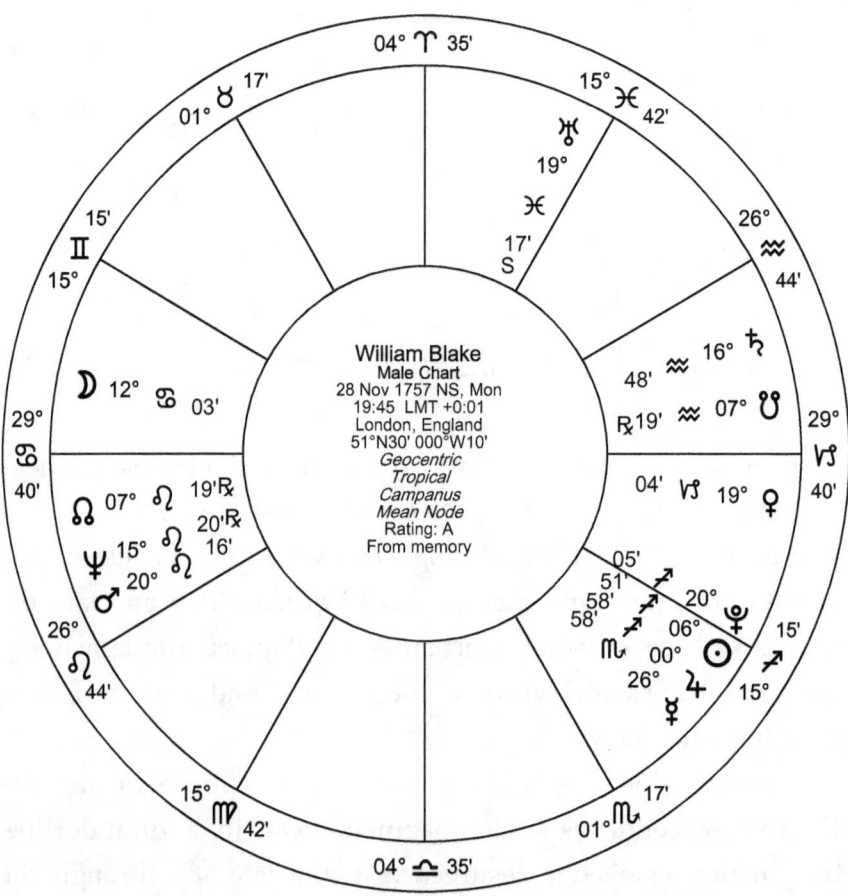

Imagination, Astrology, and Deepening Your Practice

Let's look at Reason and Imagination and their respective fruits while keeping Saturn and Neptune close to our hearts.

The triumph of Reason has cast a long shadow behind it that will be helpful to examine to get a sense of the need for the revalorization of Imagination. The cultural dominance of Reason as a way of inquiry into the world has engendered alienation and disconnection that comes about via Reason's necessity to divide the world into subject/object. We are immediately separated from the environment. Home is elsewhere, we become disconnected from ourselves, our community, and our planet; they become objects and we begin to feel like strangers in a strange land. Once we objectify the world, de-animating it, withdrawing its subjectivity and interiority, we award ourselves and posit humans as the only beings with soul, with consciousness, with depth. This is problematic.

Secularization refers to the increasing disappearance of the Sacred or Divine from everyday life. The British Isles and Indigenous America have sacred places but are rarely recognized as such by the dominant culture. In modern America, we honor no natural sacred spaces; no sacred rivers, wells, glades, groves, or mountains toward which to pilgrimage. Space is homogenous, every place is the same, one McDonalds or Hilton hotel is as reassuringly the same as any other.

As a culture, we have no sacred time; one day is like any other day. Holidays float on the convenience of Mondays. Sundays once reserved as holy days now mirror any other day for working, shopping, or buying alcohol. Events once special, once in a lifetime occasions, and participatory in nature, can now be recorded for viewing later on DVR or streamed into households and thereby trivializing their individual and unique particularity by making them endlessly available to re-experience.

Astrologers, however, are imbued with the fantasy of the heterogeneity of space and time; particularity matters, this space is qualitatively different from that space, this time from that time, events are special, and they count for something. The sacredness of place and moment are fundamental to the nature of the birth chart and are not trivialized.

Reason also provides the tyranny of objectivity referring to our willingness to dismiss or discount our own subjectivity in deference to the other end of the polarity; objectivity, the way authoritative cultural dominants say things really are. We may experience that the sun rises and sets but in literal reality it's the rolling away of the horizon due to planetary rotation. We don't see an angel or hear the voice of a departed loved one, we experience hallucinatory phenomena, nor do we witness a UFO, it was Venus, or the Moon or a weather balloon. Our cultural institutions (academia, technology, and science) will tell us what we really experienced despite our own explanations.

Culturally we have traded the notion of personal destiny for statistical probability. We are all interchangeable. We each have the same chance of winning the lottery, having our homes robbed, becoming victims of violence or similar likelihoods of having a heart attack as anyone else. Yet, it's doubtful any astrologer believes this. It is my thinking that as astrologers we are charged with the responsibility to stand against these positions and champion subjective, imaginal, and metaphorical realities. Imagination has been discounted for too long by the Age of Reason.

Imagination can be best understood perhaps with a sideward glance rather than head on. Literal Saturnian reality requires hardheaded encounters, a slap in the face, a punch in the gut, a stubbed toe against the unnoticed chair.

Imaginal reality as a Neptunian referent is often viewed out of the corner of our eye, in the shadows, during twilight, slipping just around the corner, in the margins of culture, peripherally, indirectly, and obliquely. Let us begin to circle our images, astrological and otherwise, hoping to arrive at a new yet familiar shore. The poet Emily Dickinson wisely wrote "Tell the truth but tell it slant."

Imaginal realities are elusive and hard to grasp – UFO's, Bigfoot, ghosts, auras, chakras, subtle energy bodies, fairies, Loch Ness, crop circles, and angels. All these are hard to substantiate. Imaginal disciplines are equally difficult to make literal, to make empirical – homeopathy, crystal and gemstone healing, channeling, Reiki, flower remedies, prayer circles, ceremonial magic, energy psychology, reflexology, alchemy, and of course, our beloved astrology.

These imaginal realities and modalities are viewed with suspicion in a skeptical age because they won't sit still under the harsh light of Reason and allow themselves to be nailed down, pinned to the mat, dissected and analyzed. Failing to be captured in the boxes of empiricism, these disciplines hold little value for the dominant culture. We hear phrases like - 'It's just your imagination." "You're dreaming,'" "It's only a story," "That's a myth," "It's all in your head," or "That's crazy." These remarks are value statements intended to be dismissive of personal experience and discrediting of imaginal realities. Attributed to the late Gore Vidal, "It is the spirit of the age to believe that any fact, no matter how suspect, is superior to any imaginative exercise, no matter how true."

Remember one of the opening quotes about myth had to do with the confusion between literal truth and symbolic, imaginal, psychological truth. One of the definitions of myth I've enjoyed is a narrative or story that never happened but is always true. An example, recall the Greek tale of young Phaethon, son of Helios. The Sun god, Helios, wished to show his son some fatherly affection by granting his son a wish. Phaethon's desire of course was to grab the reins of the sun chariot and drive it across the sky. Reluctant, as any father would be, he granted this wish with much hesitation giving his son some needed instruction about handling this solar rig. When Phaeton took his place and said, "Giddy up," there was simply too much horsepower and the chariot flew too high, gashing a scar in the heavens that became the Milky Way and then fell way too close to the earth scorching it, causing a damaging drought to result, and burning people, darkening their skin.

Now, this is not literally true, and yet it happens every day in America. "Mom, can I borrow the car," and damage or an accident occurs because a naïve, impatient youth has not the skill to successfully manage a vehicle as a practiced driver. You might also imagine this as an interaction between the astrological Sun and an impetuous, youthful Mars.

As Joseph Campbell noted, to misread myth is to insist, for instance, that the Bible is literal history. This is the basis of religious fundamentalism; the unassailable certainty of the words brings great comfort. Literalism demands the simplest and nonfigurative explanation, generally with a singleness of meaning. Have you noticed that with the release of just about any science fiction film, commentators line up to demonstrate where it literally failed in its science.

One of the literalisms in astrology is to insist that planets really influence or cause human events; another is the prediction of specific future events. Literalism abruptly stops the flow of imagination when we insist on only one or few meanings in astrological factors. I think, however, this is changing, and astrologers are becoming more aware of their own deterministic language. Our work I would argue is primarily about language and imagination though we also need to include reasonable and common-sense thinking.

Here is the reality of Imagination. <u>If</u> Neptune is intimately associated with Pisces (reputed to be the dustbin of the zodiac), there might be a reflection of submission, surrender, resignation, sacrifice, confinement, dissolution, confusion, delusion, fiction, fantasy, ecstasy, reverie, and transcendence. And the 12th house, which shelters the dispossessed, the disenfranchised, the disempowered, even the disembodied, being the repository of various odds and ends, the collector of the leftovers within society; nursing homes, hospitals, mental health facilities, prisons, monasteries; people who are ill fit to culture and need to be closeted, <u>then</u> Imagination, the embodiment of Neptune, is quite naturally regarded as possessing little recognized value and worth in society. Now, is it possible to revalue Imagination both personally and collectively so it becomes integral to a life well lived? Let's unfold Pisces a little.

In Neptune's association with Pisces, we can never overlook that Pisces is the matrix out of which something new arises to birth. It is the fecund chaos present at the creation of the world found in creation myths. It is the *massa confusa* of alchemy. It is that pregnant moment just prior to the bursting forth of an insight or revelation. It is That out of which the Big Bang flared forth. The Piscean moment before manifestation, before birth, is the ultimate uncertainty and it is potent. Whereas Neptune is the focus of Pisces, Pisces is the great field of Imagination out of which everything manifests. In other words, Imagination precedes perception and thought.

As Neptune is the agent for fulfillment of our Piscean need for transcendence, unity, ultimate beauty, and what historian of religion, Mircea Eliade, called our nostalgia for Paradise, we recognize Neptune as transpersonal, something that reflects our submission to the way of the world and delicately cradles our longing. It allows us indirect glimpses of Paradise, something seen through the mist or fog, something that doesn't require the bright beam of a spotlight consciousness i.e., the keen critical eye of Virgo but rather, the diffuse illumination of a floodlight awareness, where we attend to the background. Here we are able to make out the vague landscape of Imagination, the night world of the unconscious where images, stories, and memories arise, rather than the foreground of our orderly experience, the day world of Reason.

Imagination once held great value to culture, perhaps most so during the Renaissance, was eclipsed in the 16th, 17th, and 18th centuries throughout the Age of Enlightenment, then later, rose again with the Romantic tradition in the figures of Goethe (Neptune in 9th trine Jupiter), Wordsworth (Neptune in 9th conjunct MC), Coleridge (Venus/Neptune conjunct in 9th), Byron (Neptune prominent with four trines, three squares being part of a Grand Trine and apex planet in a T-square), to mention some of the more significant Romantic figures and then that Romantic holdover, Jung in the 20th century.

Jung, a champion of Imagination, with his Sun in Leo squaring Neptune in Taurus suggesting giving body to image, writing, "What appears to us as immediate reality consists of carefully processed imagery... we live immediately only in a world of images." And elsewhere, "Image is psyche." Or rather we can understand this as image: psyche : anima : soul : imagination.

The imaginal realm has also been referred to as the collective unconscious, daimonic reality, the world of Faery, the Otherworld, and the Soul of the World. In essence, is it possible that these are the variety of ways in which Imagination attempts to imagine itself?

Our lives are brimming with images, fantasies, reveries, apprehensions, figures, constructs and impressions. Whether we are discussing the political climate, the tenets of a particular religion, the theory of dark matter, or explanations of the state of the economy, we are deeply engaged in imagining, fantasies of how and why things are, productions of psyche, poetics of soul. Whether worldviews or mythologies, we are constantly bathed in images. Oddly enough, I once heard Dr. Memet Oz suggest, "We live in a world that is 99% pretend and 1% real." Though I doubt he was aware of the import of his statement.

Imagination is central to our lives and recognizes all realities as primarily symbolic and metaphorical. Borrowing from the Unitarian minister, Doug Muder, the world presents itself to us in a bewildering and dazzling display of shapes, colors, sounds, smells, pressures, temperatures, textures, etc. It does not present people, things, and circumstances. We construct and co-create our world from this input via Imagination.

If we stopped imagining the world; the people, things, and situations in our lives would dissolve into an amorphous cacophony of noise, shapes, and colors, before our eyes. This helps explain why blind people given sight for the first time see chaos. A different example, hallucinogenic substances can be frightening as they open imagination in totally unfamiliar ways and we are unmoored from our usual anchors of understanding the world.

Psyche or soul is that part of us that imagines the world on a daily and moment to moment basis. We can imagine well or poorly, live in a two-dimensional doodle or in a landscape of great richness, depth, and texture. We can weave a life of simple unadorned broadcloth or one of an elaborate tapestry. Imagination is reality, our guiding fantasies shape our relation to the world and how we act in it.

For example, do I imagine myself as a man of action or an aging fellow past his prime? What fantasies do I have about my spouse and children? How do I imagine my home life or my workspace? Is my physical complaint a tension headache, a neurological migraine, an aneurism, or brain tumor? Is my depression the harvest of a past life, the curse of the stars, a biochemical imbalance, a learned behavior, negative self-talk, or a rotten childhood? Do I constrain and imprison myself by imagining that I'm a loser, an underachiever, a conservative, an alcoholic, or what?

If we deliteralize these identifying labels, then imagination opens us to the world to dream the dream forward, to follow the myth, to penetrate the symbols, to create a new story or self-narrative. Who has not at one time or another been deeply moved by a dramatic presentation, enriched by poetry, caught up in musical ecstasy, entranced by art, or enchanted by ritual? When we experience our environment, are we walking through the great forest or simply a stand of timber, admiring a beautiful lake or our town's water supply? Are we co-habiting the landscape with our fellow beings, the cow and pig or is it simply beef and pork for our consumption? How one answers these questions makes all the difference in the world.

If as Jung, Hillman, and others believe, that psyche or soul is image and that we live immediately only in and through images, then cultivating images is soul-making and creates psychic space within us. I claim this is what astrology can do. Cultivating images in the chart helps enrich a life. Give clients a possible meaning of an astrological factor and ask them to unpack this image through more image making. Our sessions become rich aesthetic moments rather than information-giving occasions. Do not underestimate the healing power of beauty.

Imagination, Astrology, and Deepening Your Practice

As a parallel to astrology, consider poetry, it takes an ordinary event and through reflecting upon and working the image, it deepens the event into a more meaningful experience for the poet and the reader. Here is an image. Take a moment to experience this. We are visiting the zoo and word has spread that there is an escaped gorilla. Our immediate, visceral response might be fear or danger. We think to ourselves, round up the children and get toward the nearest exit.

I've offered an image - escaped gorilla - I've taken and moved it toward fear and concern for safety. Now, that is one bit of imagining the image forward, but let us not stop there; here is another. This is a poem by David Wagoner from his book, *A Map of the Night* titled "The Escaped Gorilla"

When he walked out in the park that early evening
just before closing time, he didn't take
the nearest blonde in one arm and climb a tree
to wait for the camera crews. He didn't savage
anyone in uniform, upend cars
or beat his chest or scream, and nobody screamed
when they found him hiding behind the holly hedge
by the zoo office where he waited for someone
to take him by the hand and walk with him
around two corners and along a pathway
through the one door that wasn't supposed to be open
and back to the oblong place with the hard sky
where all of his unbreakable toys were waiting
to be broken, with the wall he could see through,
but not as far as the place he almost remembered,
which was too far away to be anywhere.

See how we have taken the image in a different direction, perhaps even a richer one, disclosing a different psychological truth?

Let's stick with the primate image and extend it. Here is a related image of King Kong and the scaling of the Empire State Building, an image with which we're all likely familiar.

This poem is titled "A Letter From the Empire State Building to the Ghost of King Kong." I do not know its author but it appeared in a magazine called *Rags* in the early 1970s.

Dear Mr. Kong,

Forgive me for writing
but as your death place
I feel I know you
and I know what it is to be a monster.
I just want to say that
I'm sorry I wasn't high enough,
sorry I wasn't a gold ladder
you could climb
up into the clouds and escape
with your blonde girl
into some celestial jungle.
Your death – the mosquito airplanes
made me feel so short
I'm sorry. I miss the touch
of your hairy body.

Now it is easy to simply say that the poets are anthropomorphizing the primate and the building giving them human feeling and desire. Yet the poet is also cosmicizing the reader, dissolving the boundaries between human and world and bringing a unity, reanimating the world, not unlike what we can do with astrology.

Note Rudhyar's thinking on this same matter when he discusses the meaning of the Sabian Symbol of seven degrees Leo. He writes, "If man [sic] projects his basic human nature upon the star-filled night sky, is it not just as logical to say that the universe projects its own forever-evolving patterns of order upon human nature?"

If as Rudhyar suggests that there is another intent in our lives beside our own, it is that of the cosmos or the Soul of the World, this brings the notion of necessary uncertainty into our lives; the will of the gods.

Wallace Stevens wrote in *Opus Posthumous*,

> "Things that have their origin in the imagination or in the emotions very often have meanings that differ in nature from the meanings of things that have their origin in reason....In short, things that have their origin in the imagination or in the emotions very often take on a form that is ambiguous or uncertain. It is not possible to attach a single, rational meaning to such things without destroying the imaginative or emotional ambiguity or uncertainty that is inherent in them and that is why poets do not like to explain."

Writing poetry is a form of cultivating images or soul-making and is about differentiating the middle ground between mind and body, between spirit and matter, between the abstract thought and the concrete actuality, between the event and the experience. The 13th century Islamic philosopher, Ibn al 'Arabi, described Imagination as the intermediate world of which the soul is woven, an intrinsically ambiguous isthmus between the spiritual and the corporeal worlds.

Marsilio Ficino in the opening pages of his volume, "On Obtaining Life from the Heavens," (Volume three in his *Three Books on Life*) noted that Soul is the middle factor between Intellect and Body. For Jung, soul or psyche as the mediating reality is the "betweenness" holding together heaven and earth, the interpenetration of subject/object, mind/matter, and the glue between self and other. This is the perspective we use with composite charts. The reality of relationship, the soul of the relationship, is the betweenness of the two individual's charts.

This betweenness, this psyche or soul for Hillman (Introduction to *Re-Visioning Psychology*) is not a thing but rather a perspective, a perspective that is reflective, mediating events and making differences, a way of seeing through the literal to the metaphorical, it's the imaginative possibility in our natures that deepens events into experience. Psyche is both us and more than us, self and other. Hillman further notes, "It is as if consciousness rests upon a self-sustaining and imagining substrate – an inner place or deeper person or ongoing presence – that is simply there even when all our subjectivity, ego, and consciousness go into eclipse." This for me is the root of psyche and the foundational image that a natal chart expresses.

Astrology can be regarded as an imaginal discipline in which we fantasize life as a meaningful journey into the depths and heights of living, using imagination, attention, and acceptance, and this is where astrology moves back into our conversation. Astrology allows us to create this psychic space, to enrich and deepen our experience of ourselves through endless imaging with the metaphorical language that is our craft. Astrology is a marvelous tool for soul-making or psycho-poiesis.

The most obvious example of this is the natal chart itself, literally a map of the sky as viewed from the moment and place of birth. But for astrologers, it is also an imaginal map of our interior landscape. Talk about creating psychic space, we are placing the entire cosmos within us. Conversely, we are also placing ourselves in the cosmos and returning our lives to the gods. In so doing, the world is re-animated; there is recognition of the *Anima Mundi*, the Soul of the World.

I tend to think of the structure of a cycle as archetypal; be it mirrored in the foundational solar year of the zodiac, the daily round of houses, lunations and planetary cycles, the meaning of aspects, etc.

Our zodiac, our houses, our aspects are all fantasies, having all the reality of lines of longitude and latitude, that imaginary net that we cast over the landscape in order to wrestle it into organized submission. We tend to forget these are imaginal realities wonderfully efficacious for orienting us to the world. The zodiac provides a series of guiding fictions for us, the fantasy of Capricornian perfection, of Leonian pride, Taurean security, Virgoan competency, Pisces blissful at-one-ment, etc.

The planets that so concern us are not singularly out there in the heavens but in here, within each of us. The nodes - intersections of imagined circles, midpoints, progressions, composite charts, eclipse points, Black Moons and Arabic parts - are all mathematical points, condensations of nothingness. Are they literal actualities? No. Should we take them seriously? Yes. Are they real? Between real and unreal, they inhabit the imaginal world, betwixt abstract concept and concrete actuality.

The chart of course is a literal map of the heavens and also an imaginal map of the hidden architecture of the moment. Remember Blake's earlier words – "And twofold always, may God us keep, from single vision and Newton's sleep."

Indeed, the chart is both, and to see through its literalism we have to allow for a polycentric perspective, which is what astrology does. It allows for multiple points of view, and by extension, multiple layers of meaning, each having legitimacy within its own perspective. Each of the gods reflecting a different style of consciousness, competing values, modes of behavior, forms of feeling, etc. There is no singleness of truth, meaning, or morality. Our astrology becomes more aesthetic and less concerned about literal prediction and circumstances.

Many native peoples believed that the Land did not belong to them, they did not own it, but rather they belonged to the living Land and behaved accordingly. In like manner, perhaps the chart does not belong to us as much as we belong to it, to the cosmos. The question then becomes what Life wants of us, not what can we get out of it. Asking how we can manipulate the gods to do our bidding for a happy marriage, a successful career, or winning the lottery furthers the heroic stance and trivializes astrology. When we enter the chart, we enter the Otherworld or Underworld as did the archetypal hero, Hercules, for his last labor. He entered without initiation into its ways. He muscled his way in with a club, without respect for its denizens; he literally brutalized his way through the underworld even wounding death, Hades himself, in the effort to triumph in his task. He took the heroic approach not unlike European expansion in the 15th century onward.

As an imaginal language, astrology is neither true nor false or perhaps it is both true and false. The important quality is its functional validity. Is it useful, opening us to the world, awakening us to a living cosmos, allowing us to listen to the claims that life has upon us? As Hillman noted, these planetary gods are not to be viewed theologically and believed in, but rather viewed psychologically and imagined ever more fully as the various potencies of life that flow through us. They are givens in the very nature of being. Our work is to incarnate these gods, differentiate them, see their imaginal presence in every moment. They are both us and other, foreign and familiar, archetypal and intimate. In this manner, I am called to affirm that my personal life participates in a larger context of cosmos.

What does this shift of vision do to our consultation style? Well the first thing is that it does not require that we 'do' differently but rather that we 'see' differently; no need to add asteroids, midpoints, Arabic parts, fixed stars, shift house systems, etc. In fact, this desire to add more things, techniques, and methods suggests at least two concerns; First and foremost, it suggests that psyche loves to imagine, to elaborate the warp and weft of astrology, adding more color, texture, and pattern, dreaming the astrological myth forward, complicating it.

I rarely hear astrologers talk about methods that don't work for them. It seems that all techniques and methods work for those who use them. It's similar to painters who use different paint media; acrylic, oil, water, tempera, different styles, sizes, and material for brushes, and to paint upon canvas, paper, wood, metal, glass, etc. There is such great diversity suited to each artist and every astrologer.

Second, the desire to add more and more may also reflect dissatisfaction with our present style of practice. Our practice, however, may not be calling out for a wider approach but for a deeper one. It requests that like the poet who takes an ordinary event in his or her life and makes it into a rich tapestry of meaningful experience - the image of an escaped gorilla for instance - we transform these events from simple sounding encounters to memorable and meaningful experience. We as astrologers of the psyche are the sky poets, helping clients see through their daily events to recognize the gods at play in their lives. To see that our activities have a divine component is a way of sanctifying a life, of giving the possibility of meaning, of making the profane sacred, and the ordinary beautiful. It is an aesthetic astrology.

The fantasy of 'seeing' differently in consultation has also to do with the notion of seeing or reimagining the fantasy of 'growth' differently. I will borrow generously from Hillman's *Kinds of Power*. Now this is key, as most astrologers that I know are concerned with helping their clients in their efforts at personal or spiritual growth. Growth usually refers to expansion, accretion, building up, getting bigger, increase, accumulation, etc. Typically, the image of personal growth includes various elements of self-evolving, increasing happiness, expanding consciousness, improving conditions, becoming better, and incrementally moving toward maturity. It's easy to understand why astrologers would idealize these factors.

These are certainly productive aims but let's imagine growth as a Persian carpet and that the surface pattern has to do with improvement, making better, consciousness expansion, evolving, etc. But lifting the carpet and looking at its underside we see something quite different, the ventral weave of growth discernible below.

Deepening is an element of growth that includes rooting ourselves in a situation rather than reaching for escape in self-improvement, weight loss programs, anger management, divorce, moving to a new location, or seeking a different employer. Digging ourselves in, letting our roots grow down to be nourished by our difficulties.

Intensification may include condensing our awareness of our immediate surroundings to appreciate them, attending closely to how the world is presenting itself in this moment, speaking less and listening intently as a way to intensify intimacy with others.

Shedding, the voluntary but more likely, the involuntary, stripping away of all that is unnecessary in our lives, simplifying, trimming away the excess, leaving baggage behind, the fiery purification of the Phoenix, or following Inanna's descent into the underworld. Loss, grief, illness, and other catastrophes are ways in which much gets cleared away and we discover what really matters.

Repetition is that which includes routine and ritual, practicing, refining, kneading, polishing, and massaging the various factors in our lives. It's not so much what we do in our lives as it is how we go about doing it.

Lastly, emptying, which can be hard to grasp, but it is not until we've been emptied of ideas, beliefs, and old habits, that we can be filled anew with a fresh tasting of life. In a Christian context, this is kenosis, the self-emptying of one's own will and desire in order to be filled with Divine will. For Zen Buddhists, *sunyata* is the absence of an independent, substantial, or eternal self. We are miraculous distillations of emptiness.

Philosophically, vast cosmic meaninglessness allows meaningfulness to emerge. Emptiness cries out for somethingness; the boundaries of the jar, the walls of the jug, or the shape of the bottle giving form to the void. Nature abhors a vacuum. It is the emptiness within these items that give them meaningful usefulness, just as the gaps, yearnings, hollows, longings, blanks, and depletions give our lives meaning. Think of emptiness as the silence out of which the sound emerges when the temple bell is struck or a mirror, empty in itself, yet reflecting everything.

These Scorpionic addenda are features in a life that can be witnessed for and supported by the astrologer so the client will recognize these different weaves of growth. In considering these threads we give a more complete meaning to the term 'growth' by including both the fiery, airy expansiveness with the weepy condensations of water and earth.

When we begin with a client, place all questions about the literal 'truth' of astrology on a shelf, try to bracket this knotty distraction. Let the client know that we will proceed in the mindset of *'as if'* the astrology is true and enter the chart, their lived experience, and discover as matters move along, the value of what is being said. The consultation rather than being a technical recitation of interpretive declarations can become a work of art, an experience rather than a simple event in the client's life. It is also a ritual return to beginnings or origin point and re-enacts a creation myth, the beginning of a new cosmos that now sits before us, an opportunity for the client to experience renewal.

If we do desire to do something differently to bring imagination more deeply into our consultation, consider that if our consultations are primarily monologues with the astrologer doing most of the talking, consider shifting into more dialoguing with the client. Instead of starting by telling the client about themselves, begin by asking the client to tell their stories, by what myths are they living?

Begin with orienting questions. "What brings you here today?" "Tell me a little about your situation." "What is it you hope to get from our session?" "How do you imagine our work together will be of value?" Let them unfold their story; listen for which god is clamoring for attention or dominating the conversation. What god is speaking? Is it Luna, Mars, Saturn, who? Don't be afraid to ask open-ended questions to foster the imaginal process adding texture and clarity. Asking questions keeps the imagination flowing, giving answers can freeze imagination, curtailing the process. Consider letting the session be client centered rather than chart centered. Letting the story unfold deepens the client's experience of their life. The astrological corollaries connect them to a larger, sacred context that may provoke insight, humility, and gratefulness.

Imagination, Astrology, and Deepening Your Practice

Providing answers to clients feeds the fires of false certainty and heroic stance. Generate questions which open into other questions and lead them deeper into their lives. When we provide answers, the imaginal process stops, there is no need to proceed further. Like a thief in the night, we pilfer little bits of their lives. We cut short the experience of cultivating imagination and add nothing to the available stock of reality. If we imagine ourselves as seer, sage, or someone who has the cosmic answers for the client, it may be difficult to give up this vested role. One suggestion is to dispense with the heroic pose that astrologers can save or help them. Nurture a context in the consultation that allows the client to disclose their story, travel their path. Don't be afraid to say outcomes aren't knowable that may be imaged in the chart, in transits, directions, or progressions. It's okay, really.

Let me offer an example, Saturn in the 7th for instance isn't limited to telling a client they're never getting married, or their marrying late in life, or marrying an older person, or having a mature or pessimistic spouse, or marrying their boss, parental figure, or image of authority, or suffer a troubled marriage. Saturn in the 7th could reflect a defensiveness in relating, shyness in meeting people, and/or a preference for few intimates. It might also image a style of partnering that willfully engages the necessary effort to ensure its lastingness and success. Saturn may have graced them with a willingness to work and persistence to attain a well-polished marriage or partnership, perhaps, a sturdy and well-tempered love of solitude that may not have been possible if the person had possessed easy social skills. Perhaps there is a lifelong unfolding to discover their inner authority that necessitated a rejecting of outer authority.

But consider this, rather than telling the client how it is, talk to them about the meaning of Saturn and let the client elucidate the varied possibilities of this placement in their life. How have they actually honored this divine presence? What is their story?

I believe that stories have the power to bind us in both healthy and unhealthy ways. It makes no difference whether they are literally true or not. If there are questions from the client about the future, these reflect uncertainty or anxiety in the present. Every prediction is a fantasy, how could it be otherwise? We can create responses to encourage hope, pronounce caution in the face of possible catastrophe, or perhaps better yet, enter the story of the anxiety with the client. Give body to that imagining.

If appropriate, ask clients to consider a homework assignment, suggest a relevant imaginative excursion for them related to their concern, maybe some appropriate poetry, or listening to great piece of music, read classic literature, watch a meaningful film, see a play, or visit an art museum and then contemplate their concerns after that with greater Imagination. They may find something in their mythic explorations that resonates for them and sparks their creativity. There are a lot of resources out there to guide us in our choices along with our own discernment. Or better yet, ask the client to offer several activities or ideas related to the god who is asking to be attended.

I would be remiss if I didn't round back to the notion of astrology as healing fiction. A healing fiction is a modality that sees through the literalisms in life to the metaphorical actualities. Astrologers may wish to focus less on strengthening the client's ego and more on dethroning it from being the only center of power and consciousness within our being. It is a move toward healing to help clients deepen their sense of identity to include the entire pantheon of their inner figures to be an inclusive community of selves rather than a singular isolated ego adrift in an uncaring and meaningless universe. The ancient Roman playwright, Terence, wrote, "I am a human being, I consider nothing that is human alien to me." Being able to affirm and embrace all the features in the chart as reflections of our troubles, failings, shortcomings, and flaws is a marvelous and healing experience.

Let me reiterate an opening quote by George Quasha, "Our reality is created through our fictions, to be conscious of these fictions is to gain creative access to, and participation in, the poetics or making of our psyche or soul-life…"

To be aware of the malleability and fluidity of our lives, the polysemic nature of the natal chart helps loosen the bindings that keep us held fast to difficult problems in which we're entangled. To be capable of sitting with our uncertainties and ambiguities, mysteries and unknowns without being anxious for explanations and answers is a hallmark of a contented, rich and interesting life.

Healing or getting unstuck becomes not so much a ridding oneself of maladies that trouble, or seeking a cure, or promises of a brighter future, healing is a coming to terms with the actualities of our situation, of softening the hard places, of loosening the bindings, of thawing that which has become frozen, of arriving at acceptance, of recognizing necessity in our lives, of accepting the hidden blessings of the god at whose altar we sit. There is a rabbinic saying, "Wealthy is the person who is happy with his portion."

Each of us knows that every planetary placement and aspect reflects an almost limitless number of existential situations that can be explored together. It is an art to discern what can be changed in our lives and what need not. As mentioned earlier, how we imagine our lives is fundamental to how we live them. Question, question, question! Avoid giving clients answers or coming to conclusions about their situations; that move curtails creativity, aborting imaginal process. A successful consultation complicates, adds textures, enriches and deepens a life. Clients leave not being buoyed by answers but rather enthused about new sets of questions to ponder, new paths to explore.

This may be a different approach to consultations but give it time to sink, settle, simmer and see if something of use rises to the top.

3

The Dark Monastery

"Where there is Sorrow there is holy ground."
Oscar Wilde

I worked daily in the underworld for three decades. It had been both challenging and rewarding. I worked in prison mental health with men who had abused drugs, molested children, thieved, raped, assaulted, and murdered. Prison is a real place and not the Hollywood stylization that many people hold as an accurate reflection. It is highly structured toward uniformity and intended to disempower its residents, in essence, to make individuality invisible.

Some of the men with whom I worked were so psychologically misshapen that they were beyond the reach of any human agency. They tended to be poorly educated, under-socialized, survivors of abuse and neglect, and viewed violence as a solution to most problems. There are histories of sporadic employment, strings of failed relationships, problems with impulse control, difficulties delaying gratification, and perhaps most importantly, an image of themselves as 'victims' in this life. They need not worry about food, clothing, and shelter and have few concerns about paying bills or working a 40 hour week. Many will spend much of their lives moving back and forth between freedom and captivity.

The men I found most rewarding to work with, however, were those who were likely to not leave prison and may spend the rest of their lives within the grey belly of that Leviathan. It is a powerful thing to be invited to journey with them (as therapist) from their valleys of despair to the hopeful plains of significance. To engage a person as they attempt to discover or construct a meaningful life for themselves, a life worth the candle in this darkness not only changes them but also changed me. Through them I saw my own darkness, was forced to confront my own projections, become aware of my own craziness, my fears, my uncaringness, my own capacity for evil, and I was constantly humbled by this. In the same manner that playing with a child tethers us to our own innocence, working in prison nurtures the dark intensity in our souls. There is something deeply and strangely nourishing for me there as reflected in my closest natal aspect: Moon/Pluto opposition in Aquarius/Leo from the 12th to the 6th houses, 27 minutes from partile, and Jupiter, the significator of the 10th in Pisces in the 12th.

My fantasy about prison is that for a minority of those incarcerated it can be imagined as a dark monastery, a place where a person can encounter the possibility of spiritual and personal transformation. But monasteries in the underworld are a bit more difficult than the ones in the world we inhabit.

In a typical monastery there are certain values and virtues esteemed as most worthy. These would include the practice of charity, poverty, hospitality, patience, humility, kindness, generosity, honesty, and compassion. These are supported by the monastic community. However, in the domain of the underworld, these virtues and values are inverted as one might expect. Each of these, in the context of the prison environment, is seen as undesirable and viewed as weakness. Men who still value these monastic virtues are easily consumed by this dark, predatory beast. In the underworld, you keep to yourself, you hold what you have, you get what you can, you mind your own business, and don't lend a hand. That is the way this community functions. There are however a very few who are motivated to change how they imagine themselves and may discover that prison experienced as monastic can be a cauldron of transformation for them.

Though I am not a researcher, I would like to offer some observations about these denizens of the underworld that may be informative for those readers who prefer to travel only in circles of light. Traditionally, prisons are associated with Pluto, Scorpio, and the 8th house and Neptune, Pisces, and the 12th house. As I use astrology in my counseling work, it is not uncommon for me to notice an emphasis on one or more of these reflections in my client's charts.

One man, Jim, in his mid-fifties, is serving 20 years for rape. He is a somewhat passive fellow and led a fairly nondescript life until a few years ago. Natally, he has the Sun and 3 other personal planets in the 12th house opposing Neptune. Saturn, the most elevated planet in the chart, is near the MC in Pisces squaring his natal Sun. There is certainly the suggestion here that removal or retreat from society may be a feature in his life at some point. These sorts of configurations are not all that uncommon. Several others follow.

Another man, Leroy in his late fifties, doing 14 years, has Aquarius rising with its ruler Uranus conjunct Pluto. Scorpio is on the Midheaven and his Sun is conjunct the 12th house cusp. His Moon, the apex of a T-square, is in the 8th squaring Saturn and Jupiter in the 12th and Mars in Cancer in the 6th.

George is serving time for rape and is sentenced indeterminately from 15 to 50 years. Neptune in the 2nd has prominence in his chart by being the only unaspected planet. Mercury, the ruler of his Ascendant and Midheaven is exactly conjunct the 8th house cusp opposing his Moon in Scorpio in the 2nd.

Dark Skies

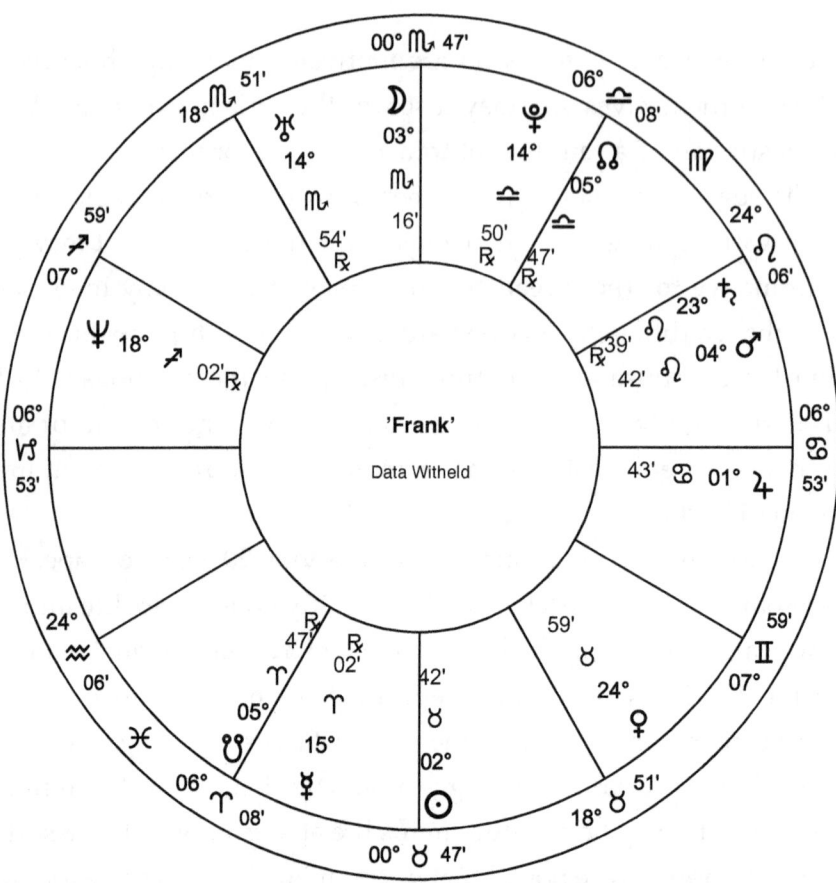

Frank (above, private data) is sentenced to life for the murder of his parents. He has Moon conjunct the MC in Scorpio opposing his Sun in the 4th which are both in a T-square relationship to Mars in Leo in the 7th. He has Pluto in the 9th opposing Mercury in the 3rd, a reflection of his past satanic beliefs and his present nihilism. He also has a certain intellectual relentlessness spending his time pursuing religion and philosophy.

Alan in his mid-fifties is serving big time for a sexual offense. He has lived a very sheltered life and presents as overly concerned about what others think of him. He has the Sun conjunct Venus in Leo in the 7th, four degrees away from the 8th house cusp and opposing Saturn in the 2nd. This aspect is part of a T-square configuration with Neptune in Scorpio in the 10th, the most elevated planet in the chart. Neptune is also quincunx Jupiter which is the ruler of the 12th.

Charlie (below, private data) is serving life in prison for killing his mother. He is in his late fifties. He never was quite able to truly emancipate himself from her. He has spent most of his adult life in and out of alcohol rehab. When he thought he was finally getting his life together, his mother pulled the plug on an arrangement that they had made that sent him into a downward spiral of several days of drinking, doing crack cocaine, and avoiding sleep. He inadvertently accosted his mother in the early morning hours of the third day of staying high, they argued, and she died by his

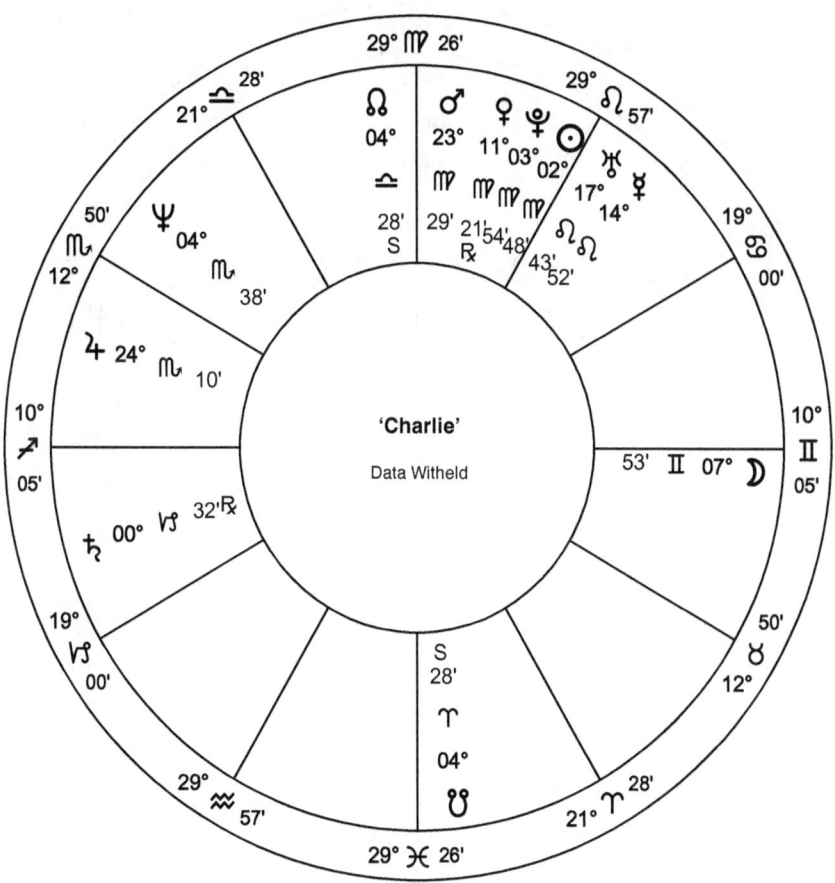

Dark Skies

hands. Charlie has Sagittarius rising with Jupiter in Scorpio in the 12th house. He also has a tight Sun/Pluto/Venus conjunction in the 9th all squaring the Moon conjunct the Descendant. Virgo is on the Midheaven with its ruler conjunct Uranus in the 8th. Once again we have a chart that images a life deeply involved with the transpersonal dark lords. He has struggled mightily to try and come to terms with the enormity of his act and find some sense in it all.

Not every chart is so obvious in its connection to the underworld. Sam (below, private data) serving life for the killing of a child had always wanted to make something of himself. He was serious in his ambition and had achieved enough by early adulthood to buy his first house (Taurus ASC, Venus conjunct Saturn in the 2nd,

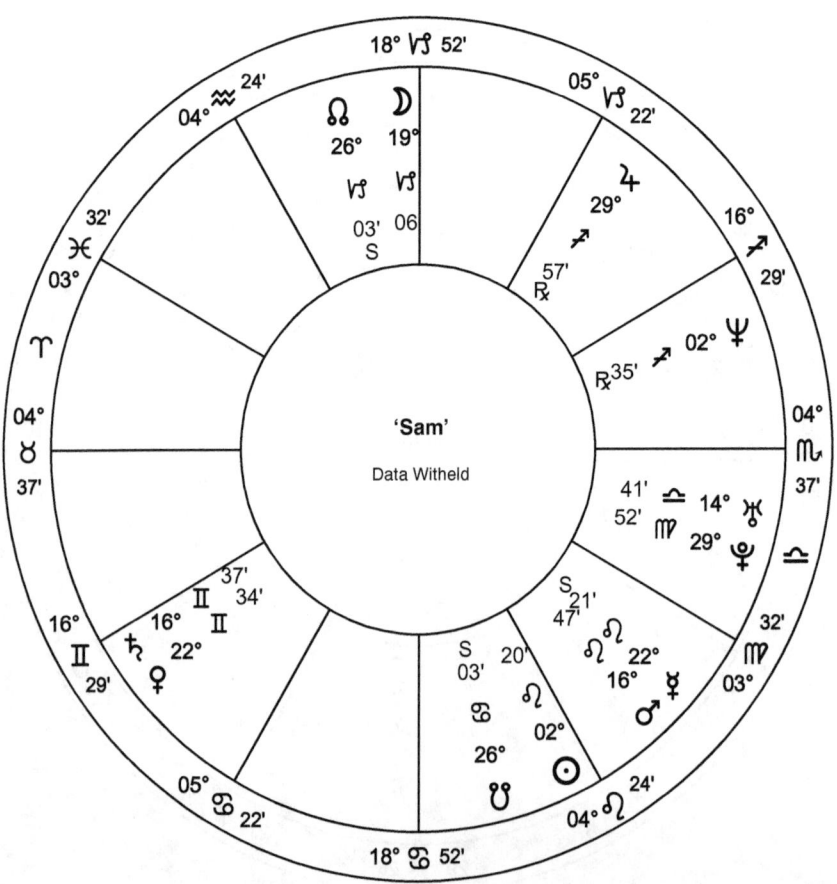

Moon in Capricorn on the MC). He views himself as playful and magnanimous, easily hurt by slights, and responds angrily to any sign of disrespect which he perceives as an invalidation of himself (Sun, Mars, Mercury in Leo in the 5th). He describes his father as an unpredictable and harsh disciplinarian and his mother as a free spirit with multiple marriages who believed in free love, drugs, and rock and roll. She proved less than reliable and did not provide stability in the home (Moon in Capricorn in 10th square Uranus in Libra in the 7th).

His most important goal had been to be a father and have a family of his own (Moon conjunct MC). His Moon (apex planet of a 2nd, 5th, 10th house yod) is highly stressed by the Uranus square, the Venus/Saturn conjunction quincunx the Moon from the 2nd and Mars/Mercury conjunct are also quincunx the Moon from the 5th. He also has a T-square with Venus in the 2nd opposing Jupiter in the 8th, both squaring apex Pluto in the 6th.

There had been several different women he had impregnated over the years but each pregnancy had ended prematurely to his sad and bitter disappointment. These losses occurred during the period that Uranus and Neptune had been crossing his Moon and MC over a several year period. Finally, his girlfriend gave birth to a son and the couple decided to marry (Jupiter was transiting his 5th). His fiancé also had a small child from a prior relationship and it was this child (that he loved dearly as his own), who perished, perhaps accidentally, at the hands of this man.

During the time of this tragedy, transiting Mars and Uranus were on his 12th house cusp forming a yod to his natal Sun and natal Pluto. Transiting Saturn in the 3rd was approaching an opposition to natal Moon and a square to natal Pluto. Transiting Neptune was in the 11th opposing his natal Sun and Mars. Transiting Pluto was in the 8th and opposing the natal Saturn/Venus conjunction and going stationary direct in 6 days. To cap it off the transiting Moon in Gemini was sweeping over his powerful natal yod triggering that tension. Oddly enough, the transiting Sun/Venus/Jupiter were in his 5th but past triggering the yod. This amassing of transits reflect a very powerful and disturbing time for this man which continue to echo through his life. I don't believe however that anyone could have predicted this sorrowful moment in the history of the many lives impacted by this terrible blow. We had worked together for some time to help him through his grief, self-loathing, and guilt.

The guiding fiction throughout my career has been a fragment of wisdom from the Renaissance priest, composer, astrologer, physician, and psychologist, Marsilio Ficino. He wrote in his *Three Books on Life*, "There is nothing to be found in the whole, living world so deformed, as to have no Soul." This line, enfolded in my heart, is a constant reminder to this day of the things that I share in common with these men. I, along with each and every one of them, have sought pleasure in life while trying hard to avoid the pain of living, have experienced a wide range of disturbing emotions, have faced a variety of challenges and failed at some, have known illness and loss, and will someday move on to a great unknown. Suffering is the great equalizer.

Have I helped any of these men in my time? Well that depends on how one understands the term, 'help.' Are any of them less likely to act upon an impulse to rape, murder, or rob? I truly don't know. I would argue that one cannot reliably predict these things. I would like to think that there is less likelihood of that happening in the future and yet, history is biography and character then, is destiny. Approximately two-thirds of incarcerated men will return to prison at some point in their lives.

But I have been there with them, have witnessed for them, have affirmed their worth, and heard their sufferings, and walked a little along their path with them. I do not believe that it is possible for one person to heal another. Healing is something that occurs within each of us as we can open to it. There is great resistance to healing and getting unstuck due to fear of change, habit, and ignorance. When we are ready, healing occurs in its own time. Healing doesn't mean that the client automatically improves or makes progress. Sometimes it means that clients are simply able to begin the process of learning to embrace and accept themselves, their dangerous impulses, twisted thinking and emotional deformities. They may experience their lives as enriched and deepened though not necessarily better. My task had been to coax into being an environment within which healing may occur, to catch that moment when the client is ripe for change. That, at its best, described my calling to the underworld.

I would be remiss if I didn't briefly mention the group of clinicians who like Hermes, were able to enter and depart the underworld as needed. Of the seven colleagues whose charts I have, five of them have Virgo rising, one has Cancer rising, the other has Scorpio, and I have Pisces on the Ascendant. In my case, I mentioned above the tight 6/12 Moon/Pluto opposition. My Moon is also trine Neptune and my Midheaven is in Sagittarius with its agent, Jupiter, retrograde in Pisces in the 12th. Jupiter is also trine my Venus/Uranus conjunction in the 5th. The two groups that I enjoyed conducting the most were the mindfulness meditation class and the enhancing self-awareness through astrological metaphor group.

My Cancer rising colleague has the Sun in Scorpio, the Moon in Gemini in wide conjunction to the 12th house cusp in quincunx to Mercury/Venus conjunction in Scorpio in the 5th. Pluto is on the 2nd house cusp, the traditional house of income, and a Saturn/Neptune conjunction crosses the threshold of Libra and Scorpio in the 4th. One of the groups he conducted was for men with mood disorders and another of his activities had to do with victim/offender dialogues.

The Scorpio rising clinician has Leo on the Midheaven with the Sun in the 8th squaring the Moon in Pisces and opposing Neptune in Scorpio on his 2nd house cusp. We also have Mars in the 8th squaring Pluto in wide conjunction to the 12th house cusp. It's interesting that the group he conducted was focused upon violent offenders.

Of the five Virgo rising clinicians, a psychologist (below, private data) has Taurus on the Midheaven with its agent, Venus, in Pisces in the 7th house and Neptune on the 2nd house cusp.

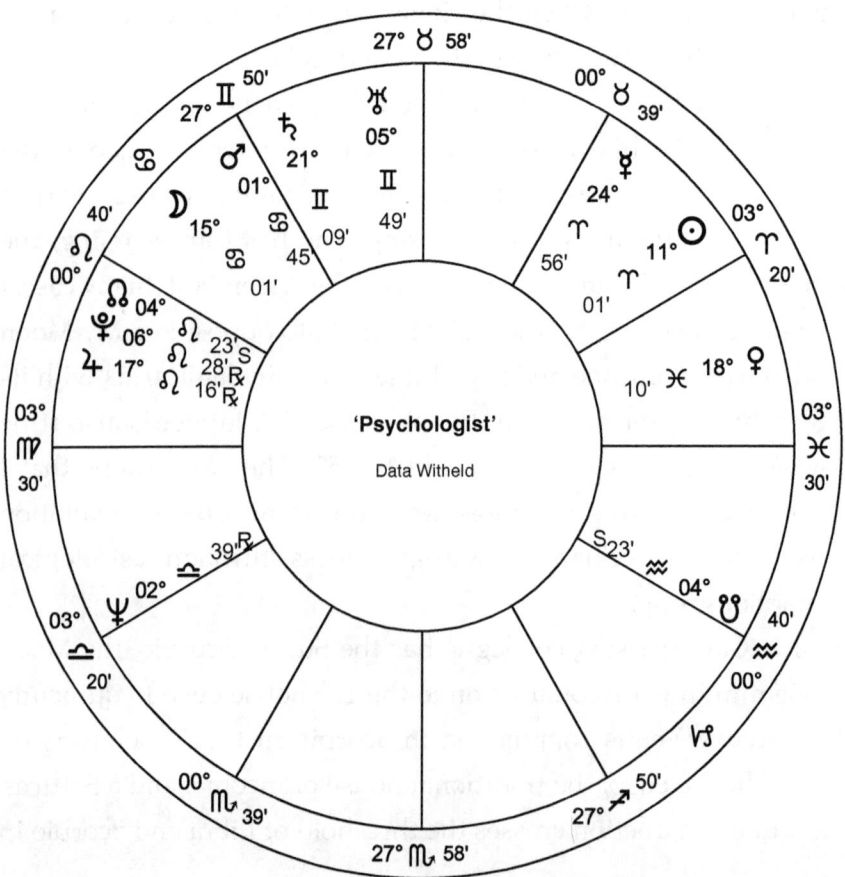

Another retired colleague has Neptune in the 1st (6 degrees off the 2nd house cusp) opposing the Moon in Pisces in the 7th and the ruler of his Midheaven and Ascendant in Cancer. He also has an apex Pluto on the cusp of the 12th in T-square with Mars opposing Jupiter. He conducted the anger management group for a number of years (below, private data).

One therapist has a Pluto/Uranus conjunction in the 1st in quincunx to an 8th house Sun and square a 10th house Moon in Gemini. She conducted a feelings identification group and one on anxiety management. With Taurus on the Midheaven, its ruler Venus also in the 10th opposes Neptune, the most highly aspected planet in the chart.

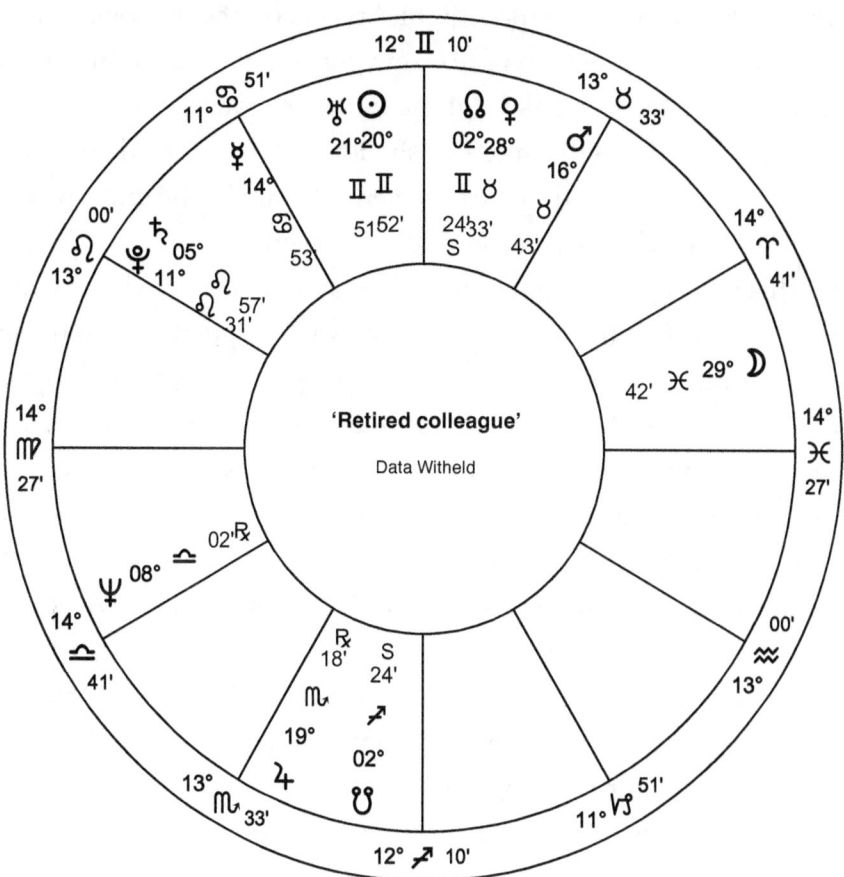

Another psychologist has that Uranus/Pluto conjunction closer to the Ascendant, quincunx a wide conjunction of the Sun and Mars in the 8th house. This Uranus/Pluto conjunction is also square Venus conjunct the Midheaven. He had a clinical focus based on intimacy and relationships recognizing that wounding in this arena can have terrible consequences including social alienation, poor relational skills, and a disregard for the rights of others - all warning signs on the road to imprisonment.

Last is a therapist with Pluto in the 12th squaring Saturn in Scorpio in the 3rd. Additionally, he has a very tight Sun/Jupiter conjunction in the 12th in wide opposition to Mars in Pisces in the 7th. His Mars is the handle of a bucket chart, the only planet in the western hemisphere. Mars' sign of Aries is on the 8th house cusp. This clinician spent much of his time putting out fires doing crisis management. He also has Neptune in the 2nd house.

As the reader will note, the shadows of the dark deities are prominent not only in the charts of men who inhabit the underworld but also in the charts of those who work there.

This brief tour of the underworld may not be as foreign as one might suppose. If the reader thinks my work applied only to those who are incarcerated, I offer this: the image of the prisoner is an apt metaphor and concise embodiment of what it means to be human. Though we profess a love for freedom and self-direction, there are many ways in which we weave restraint and binding into our being. That ancient mortician, Saturn, firmly announces his presence when we find ourselves locked in by our own fears, buried by family obligations, stuck in meaningless occupations, or held captive by our own inadequacies. In this, then, we are all doing time in prisons of our own making and it's terribly hard to see our way through to freedom. When we are chained to our ideas and beliefs, beliefs that keep us back, press us down, limit our sense of the kinds of power we actually possess in life, we are incarcerated. In moments of clarity, we may realize the frenzied grasp of a relationship that has exhausted itself yet will not release us, or the moth to flame compulsiveness we may have for another, knowing full well that it would never work out. Sometimes we confuse doing with being, and are so attached to what we do that we come to believe it is who we are and we become bound to that identity, facing crisis should we not be able to continue this work. These are all traps we set for ourselves and are surprised when they're sprung and we're recaptured, held fast, becoming again, our own jailers. These limitations, boundaries, and suffering are as much a part of the human condition as are expansiveness, freedom, and joy.

Even though we may not have to literalize prison by being actually incarcerated, we each carry the underworld as constant companion. Many of us deny these denizens of the dark, hiding them away, concealing their existence, but this seems a recipe for disaster. When we no longer recoil in shock and disgust at these morally reprehensible and socially unacceptable inner figures but instead greet them as kin then we may discover that our self-imposed prison has transformed into the dark monastery. In this stygian abbey we learn that we may with difficulty practice kindness, humility, hospitality, and patience. We discover that previously despised elements of our being blossom from the humus of this dark soil. Our suffering engenders compassion not only toward ourselves but also toward the Dark Others that we encounter in the world. Beast becomes Beauty, fiend becomes friend, and the boundaries of identity soften and expand to include ever more of what we thought was alien and foreign born.

The poet, Rilke (Bly translation) wrote,

Dark Skies

I live my life in growing orbits
which move out over the things of the world.
Perhaps I can never achieve the last,
but that will be my attempt.
I am circling around God, around the ancient tower,
and I have been circling for a thousand years,
and I still don't know if I am a falcon, or a storm,
or a great song.

I left this dark monastery in 2012 after three decades and every now and then I recall those occasions when the client and I were able to open and notice that we had found the moment and caught a glimpse of the darkness that is illumination.

4

In Praise of Melancholy

"Without Contraries there is no progression."
WILLIAM BLAKE

"From the strain of binding opposites comes harmony."
HERACLITUS

"Crisis is the crucible that burns away all that is inessential and reveals to us our vital core."
E. G. WILSON

"Taught by suffering. Drop by drop wisdom is distilled from pain."
AESCHYLUS

The statements above suggest strife, tension, crisis, and suffering are springboards to a life filled with progress, harmony, vitality, and wisdom. All that may be required is to embrace the necessary. The Greek notion of Necessity (Ananke) is that which opposes human purpose and is beyond not only human manipulation but also beyond the control of the gods. Necessity is contrary to personal desire. Hillman writes in *Facing the Gods* that Necessity in the Greek sense means "a physically oppressive tie of servitude to an inescapable power." Necessity seems woven into the fabric of Saturn and Pluto. What are we to do with such an anti-humanistic dynamic that flies in the face of our reaching for the brass ring in life? After all, shouldn't we be free to not only pursue but achieve happiness? We might also consider the notion of Fate, perhaps a sister to Necessity, that I prefer to define as the 'given' in which we are situated. Necessity and Fate seem to deny our autonomy, our self-expression, and the American birth right.

Americans are an interesting and curious people and I am quite fond of the Sibly chart for America with its Sagittarian Ascendant. I believe that it nicely reflects the American character as a nation in pursuit of happiness and filled with a confident optimism that there are few limits to what we can achieve. It was our manifest destiny to expand westward across the continent and then take a vertical turn straight to the Moon and beyond. We comfort ourselves with the fantasy that America is *Numero Uno* and attempt to export this notion to the rest of the globe. With recent exception (fill in the blank), who doesn't want to be an American? To hear our president speak, groups are out to destroy America because they jealously want what we have; freedom and especially democracy.

Our psychological orientation via the humanistic/transpersonal perspective is that we should spend our lives enthusiastically committed to seeking personal growth, self-actualization, peak experiences, liberation (i.e., expanded perspective), and with the recent emphasis on positive psychology, happiness. This manic search leaves us with a lopsided vision of the world. I might argue that life is too precious and brief to exhaust it seeking enlightenment. As a nation I suspect we easily identify with America's Sun/Jupiter/Venus conjunction and struggle with the nature of Saturn's claims upon the soul of America in its square to the nation's Sun. I think this can perhaps be read as a shadow issue, as an easy denial of and a cultural unconsciousness toward Saturn. Additionally, America may find it easier to own the Mercury end of the Mercury/Pluto opposition and deny or bury all that is Pluto in our culture.

The *Danse Macabre* is a medieval allegory of the universality of death; dancing skeletons remind us of the fragility of life and its inevitable outcome. It is a form of *memento mori*, a Latin phrase for a genre of art popular in medieval and later times meaning "Remember your death." It is a promise that evokes immediacy in living and full awareness to the moment. It humbles our arrogance and keeps us fully situated in our ecological niche rather than seducing us with the hubris of believing that humanity is the crown of creation. Its very nature is Saturn, sobering and grave.

Liz Greene notes in *Dynamics of the Unconscious* that there are two signs that are particularly prone to depression, Scorpio and Capricorn. Their agents, Saturn and Pluto, both image different facets of death and suffering. Saturn is classically associated with death as boundary and finality, and in our modern time Pluto has been imaged as the necessary extinction preceding new birth if the cycle of life is to continue. It is death in the service of life. Life is able to proceed by consuming itself as in the archaic image of the snake eating its own tail; the *Ouroboros*. Those who have a dominance of Capricorn or Scorpio with strong Pluto and Saturn presence may be gravely blessed with a sensitivity to these matters, but I think it is necessary to hold in mind that we all have Saturn/Capricorn and Pluto/Scorpio somewhere in our charts. No one here gets out alive.

Saturn, that old minion of mortality, of finitude, and limitation gets no cultural respect. When Saturn tugs at our lives, he wants our attention, our acknowledgement, our affirmation. When his claims upon us are ignored, we may be visited with sad mood, emptiness, a sense of being burdened and contracted, feeling alone or aged or worn out.

Pluto, Lord of the Underworld, minister of Death also keens for our attention. He wishes us to affirm and accept the darker aspects of our existence, our shadows, our destructiveness, our perversities, our unacknowledged companion; the grim reaper, and the grave loss of what we hold dear and to which we cling.

When Pluto comes knocking, we need to courageously and with faith answer the door.

Is it possible that the pervasive presence of depression in our nation is the inevitable voices of Saturn and Pluto trying to be heard in a culture bent upon endless growth while denying both decline and demise? It has become almost sinful to get old when there are cultural strategies in place to ward off aging and death. Let nothing show its age; tear down the old architecture, replace the two year-old cars with the newest models, dress in the latest fashions, purchase age defying cosmetics, surgically remove the wrinkles, tighten the bags, flatten the belly, lift the breasts, store the elderly out of sight, and for god's sake, hide the dead from public view. When we ignore or deny the Saturn/Pluto realm of experience and overcompensate with the more Jupiterian aspects we are in trouble, Jupiter is free to run wild. And to borrow a phrase attributed to eco-philosopher, Edward Abbey, "Growth for the sake of growth is the ideology of the cancer cell."

I do wish to make a distinction between major depression and the melancholy of whose praises I sing. Putting it rather simply, though closely related and appearing the same initially, the inner dynamics differ. Major depression strikes so deeply to the bone that the person often becomes psychologically paralyzed; apathetic, numb, without feeling, with an inability to think or concentrate. Interest and energy is fully withdrawn from the world. People become psychically shriveled to such a degree that their world has collapsed in on itself like a dying star. Medication is certainly called for in these situations to help move the person to a more functional region. On the other hand, melancholy produces a great dissatisfaction with the status quo, a deep sadness with present matters, a longing for new life to lift the gloom, and a concomitant sense of stagnation and fixity. It can feel like a crucifixion. I believe it to be less disabling than major depression and more likely to portend a creative chaos out of which new life may emerge.

An estimated 26% of Americans of ages 18 and older -- about 1 in 4 adults -- suffer from a diagnosable mental disorder in a given year according to Johns-Hopkins Medicine, and it is major depression and bipolar disorder leading the way. That is not to mention those millions of Americans who episodically have the blues, feel down, lack enthusiasm, or experience a malaise but do not meet the diagnostic criterion for mental disorder. These are the stuck, turning slowly on the lathe of melancholy.

Our cultural response to this is to mount an attack against depression, to medically combat melancholy, first by renaming it a disease rather than a divine visitation in the classical sense and second, to redouble our efforts to eradicate it (via pharmaceuticals) as we would a noxious weed. Do I intend to say that people should not seek medication to help alleviate depression? Of course not, some people are so severely depressed that they can no longer function adequately enough to live reasonably. It's been estimated by the National Institute of Mental Health in the U.S. that 21 million Americans had at least one episode of major depression in 2021. During that year 337 million prescriptions were written for antidepressants in America. What I am saying is that the number of prescriptions written for antidepressants far exceeds the number of people diagnosed with major depression. Many of the walking wounded are attempting to extinguish the underworld. And yet, these darker sufferings of anguish, emptiness, dryness, gloom, failure, guilt, and impotency constitute a large portion of what it is to be a full human being. Melancholy and its siblings are sacred vessels able to carry us away from a partial existence and toward a new horizon.

In wanting to kill off these elements in our lives, we throw ourselves out of sync with the vast cosmic rhythms of existence. We want the high of riding the crests of the waves of life without experiencing the troughs. We want dawn without dusk, sun without storm, expecting to find full self-actualization with only a partially lived life. Must we remember that enlightenment requires endarkenment? In *Alchemical Studies* (CW13, pt.1) Jung wrote, "One does not become enlightened by imagining figures of light, but by making the darkness conscious. The latter procedure, however, is disagreeable and therefore not popular." But it is the engagement with the melancholic aspects of living that brings a depth and richness to life. We will want to keep in mind the unexpressed and invisible promise of both Pluto and Saturn. Pluto, whose name also means 'wealth' and Saturn's mythological golden age suggests the possibility of discovering gold within the dross of human experience.

Just as the field of psychology since the 1960's has been increasingly focused upon helping clients get what they want, astrology has followed suit in its efforts to assist clients find happiness, success, health, wealth, and reassurance that they are living their lives in a manner that will get them what they want. This narcissistic focus has brought about a loss of soul, a dismissal of Fate, and a secularizing perspective to astrology. In my thinking, there is a certain hubris and shame in the idea of using the vast pulsating energy of the cosmos, the very power of the gods, as a tool for satisfying egoistic desires for personal comfort and gain. It also demonstrates a tremendous lack of faith in the way of one's life as an expression of the cosmos, thinking that we somehow need to intervene to make things right in our lives. I am well aware that readers may be so deeply enmeshed in the dominant paradigm that my words may not make great sense so I can ask only that you bear with me.

A Daoist perspective on astrology would suggest that we are never out of accord with the way of the heavens. Life consists of both harmony and dissonance and the only constancy is change. This suggests that the yin and the yang of any situation are always in dynamic process, enfolded in each other and unfolding each in its own time and manner. In the 29th chapter of the Dao de Jing we read:

> Do you think you can take over the universe and improve it?
> I do not believe it can be done.
> The universe is sacred.
> You cannot improve it.
> If you try to change it, you will ruin it.
> If you try to hold it, you will lose it.

This is a tremendous faith statement; the given in which we are situated, the Fate of the moment, is complete as it is and in perfect accord with the heavens. As I've said elsewhere, just because life feels out of our control, doesn't mean that it *is* out of control. There are larger guiding factors at work in the world, call these God, Dao, guardian angels, daimons, spirit guides, the Self, or what have you. It is a matter of trust and faith in cosmic process, that it conspires for your benefit, and that there is an inherent goodness in creation despite the necessary presence of violence, suffering and death. Saturn and Pluto show us, as Eric Wilson writes in *Against Happiness*, that "our demons---the dark parts of our hearts, our agitations and our loathings, our cynicisms and our acerbities---are integral parts of ourselves, absolutely essential."

When clients come in depressed, anguished, lost questioning, it is not always in their best interests for us to help by trying to answer their questions and reassuring them that everything is going to be okay. I realize that the whole enterprise of astrology is founded upon clients wanting answers to questions that are conventionally unanswerable, "When will I marry?" "Will my parent recover?" and of course, "What do the stars say about my future?" These questions all reflect a certain discomfort and uneasiness with their present circumstances. Clients are trying to slip out of the noose of their lives into a future not yet arrived. Answering these questions may not be the most effective use of astrology.

It is my belief and my practice that we as astrologers should deflect these kinds of questions and encourage our clients to explore their melancholy (or anxiety) to find the seed of transformation buried within it. It is in the very grasping for something more or different (the brass ring) that contributes to our malaise. Exploring present circumstance may stir up matters enough to foster an alchemical process that will simmer and bubble so that in time the hidden issues can ferment to a state of readiness to transform on their own, granting the client a ripeness bringing forth a new sense of contentment with their situation.

Many clients seem to me to be estranged from their lives much like Joyce's character Mr. Duffy in *The Dubliners*. "Mr. Duffy abhorred anything which betokened physical or mental disorder…. He lived at a little distance from his body, regarding his own acts with doubtful side-glances." Is this the postmodern condition, distrusting of and distant from our own being, split and conflicted? Are we cut off from the life-giving sustenance of spirit? Have we suffered the loss of soul by this endless chasing for that which we do not believe we already possess? Do we abjure our essence, seeking something better and grander than what we presently experience?

In Praise of Melancholy

There is a story in the Hindu tradition. A long time ago human beings were actually gods but they so abused their divinity that Brahma, the chief god, believed that their divinity should be taken away from them. He called a council to discuss the matter and pose the question of where he should hide the divinity of humanity. Some said that it should be buried in the deepest part of the earth but Brahma objected stating that humans would dig deeply into the earth and someday find it. Another suggested that it should be tossed in the ocean to be hidden on the bottom but Brahma said that human beings would eventually go to the bottom of the sea and reclaim it. Another said then let us secure it on the top of the highest mountain and again Brahma objected saying that humanity would scale all the mountains on earth and recover it again. Finally, after much thought, Brahma stated that he would sink it deep into the center of each human being for they would never think to look for it there. And since that time, humanity has been digging, diving, climbing, and looking over the whole earth seeking for that which is already within. Our incessant grasping for that which we believe we do not possess befuddles us to no end.

It seems, like Mr. Duffy, we suffer a dislocation in time and space; living somewhere in the future or the past, anywhere but here and now. But it is in the present moment that we make the painful discovery that the presence of death and suffering are deeply and inextricably entwined with life and joy. The , contraries, as Blake called them go hand in hand. To embrace one and deny the other fractures our wholeness. Birthing and dying, the two polarities of life cannot be separated. We have been dying since the day we were born and being birthed anew in each rising moment. Like the yin/yang symbol, there is a secret sorrow in our most profound joys and a joyful blessing residing at the heart of every sorrow. *In Against Happiness*, Eric Wilson writes:

> In feeling fractured and fragmented, isolated and bereft, one actually comes to experience wholeness and unity. To suffer melancholy is also to understand its polar opposite, joy. Lacking joy, one broods on it more deeply than when one possesses this state.... In vacillating between sorrow and joy, one grasps the secret harmony between these two antinomies. Doing so, one apprehends the rhythms of the whole cosmos, itself a dynamic interplay between opposites.

When we try to escape suffering, failure, defects, and disappointments, we are only half alive. Plumbing our charts places us firmly in the immediacy of our lives. The archetypal images can be slowly explored in ways that can be painful but also meaningful. If we can fully embrace the rhythms of Saturn and Pluto and immerse ourselves in their *Danse Macabre* knowing full well and gracefully accepting that we are not the lead partner, then we are truly dancing with the stars.

Study Saturn, study Pluto, and in fact contemplate all the planetary gods in the chart, not in order to figure out how we can gain the advantage of their presence but rather to discover what their claims upon us are and what is the nature of our true being.

5

Empowering People, Not Planets

At various times there have been discussions about ethics in the astrological community. One area in which I would like to add to the discussion is in the ethics of helping. What in fact constitutes the nature of helping and to borrow a phrase, is help helpful?

There are numerous factors which lead a person to seek out an astrologer. A client may have some insecurity about an upcoming situation and desire some reassurance from the astrologer that they are on the right track in their planning, or they may naively want the astrologer to tell them their future. The client may be seeking comfort from emotional pain believing that if they can see that their pain is connected to a larger context it may be more bearable. He or she may be looking for some validation or approval from the astrologer that they're okay. The client could be searching for a solution to a problem or hoping the astrologer will make a decision for them regarding a life circumstance. They might be casting about for relationship or financial advice or expecting the astrologer to provide medical recommendations. It's possible a client is inquiring about relocating or career counsel. They might even be pursuing self-improvement, believing that astrology holds the key. I'm guessing that there are many more reasons for going to an astrologer and it is important for astrologers to carefully sort through client requests to determine what is and is not feasible. If a client request exceeds our area of skill, whether an electional question or mental health issue, it is incumbent upon us to refer clients to those who practice in the areas of question.

When in the helping professions, it can be extremely useful to examine our own motives for helping. What do we as astrologers get out of it? I suspect that very few of us are in it for financial rewards. Is it a way to express genuine concern for others, a path to feeling useful, a practice which helps give meaning to our own lives? Could it be tainted by a desire to be in control and express power over others by assuming to know what another person needs in their life? Is it possible that we engage astrology to create dependency in others, to keep them coming back? Do we fill a private need to gain status in the eyes of others by demonstrating specialized cosmic knowledge? Could we be seeking to obtain gratitude from others and induce their indebtedness to us? Are we desperate to be liked by others and do we feel obligated to make people happy? Doing some soul searching about our own motives can be a productive enterprise, whether this is done privately or in the context of our own counseling or therapy. Once we are clear about our own motivations for helping, we are better able to hold these in awareness, not letting them tug us in unhealthy directions.

When people come seeking help from others there is always the potential for less than desirable outcomes. Depending on our own attitudes toward helping, our willingness to really listen to clients, our philosophical orientation regarding astrology, and the kind of language that we use, outcomes can vary widely. For example, if our orientation to astrology engenders a lot of traditional language or the objectifying of the planets as causal agents, clients may leave the session feeling victimized by the 'stars', unable to change, touched by the finger of Fate. As astrologers, we end up empowering planets, rather than people. Depending on how information is presented, clients may become more helpless and more dependent upon us for guidance as to how they should conduct their affairs. They may feel less able to make decisions or less willing to take risks in life without first having a consultation.

In the broadest of brushstrokes, "If you give a man a fish, you feed him for a day. If you teach a man how to fish, you feed him for a lifetime." I trust there is no one reading this who would disagree with the common sense wisdom of this statement. This popular maxim defines for us two levels of helping others, the short term immediate form and the long term growth inducing form, respectively.

Short term help attempts to offer immediate aid, provide relief, and alleviate crisis. It supplies assistance and brings partial or full remedy to a condition or situation. It tends to be topical and is oriented around symptom removal and problem solving. This is the Western heroic approach. It is the manner by which much of the mental health industry operates today after which some astrologers want to model themselves in an effort to gain cultural legitimacy. It is certainly an approach which is supported by the insurance reimbursement industry in the States. It can be efficient and time saving but can also leave the client feeling like it was a fast-food encounter. It has more of a Band-Aid feel than a quality of depth about it. The person may leave with the feeling that he or she has not been known.

The long term approach to helping is intended to awaken clients to the growth processes within. Symptomatic complaints may or may not disappear. The "long term" quality does not necessarily refer to the number of encounters a client has with the astrologer but rather to the notion that quality growth takes time; ask any forester or vintner. Why do we value and try to protect old growth forests? Because we perceive a higher value (quality if you will) in them than in the quick growth paper mill forests. If a vintner tries to coerce his wines into hastier transformation, he ends up with an inferior product.

Long term help by its very nature has a lastingness to it. It is often more alchemical or Daoist in flavor. There is attention, patience, observation, and allowing the process to unfold, heat up, simmer, and ferment. Healthy change takes time. In fact trying to force it may hinder or abort it. The kind of growth that we are talking about can be defined as an increase in the person's capacity for self-support replacing environmental supports. This reduces the person's need to manipulate and maneuver others into doing for them what he or she is capable of doing for themselves. We would hope to see an increase in a client's acceptance of and an openness to themselves and others. The client would possess the ability to experience and accept a full range of feeling states. There could be a gain in trust in themselves and life with a concomitant loosening of the need to be in control of things. Additionally, there would be an enhancement of feeling an at-homeness in the world. These can be considered if you will, symptomatic of growth and development.

There are different styles of helping interventions which in the immediacy of the situation may be helpful but do little to foster the kind of growth which has been elaborated above. Several of these have been adapted from consulting psychologist, Jack R. Gibb, in an article that appeared in *Theological Field Education: A Collection of Key Resources* (Vol.1, 1977) titled, "Is Help Helpful?"

The first problematic intervention is instructing versus collaborative learning. Piscean Age thinking tends to promote a savior/sinner, rescuer/victim, expert/novice style of approach to matters. For a client, something outside of him or her has the power to save them, rescue them, redeem them, make them better, show them how to improve, etc. An Aquarian Age ethic would decentralize power and authority placing it firmly in the hands of both participants who make joint inquiry and learning together a priority. We see this slowly happening in the bastion of medicine where doctors no longer wear the mantle of ultimate authority but have been divesting themselves of this status and attempting to foster a well-informed patient who becomes their own authoritative decision-maker regarding their own healthcare. This moves a client's responsibility for their own life path back into their own hands, a step towards growth. Though we as astrologers possess specialized knowledge, it is the client who is the expert of their own life, something that we should not forget.

The second intervention is advice giving versus shared problem solving. In this scenario, the astrologer does all the work even though the client is quite capable of doing their own dirty work. Client growth is limited when the astrologer provides the solution through advice giving to a client thus cheating the client of the opportunity to develop their own problem-solving skills. When the two participants in a joint effort mutually engage in exploring the problem this returns responsibility back to the client that can also contribute to enhanced self-esteem.

The third style raises the issue of covert agendas versus openness. If the astrologer or client is using the other for his/her unstated needs, help is not likely to occur. Honest communication and feedback are difficult if one of the partners is focused upon a hidden agenda. For example, the astrologer has the hidden agenda of wanting to be liked and therefore finds it difficult to be honest with the client when there is a need for the astrologer to confront the client on a particular issue. Both participants must be able to be open to honest responses from each other if the exchange is to be productive.

Assessment versus mutual growth is the fourth problematic intervention. Help is most effective when the participants are focused upon opportunities for mutual growth rather than the astrologer telling the client what they need, attempting to remedy defects, correct the client, or fix them according to some preconceived ideal. Carl Jung (CW 10, para. 867) wrote, "It is presumptuous to think that we can always know what is good or bad for a patient…. Perhaps fate, or the unconscious, or God… had to give him a hard knock or roll him in the dirt, because only such a drastic experience could strike home, pull him out of his infantilism, and make him more mature." It is simply not within the province of anyone's knowing to speak of what another needs to move their life in the direction of growth.

The fifth intervention issue is that of coaching versus autonomy. Coaching appears to be gaining in popularity in the counseling profession and with astrologers. Coaches will guide, mold, and steer a client in a certain pre-established direction. Clients are subtlety encouraged to maintain a respectful dependency toward the coach, put trust in him or her, and not challenge their authority. The client may indeed increase in a particular skill but is not likely to experience much in-depth growth.

Reassurance versus tentativeness is the sixth intervention. When an astrologer reassures a client that everything will be alright, he or she is overstepping the boundaries. One simply cannot know the outcome of events with certainty and may be planting unnecessary anxiety or false hope in the client. More in order would be a realistic appraisal of the situation and a supportive stance toward tentativeness of outcome. Helping a client to increase his ability to stand in the uncertainties of life is a move toward growth. Let me paraphrase a Chinese story I heard from Alan Watts (circa 1970) that illustrates this well. Once there was an old farmer with two horses to work his farm. One day one of the horses ran off, not to return. Several of the farmer's neighbors gathered round him to offer comfort and condolences for his bad luck. The farmer offered his thanks to his neighbors and said, "We'll see, we'll see." Two days later, his horse returns and brings with it three wild horses from the outlands. His neighbors return to offer him congratulations for his good fortune for now he owned five horses. He replies, "We'll see, we'll see." The next day as the farmer's son is attempting to break one of the wild horses so that it is rideable, he falls from the horse and breaks his leg. The neighbors come round to see if they can help and to commiserate with the old farmer for this bitter stroke of fortune. With a twinkle in his eye, he says, "We'll see, we'll see." The next day government officials come round the village seeking young men to be conscripted into the army to fight but alas the farmer's son is of no value to them with his injury. The neighbors once again come around to congratulate the old farmer on this bit of good news. I believe the reader knows how the farmer responds. The story could go on but I think the point is made. The farmer lives comfortably with a tentative attitude toward matters, what the poet John Keats termed, "Negative Capability," described as the ability to live in uncertainties, doubts, and mysteries without any irritable reaching after the fact and reason. This is also an attitude that exemplifies faith in the doings of life, an attitude where one does not complain about the hand one's dealt, feeling cheated, and wishing for a better hand, but plays the only hand he or she has to the best of their ability.

Lastly, in external conformity versus inner discovery, when the astrologer helps clients achieve some external standard, social criterion, or pre-agreed goal, the process is tightened to a degree that novelty, spontaneity, and new directions may not arise.

This cuts clients off from their own creativity and short circuits the imaginative process where they may discover new insights about themselves. When this happens clients are cheated of the opportunity for enhancing self-awareness. Dharma is a Sanskrit word which has as one of its meanings, sacred duty. When we can help clients discover their sacred duty, their inner law, their path, then from where I sit, that effort is right livelihood as the Buddhists say, and fosters growth and development in both astrologer and client.

The following is a brief reconstructed session illustrating one among several ways of working with clients where questions predominate more than answers and the client is continually thrown back upon his own resources. The client is a 29 year old single man who complains of numerous short-lived (less than a year) relationships. He is a handsome man and presents in a likeable manner. He doesn't know why he has been unable to sustain a long term relationship. He states that he would like to settle down with a wife and family. He was raised as an only child by adoptive parents. He is somewhat familiar with astrology and is interested in finding out if his chart will offer some opportunities for insight into his situation.

Since the focus of the session is on the relationship issue, attention is paid to Venus in the chart in conjunction with the Moon and Neptune, all within 8 degrees of one another. One hypothesis I draw about this client is that he has a very unformed and romanticized image of relationship. There is a strong element of glamour and idealism in his meeting with women that apparently diffuses and dissolves over time. When this occurs the bloom fades from the rose and he desires to move on to a new attraction. A deeper fantasy envisioned is that there may be a fear of abandonment (Neptune) related to his early mothering (Moon) experience. The client may unconsciously initiate the end of these relationships in order to leave them before they leave him and thus avoid the painful feelings of abandonment, replaying a possible childhood scenario.

Astrologer (A): I understand that you know a little bit about astrology. Here is a copy of your chart. Can you give me a sense of what you see?

Client (C): Uh huh, let's see. I see the symbol for Mars on the Western horizon and I've got these planets up here, one of them's the Moon, at the top of the chart.

A: You're right. There's the Moon and Venus and Neptune. Venus and the Moon reflect a lot about how we relate to others. Venus images our capacity for relationship, our interpersonal desires. The Moon reflects our capacity for nurturing and being nurtured, the way we might respond to those in need and our own experience of being mothered. Neptune has to do with the way things dissolve and melt away. There is a kind of foggy, confusing quality about it. It also has to do with some of our deepest unformed yearnings.

C: Confusing, that's certainly the way I feel about relationships right now.

A: Would you tell me more about that?

C: It seems that every time I get involved with a woman, we'll date for some time, you know even go together for a while, then 'spffftt', something changes, then it's over.

A: What's the 'spffftt'?

C: I don't know, it's like it's just not gonna work out.

A: Who ends the relationship?

C: Sometimes it's me, mostly me, sometimes it's them. It just seems the energy goes out of the relationship.

A: One of the fantasies that I have about this is that whenever we mix that Neptunian part of ourselves; that part that is fond of glamour, illusion, and bliss, with the lunar mothering part, and our Venusian relating part, it can suggest a particular desire to find a woman who can answer our every need, a woman who is both the perfect lover and the perfect compassionate caregiver. In some ways, she can be a savior for us. The difficulty of course is that real women, flesh and blood women, can never measure up to these fantasies of this great goddess.

C: I often feel like I've really been fooled by a woman or maybe I'm deluding myself with my expectations.

A: Can you build on that for me a little?

C: Sometimes it's hard to figure out whether it's her or me, that's all. I meet these really great women, we date, it's very romantic. I like flowers and dinners, small gifts, tokens of affection, but after a while it fizzles. I start seeing things in them that put me off.

A: For instance?

C: They'll say really stupid things or they come from these horrible families. I don't know, it just bugs me.

A: I'm wondering, are you dreaming the impossible dream here, trying to attain that which cannot be attained?

C: I just have this nagging feeling that there is a woman out there for me. When we meet, I'll know it.

A: If I understand correctly, you've had this "when we meet, I'll know it" experience with several of these relationships already?

C: Ah, yeah but….

A: So you haven't been able to know it?

C: Ah, yeah but it's different.

A: How is it different?

C: I don't know, it just is.

A: Listen, on one hand you say that you want to settle down, start a family. On the other, you've got a history of numerous unsatisfying relationships. Is it possible that the issue of commitment is related to this search? To accept a less than perfect relationship restricts you from being available for that damsel in distress around the next turn, down the bend, or over the hill where the goddess awaits.

C: You know I feel that way sometimes. I just really want to find Her. I've got this "someday she'll come along, and I'll be ready" attitude.

A: What does it mean to be a knight in the service of a Queen who never arrives?

C: It means an unsatisfying life.

A: Go on.

C: It means it's difficult to be deeply involved with someone while I'm distracted by this longing for Her. It means sacrifice. It means f***ing frustration, man!

A: I wonder if you could own that frustration, say 'I' rather than 'it'?

C: I'm f***ing frustrated.

A: Uh huh, the errant, solitary knight seeking the grail.

Notice that the majority of the interventions by the astrologer are questions. Also note that the session is characterized by dialogue replacing the traditional unidirectional performance of the astrologer telling the client about themselves.

In closing, a worthy astrologer has to constantly address the ethical dilemma of helping people grow versus allowing a dependency to establish itself within a client who becomes fearful without the astrologer's guidance. This dependency could be upon the astrologer, upon astrology, upon fate, upon anything that literalizes the idea that something outside of themselves comes to their rescue. The astrologer then becomes indispensable to them thus assuring the astrologer's continuing livelihood. In contrast, I want to work myself out of a job and hopefully get referrals for new clients from previous satisfied clients. I would hope that clients would be interested in increasing their interdependence and autonomy while seeking to experience a modicum of growth.

The orientation which I favor is that astrology is best used not for providing answers to client's problems but rather to generate questions by which clients are provoked to seek out their own answers which may come in the form of more questions, in other words, a quest by which they may discover the shores of their own uncharted territories. A quote from the poet Rilke that I frequently use is from *Letters to a Young Poet*. I believe it to be indispensable to therapeutic work.

"... I would like to beg you dear Sir.... To have patience with everything unresolved in your heart and to try to love the questions themselves as if they were locked rooms or books written in a very foreign language. Don't search for the answers which could not be given to you now, because you would not be able to live them. And the point is to live everything. Live the questions now. Perhaps then, someday far in the future, you will gradually, without even noticing it, live your way into the answer."

Our question resounds for us at the end of this excursion as it did in the beginning; do we give our clients a fish and feed them for a day or do we teach them how to fish and feed them for a lifetime? The choice is ours.

6

Astrology and Grief

Astrology and grief; we cannot speak about grief without speaking about loss and we cannot reference loss without raising the specter of Death, one of the deep mysteries in Life. Death despite the suffering that accompanies it discloses four distinct givens in Life.

The first is, the nature of the world is impermanence, everything is here for a while, then it departs. This transiency brings value to our experience allowing us to recognize the preciousness of people, things, and events; we realize how fragile and ephemeral life is.

Second, plans go awry. Regardless of our intention or desire, life has other designs. This interruption and seeming errancy brings the possibility of discovering the new and the novel that may lead us down an entirely different path or push us in a much needed new direction.

Third, life isn't fair, children become ill and die, the innocent are harmed, disaster occurs. When unfairness makes its appearance, we can learn the dead end of anger, blame, and retribution and try instead, justice-seeking, restoration, and commitment to a new strategy.

Fourth, pain is a part of life. So many people believe that pleasure is to be regarded as a reward for doing well and that pain is a punishment for the commission of some wrong. We unnecessarily moralize our existence instead of acknowledging that pain and pleasure are simply features in the human landscape.

It is also important to recognize that death does not so much stand in opposition to life as it stands as a complement to birth. Birthing and dying are contained within the category we call Life in the same manner that exhalation and inhalation comprise the breath, as yin and yang comprise a single totality.

Despite the seeming opposition of birthing and dying, they are intimately entwined in such a way as to be inseparable. They are essentially two sides of the same coin of existence.

Loss stands against gain in the same manner as dying does birthing. We cannot have one without the other and yet we live in a culture that educates its members in the work of accumulation (2nd house) with nary a word given about loss, losing, and letting go; in fact, in many ways this is a taboo arena (8th house). Let me collect and hoard my toys, clothes, cars, houses, and assets, but there is great difficulty when these attachments are severed and I am forced to let go. It is at these turning points of loss that grief arises.

Grief can be regarded as the normal and expected response to a significant loss, whether it's the death of a loved one, the end of a career, the decline of vitality, the sudden demise of status, the slipping away of youth, or the loss of a cherished way of life.

There are several styles of grieving: normal grief, complicated grief, delayed grief, anticipatory grief, and distorted grief. There are several tasks that need to be accomplished to complete our grieving and this process may last anywhere from several weeks to several years.

Some people embrace Kubler-Ross' stages of dying which were later transposed by her to stages of grieving that include denial, anger, bargaining, depression, and acceptance. My own preference is for William Worden's model of the tasks of grieving. These have more of an action orientation helping to empower the bereaved.

The reason this is important is because we do not have grief, rather grief has us, and we are in its maw. The tasks include (1) accepting the reality of the loss, (2) experiencing the pain of grief, (3) adjusting to the environment in which the cherished object is absent, and (4) withdrawing emotional energy from the loss and reinvesting it in other relationships.

Last, there is no timetable for grieving; everyone will grieve in their own way. Grief is the price of attachment.

Now in astrology, what planets do we typically associate with grief, loss, and death?

Saturn: traditionally the grim reaper, reflects the contraction of reality so densely that the presence of the absence is a palpable reality expressing crystal clarity. The loss is real. Despondent, brittle, and heavy hearted, paralyzed, fixated upon loss, stuck or frozen in grief.

Uranus: echoes the shattering of the assumptive world, upsets reliable routine, overturns the status quo, shocks us to numbness, and fractures comfort zones leading to breakdown or breakthrough not unlike the biblical Job or the Bhagavad Gita's Arjuna.

Neptune: the erosive solvent, dissolves the very rock upon which lives are built, pulls the rug out from under us, glamours a confusion, slips us a mickey, then casts us adrift in a rudderless craft similar to the tale of Tristan.

Pluto: one of his Roman names was Dis and this god of the underworld will dissever, disrupt, disable, dishearten, distress, dismantle, dispirit, and dismember a life as reflected in the stories of the Greek Persephone and the Mesopotamian Inanna.

It is my opinion that when significant loss occurs in a person's life that we round up the usual suspects. I can generally find a complex of transit activity reflecting this. This is however, anecdotal and not research. Many astrologers believe that transits are more likely to mirror events in life than progressions or solar arcs. I don't know if this is accurate but I suspect that current conditions in a life are likely layered throughout all of these methods if our lives are a reliably holistic affair.

But before we even consider transits, it seems important to examine the natal chart to gather a sense of how an individual might respond to loss. There may be numerous indicators of attitudes toward loss in the chart depending on the creative imagination of the astrologer. Let's look at several.

Let us imagine a dominant element in the chart. Dominant fire might respond to loss with bravado, action, finding meaning, and desiring moving on. Earth may respond by digging in, resisting, being pragmatic, and useful. Air could intellectualize, rationalize, socialize or detach. And water perhaps responds with depth of feeling, seeking solitude, or escape.

With the modalities we might expect Cardinal to respond with action, wanting to meet the challenge and be proactive. Fixed could likely make an effort to maintain and preserve the status quo. There is a possibility of difficulty letting go. And Mutable may discover built in resiliency, adaptation, or conversely, may engage avoidant behaviors.

Perhaps even more importantly, however, may be the **Moon**; our capacity to respond to immediate and changing circumstances (Rudhyar's image). The Moon is how we nurture ourselves, how we self soothe, comfort, and protect. It is our recoil response. It may reflect much of how we respond to loss in our lives.

When the Moon is in a particular sign or in natal aspect to that sign's agent we might see the following:

With the Moon in fiery Aries or in natal aspect to Mars, it wants to do something, anything, take action, act out, break something, rage, scream, start an argument, pick a fight, exercise, compete and contest.

With the Moon in radiant Leo or in natal aspect to the Sun, the Moon may offer some false bravado, seeing the loss as part of a larger drama, behave royally and appropriately, that which is consistent with self-image, as its feeling is closely tied to its sense of identity. This loss may feel like a blow to a fragile ego, a narcissistic wounding.

With the Moon in expansive Sagittarius or in natal aspect to Jupiter, we may see it trying to avoid pain by seeking how to regard the loss philosophically, as being all for the best, the deceased is in a better place, the loss is an opportunity for growth, responding optimistically that it can get through this.

With the Moon in earthy Taurus or in natal aspect to Venus, the Moon may wish to resist the reality of the loss, dig in, stonewall it, maybe indulge the senses through sexual activity, overeating, shopping sprees, getting tattooed or piercings, self-mutilation, physical stimulation of some sort.

With the Moon in pragmatic Virgo or in natal aspect to Mercury, it may be looking to be of help, for something useful to do, may engage in ritualized and repetitive tasks of straightening and cleaning behaviors, wanting to make things better, or invite guilt.

With the Moon in well-formed Capricorn or in natal aspect to Saturn, the Moon may wish to manage the moment, take charge, suppress feelings and accomplish tasks, present the stiff upper lip, emotional coolness, stoic affect, and controlling behaviors and situations similar to the Mary Tyler Moore character in the film, *Ordinary People.*

With the Moon in the airy Gemini or in natal aspect to Mercury, it may move directly into the head converting feelings into aimless talking, restlessness, unfocused behaviors, may go out and buy books on grief and approach it in that manner.

With the Moon in well-spaced Libra or in natal aspect to Venus, there may be seeking increased support from its social network, reliance on interpersonal relations to help, behave appropriately and with grace, smooth over its own and others discomforts, also a tendency to intellectualize the feelings to avoid the harshness and unpleasantness of the situation.

With the Moon in heady Aquarius or in natal aspect to Uranus, it may rush to remove itself, to dissociate and withdraw from its feelings appearing aloof and detached, even out of touch with feelings. Internally there is likely a stunning numbness in place to keep from being overwhelmed by the loss.

With the Moon in watery Cancer there is feeling, emoting, moodiness, or collapsing, and wanting to be taken care of, coddled, cuddled, comforted, may seek relief in memories or may in turn, nurture others, feed others, accept others.

With the Moon in the well of Scorpio or in natal aspect to Pluto, it will experience the loss intensely but may not disclose it, controlling its public display so as not to show vulnerability, and it may either fear its feeling or sink wholeheartedly into loss, probing it, feeling it all, strengthening its character, establishing its integrity.

With the Moon in oceanic Pisces or in natal aspect to Neptune, the Moon may fall apart, sensitive to the pain everyone is experiencing, moving from the particular loss to the universal; all its losses gather around this specific loss, ghosts gather to be present. This combination could seek solace in solitude and escape to altered states; prayer, meditation, alcohol/drugs, film, fantasy, romanticizing or idealizing the loss.

We might also want to pay attention to the 2nd/8th axis. The signs on the cusps and the aspects between the house significators and any planets therein reflect our orientation toward attachment and accumulation, our attitude around safety and security concerns, our holding on to that which we value. The 8th house is of course connected with letting go, loss, death, merging, regeneration and transformation. Transiting planets in the 8th or 2nd conjunct and opposing natal placements can be very telling of the period.

Some astrologers will also want to look at the 4th and 12th houses, their significators and any planets domiciled there.

The experience of grief may be reflected in a variety of ways in the chart through the mirror of the outer planets – Saturn through Pluto transiting with challenging aspects to the personal planets. Now consider the outer planets in transit that we mentioned earlier. Can we predict the arrival of grief and then its disappearance via astrology? I can't.

The Sun, when receiving a Saturn transit, can reflect reduced vitality, feelings of unworthiness, inadequacy, and fearfulness, with Uranus, a sense of being agitated, unstable, breaking down. Neptune can image a lack of direction, apathy, vulnerability, easily fatigued, and Pluto can mirror a period of experiencing powerlessness, avolition, dismantled confidence, the feeling of being torn apart, self-destructive, or possession by grief.

When the Moon is under duress from outer transits, Saturn may be reflected in feelings of sadness, depression, stuckness, or being frozen, with Uranus, perhaps stunned and anxious, Neptune, feelings of being adrift, unmoored, and disoriented, or with Pluto, feeling nothing at all as if the emotional life was abducted and plundered. There may also be a variety of somatic complaints.

When Mercury is distressed by Saturn, it can resonate with thinking that is narrowed, focused, thoughts about the world contracted, slowed down, minimal, or with Uranus, tangential, scattered, fragmented and racing thoughts, Neptune, unfocused, magical, dreamy, fantasy filled, or at worst, a psychotic break, with Pluto, dark, evil, erotic, or morbid thinking.

When it's Venus, Saturn can image the experience of anhedonia, wanting to be alone, values may seem constricting, relations restrained, Uranus, relational activities can take on an erratic, unreliable quality, pulling away from others, or becoming promiscuous, with Neptune, desire to be absorbed by others or engage in self-deception or idealization of relationship, yearning to join the deceased, and Pluto, perhaps giving in to death or seeking sexual outlets to feel alive.

With Mars, Saturn in challenging aspect may echo a lack motivation to act or do, diminished libido, in contrast Uranus feels electrified, freaking out, behaving unpredictably, completely out of character, experiencing muscle tension. Neptune, there can be the inclination toward sedatives, alcohol, and sleep aids, suppressed immunity, and Pluto; angry, upset, combative, urge for destruction of self or other, punching walls, punching others.

With Jupiter, transits by Saturn may mirror faith and hope being conceived as inadequate, faulty, and meaningless. With Uranus, beliefs breaking apart, shattering, becoming bizarre, called into question, and with Neptune, hope can be slipping away, dissolving, seen as unrealistic, or delusional. With Pluto, life can be denuded of meaning and easily annihilated by the power of death.

How might we go about working with grieving clients? Despite Gunzburg's assertion in her excellent book, *Life After Grief* that what astrology does best for the bereaved is to give a clear understanding of the future and shift their understanding into a bigger picture of their life, I have to agree with what I heard Rabbi Harold Kushner say. He believes the bereaved are not looking for explanation or understanding but consolation and caring. You can help more by listening than by trying to explain.

Now I suspect that there are astrologers who can do both well, but as I don't predict, I focus upon caring and consoling, helping the client to move through the grieving process. I want to be careful to not short circuit the grief but foster it, nurture it along, and work with its unfolding. I don't want to offer well intended platitudes or information. Stating for instance that "everything is going to be ok," "just give it time," "don't feel bad," "they're in a better place," "God never gives you more than you can handle," "life goes on," or the 'transits indicate that you'll be feeling better at such and such a time," or "perhaps you can see this loss as a growth opportunity," are not all that helpful. There is little you can say that will be received as helpful to the newly bereaved. Sometimes it's simply, "I'm sorry." It's such an awkward moment to be with the client in grief. Sometimes the most we can offer are our tears.

When meeting with a grieving client it's important to consider the following guidelines for engagement.

- Be present.

- Don't let your overall needs determine the session.

- Don't let your own sense of helplessness get in the way of reaching out to the client.

- Give the client permission to grieve (willingness to contain).

- Be careful to not deny their feelings.

- Be aware of your posture and comments; don't take the focus from the client and the legitimacy of their stance (don't pull away, don't change subject, don't ask them not to emote).

- Remember that you cannot talk away their grief.

- If their wound is too fresh, much of your responding may simply be listening, encouraging them to talk.

- Try to get some sense of their view of the loss.

- Ask them to speak of what this loss means to them, of other losses or the earliest loss they can remember.

- In the end, seed some hope.

- Refer to a mental health professional or grief or pastoral counselor or support group if it is beyond your skill level.

There are some common signs that grieving may be unfinished:

- If the client is unable or unwilling to discuss the loss.

- If in recalling fond memories, it turns painful.

- If the client is only able to speak of the person in a positive light or conversely, in a negative light.

- If the client experiences strong discomfort or fear in thinking about the loss.

In his book, *Essays on Psychological Astrology*, therapist/astrologer, Glenn Perry has written about the Moon as our listening response and I believe this is helpful stance. Though our natural style of listening to others may be mirrored by the Moon in our chart, we may be called when interacting with grieving clients to offer a more cautious response matched to our client. The simple awareness of our own style of listening can help us adapt our response to a more helpful intervention if necessary.

- Aries listens with an ear toward encouraging the client to act in their own self-interest.

- Taurus listens with an ear toward remaining calm and serene giving the impression of one who is reliable and safe, one who is solid and can hold the feelings.

- Gemini listens with an ear toward offering helpful information about loss to the client.

- Cancer listens with a sensitive ear toward being a container for all the emotive power of the bereaved.

- Leo listens with an ear toward affirming and validating the client's pain, giving them permission to grieve.

- Virgo listens with a critical ear toward identifying methods and techniques for helping the bereaved improve their working through their grief. They ask, "How can I help make their grieving process more useful?"

- Libra listens with an ear toward wanting to lighten the client's burden, making matters less unpleasant if possible, restoring some balance.

- Scorpio listens with an ear toward embracing the depths of the suffering and is willing to join them in their pain.

- Sagittarius listens with an ear toward placing the loss in the context of a larger framework.

- Capricorn listens with an ear toward offering workable suggestions for managing the pain of the client.

- Aquarius listens objectively in a nonjudgmental manner with an ear toward recognizing and accepting the uniqueness of the client's response to loss.

- Pisces listens with a receptive ear toward empathizing and expressing compassion to the bereaved.

In conclusion, how can we recognize when the person is moving well through their grieving process? When the person is able to think about and talk about the loss without wrenching pain. The person finds a place for the absence in their life and recognizes it's time to move on, yet never forgetting what it is they have lost. There can be continuing bonds. There may still be periods of sadness and bittersweet recollection, but it lacks the disabling quality of the fresh loss.

7

Parenting and Astrology

I'm certainly not an expert on parenting but I am a parent and I do have a few things to offer and lots of questions. Some of what I say may be controversial and some ideas with which you might disagree. I hope what I have to say will be thought-provoking, stimulating, and not immediately rejected.

I've spent three decades working in prison mental health and over those years people have asked me how we can reduce criminal behavior in our society. I offer two words, "Better parenting." What does this phrase mean, and can astrology be of any help in the matter?

Parents quite naturally in the Western world seem worried about parenting, about getting it right. We all turned to the experts, especially Dr. Benjamin Spock, pediatrician and social activist who was probably the most well-known of the childcare experts at the time. He influenced several generations of parents. His book, *Baby and Child Care* is still in print, has been through ten editions, translated into more than 40 languages, and sold over fifty million copies. He urged parents to trust their instincts, use common sense, and practice a gentler approach. When we see his chart (time in question) below, do we see a permissive, relaxed style of parenting message imaged here or a restrictive, controlling one?

Assuming the time to be near correct, I believe that an Aquarius (progressive) Ascendant, Uranus (liberating) in the 10th, Neptune and Moon in Cancer in the 5th (compassionate care giving) are a

Parenting and Astrology

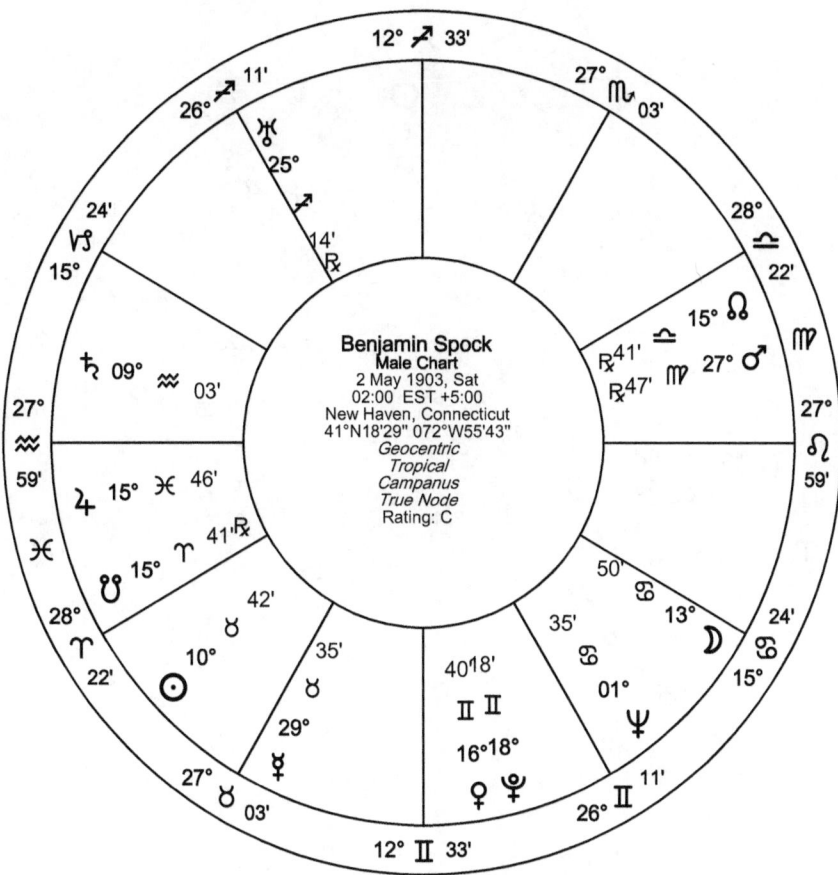

good reflection of his permissive and liberal philosophy of child rearing.

A newer kid on the block of parenting since the mid-90s is a pediatrician named Bill Sears who has become a figurehead for the attachment parenting movement. In 2012, he gained greater national attention when *Time* magazine (May 21, 2012) put a mother breast feeding her three-year-old son on the cover. The title of the article was "The Man Who Remade Motherhood." Its most populist and well-known precepts are - extended breast feeding, co-sleeping, and baby wearing. The major premise is the more time a child can spend with the mother, the better adjusted and happy it will grow

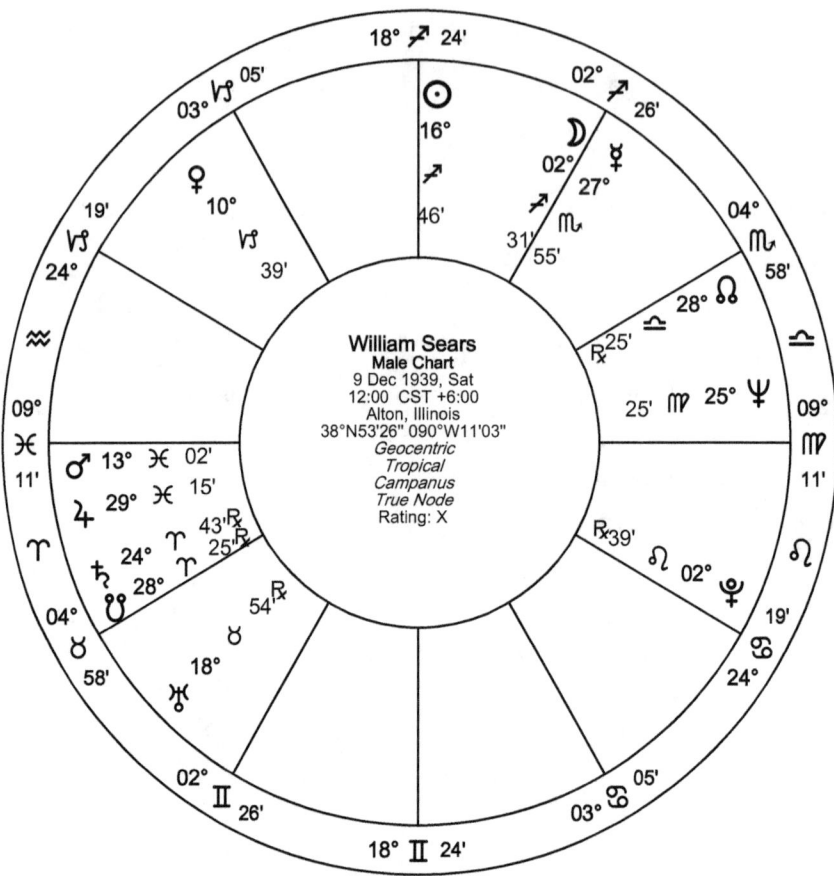

to be. This approach has come under fire from many quarters not the least of which are the sacrifices the parents must make to ensure the child gets enough attention. There are worries that parents will become way over-stressed attending to every mood and display of the child and that children will become overly dependent on external nurturing.

I don't have the doctor's birth time but even without it we can see a grand trine in water with the Pluto, Jupiter, and the Moon suggesting a somewhat taboo and revolutionary philosophy about mothering involving a continuous and ongoing merged state of child and mother.

Linguist and cognitive scientist, George Lakoff, cites the longitudinal research that's been done on how it is people flourish. Researchers looked at four kinds of families to determine what kind of family environment is most effective at helping its constituent members flourish so that the children grow to function successfully in both the personal and societal realms. These four kinds of families identified by psychologist, Diana Baumrind in the 1960s are the strict-father authoritarian family, the authoritative family, the permissive family, and the uninvolved or neglectful family. This gives us four parenting styles.

Authoritarian parenting, in which children are expected to follow the strict rules established by the parents. Failure to follow such rules usually results in punishment. Authoritarian parents fail to explain the reasoning behind these rules. If asked to explain, the parent might simply reply, "Because I said so." These parents have high demands but are not responsive to their children. According to Baumrind, these parents "are obedience- and status-oriented and expect their orders to be obeyed without explanation." This sounds thick with Saturn's style.

Authoritative parenting is a style that has a good balance of Saturn/Moon. Like authoritarian parents, those with an authoritative parenting style establish rules and guidelines that their children are expected to follow. However, this parenting style is much more democratic. Authoritative parents are responsive to their children and willing to listen to questions. When children fail to meet the expectations, these parents are more nurturing and forgiving rather than punishing. Baumrind suggests that these parents "monitor and impart clear standards for their children's conduct. They are assertive, but not intrusive and restrictive. Their disciplinary methods are supportive, rather than punitive. They want their children to be assertive as well as socially responsible, and self-regulated as well as cooperative."

Permissive parenting is more lunar in its style than Saturn. These parents are sometimes referred to as indulgent parents and as such have very few demands to make of their children. These parents rarely discipline their children because they have relatively low expectations of maturity and self-control. According to Baumrind, permissive parents "are more responsive than they are demanding. They are nontraditional and lenient, do not require mature behavior from their children, allow considerable self-regulation, and avoid confrontation." Permissive parents are generally nurturing and communicative with their children, often taking on the status of a friend more than that of a parent.

An **uninvolved** parenting style is low Moon/low Saturn and more reflective of Uranus. This style is characterized by few demands, low responsiveness and little communication. While these parents fulfill the child's basic needs, they are generally detached from their child's life. In extreme cases, these parents may even reject or neglect the needs of their children.

The authoritative, the permissive, the authoritarian, and the neglectful are ordered here in terms of the effectiveness in raising children who flourish in later life. This sort of data which seems like common sense can certainly serve as a broad guideline for successful parenting, much like for aging in a healthy fashion, people would do well to quit smoking, eat better, and get regular exercise. These kinds of statements, whether about health or parenting, are derived from research that looks at groups of people and derives statistical recommendations for improving the particular area being studied. As astrologers, however, we should all pause when we hear these kinds of guidelines, for in them we have traded personal destiny for statistical probability.

Statistical probability means that all things being relatively equal (no significant variables) that such and such is likely to be the case if you are part of a larger group with similar characteristics. That everyone who purchases a ticket has a roughly equal chance of winning this week's lottery though great the odds may be. This kind of thinking runs counter to astrology where each person has a unique and specific framework of destiny within which to construct a self-narrative.

If we as astrologers truly see the chart as intimately linked to the individual, then despite the broad recommendations for raising healthy children we should not lose sight of this astrological image reflecting a uniqueness of the person who stands before us. Now I'm not suggesting that we throw the baby out with the bathwater and ignore parenting and health research. That would simply be silly. In fact, we should hone our critical thinking skills around reading research and also in examining astrological claims; we can train ourselves to look carefully and deeply into such matters.

My own stance toward the raising of my own children was that children should be unfolded not molded. But will this stance work for everyone's children in all families under all sorts of socioeconomic conditions and backgrounds? Additionally, there are questions such as how do we know if we have been or are being successful parents? By what criteria can this be measured? And when does it stop? Are we successful parents if our children graduate high school, college, no criminal record, have a good job, no health problems, no divorces? When our children conform to the cultural myth of marriage and family; settled with 2.5 children, a house, and two cars, a dog or cat; are we successful parents then?

What are the standards of successful parenting? Often, I think the strategy many of us employ as parents is similar to the person lost at sea in a lifeboat, who begins with a prayer for rescue and then rows like hell. Although the structure of a chart remains a constant, the content of a life will change and develop throughout a life. Children are resilient; they are not simply reducible to their childhoods.

As we might expect, it's not uncommon to find sex offenders in prison who were themselves sexually abused as children. Additionally, however, there are a huge number of people who were sexually abused as children who have never repeated the behavior as adults. Can we tell this by the chart?

There are people who are raised in poverty and continue to live in poverty and create welfare generations. And there are also people raised in poverty that have climbed their way out and moved far beyond their impoverished circumstances. Is this discernible in their chart?

There are people from families where severe alcoholism existed who grow to experience alcohol problems themselves as adults. And there are people who have surmounted substance abuse environments and problems and have no difficulties in that arena or who work to heal others with these histories. Can the chart reveal this?

People are deep mysteries, Life is mystery. For the religious, God is Mystery. I taught a spirituality and mental health class in prison and one of the things we take note of is that there are times in our lives when we feel the rug has been pulled from under us, that our very foundations are shaking. And many turn to God for help only to discover what? That it is God, Fate, Life, soul, their guardian angel who is shaking their foundations, whispering, "Wake up."

Problem-free childhoods are a fantasy that all parents may desire stemming from a deep wish to protect our children from the vicissitudes of living. By shifting our imagining of childhood however and recognizing their charts are perfect as they are, we may have less need to interfere. We discover that difficulties may be necessities to spark genius, to let the creative daimon loose, to move our child toward its destiny.

Parenting is a mystery. Parenting is a spiritual challenge. Psychologist, Jon Kabat-Zinn writes in *Everyday Blessings*, "As [our children] grow, they seem to challenge every place that we might be holding an expectation, a fixed opinion, a cherished belief, a desire for things to be a certain way."

There is a book titled *Cradles of Eminence* by Victor and Mildred Goertzel. It's a book of several hundred brief biographies of people who have attained and accomplished enough in life as to be considered by the public to be eminent figures. The authors draw from areas of literature, art, politics, science, athletics, business, and religion. It is interesting because many if not most of the people had childhoods few would consider ideal, healthy, or normal. Many of the lives are filled with fractured families, broken homes, rejecting and overcritical parents, foster placements, juvenile delinquency, poor school performance, substance abuse problems, health conditions, etc.

In the opening pages of Goertzel's sequel, *Three Hundred Eminent Personalities*, we read, "Normalcy would be nothing less than an obstacle to the person who is driven to make his or her mark upon the world." If anything, deviation from the norm is more apparent than normalcy. Many of the eminent people who were examples were often criticized for being "too intense, too driven, too creative, too sensitive, too different, too nontraditional, and too self-absorbed."

We're not talking about trines here; we'd be expecting to find the growth inducing aspects, squares, quincunxes, and oppositions prominent in the charts along with some supportive aspects. These challenging patterns may reflect a consuming need, a calling, an archetypal passion. Goertzel writes, "If a child lacks this thorn in the side, this drive to triumph in some field, what should parents do? Probably count their blessings. There is no evidence that famous people are happier than people who take a more balanced approach to life." It would appear that our children's charts as mirrors of their unfolding lives are neither good nor bad, nor any guarantee of success or happiness.

So, there are underlying questions: why do we want astrology to be involved with parenting? What purpose do we have in mind in using astrology? Are we using astrology to calm our own anxieties about parenting, to settle our own discomfort? Are we using astrology out of fear and expressing a lack of faith in our child's developmental destiny?

Do we want to help them sidestep what may be painful experiences as imaged by challenging aspects that can be necessary to the flowering of their particular genius?

In current psychological thinking, the question of how much we emerge with at birth and how much is shaped by our environment, the ratio, I believe, is 60/40 respectively. Again Kabat-Zinn writes, "As every parent knows or soon finds out, each child comes into this world with his or her own attributes, temperament and genius. As parents, we are called to recognize who each one of them uniquely is, and to honor them by making room for them as they are, not by trying to change them, hard as that sometimes is for us."

This is where I believe astrology can be a tool to deepen our experience of discovering who our child is. And we might find astrology at odds with the cultural *zeitgeist*. As a nation, the United

States seems engaged in a great effort to establish evidence-based and best practice standards toward a homogenous model of child rearing and education. We seem to want uniform standards, no children left behind, everything reduced to the lowest common denominator so that it is inclusive of everyone.

When briefly surveying the astrological literature, there hasn't been a lot written on astrology and parenting that I located. We have the wonderfully articulate and pragmatic *Growing Pains* by Alex Trenoweth and Gloria Star's text, *Optimum Child*. Also, an older text, *Astrological Insights into Personality* by Betty Lundsted is an interesting work. Gretchen Lawlor has written some excellent articles on the topic, as has Donna Cunningham about parent/child relations. A non-astrological text that I imagine many readers know is James Hillman's, *The Soul's Code* in which he discusses the acorn theory of human development in which our task is to grow down into life, becoming substantially who we are at birth, the seed of that particular moment, an image of cosmos.

Is it possible to consider parenting as a spiritual path, a sacred charge? We've been entrusted with a small portion of the sky, to create a space, a vessel, an alchemical alembic if you will, within which development and transformation may occur for the child. As parents we have a responsibility to tend to this small divinity. If we can provide a safe container, contribute the right seasonings, perform the necessary heating and cooling, tempering the process, then we are engaged in fostering this child's unfolding and ripening. Children in turn, reawaken us to our playfulness, our innocence, our spontaneity, our creativity, our need for validation, and to much of our own unfinished childhood material.

Now of course, parenting is easier said than done. When I mentioned the topic of astrology and parenting to an astrologer friend of mine, she wrote, "One of the hardest things about being a parent is that your child has a chart!" Fear, dread, catastrophe, oh my! When we know our child's chart we can easily imagine the most horrid situations that may befall our children and we might torture ourselves relentlessly with pathological imaging.

Has it been noted that in the history of imagining heaven and hell that the wealth of imagery for hell is just so amazingly creative and wonderfully elaborated, albeit grotesque and perverse? Think of Bosch's "Garden of Earthly Delights." Layers upon layers of suffering, pain, ugliness, deformities, perversions, bizarre creatures, and behaviors, while our images of heaven tend to be rather staid and boring with multitudes standing around the throne of God in adoration and chorus or we envision a kind of puttering around in the clouds or some other sterile environment.

It is so much easier then for us to fantasize about terrible things happening to our children rather than wonderful things. We hear media stories from around the world that may shape the way we shepherd our child. How much more so for the astrologer parent who catastrophizes every hard outer planet transit? Know your child's chart but look at it only after the fact of lived experience. As astrologer parents we can take some solace that when our child's life seems troubled or problematic that rather than blaming ourselves for poor parenting, look to their daimon, soul, genius, angel, fate, or however you conceive this paradoxical inner other which is also intimately us. It may have other claims upon them, other plans that need unfolding. In *The Secret Tradition of the Soul*, Patrick Harpur writes, "It is a constant task to look for the angel in our children's errancy, and not be too quick to medicate, subdue, or hammer them into line."

I also encourage astrologers to not engage in forecasting with children's charts especially if the parents are imaginative and prone to anxiousness. Look at transits, progressions, or returns only

Parenting and Astrology

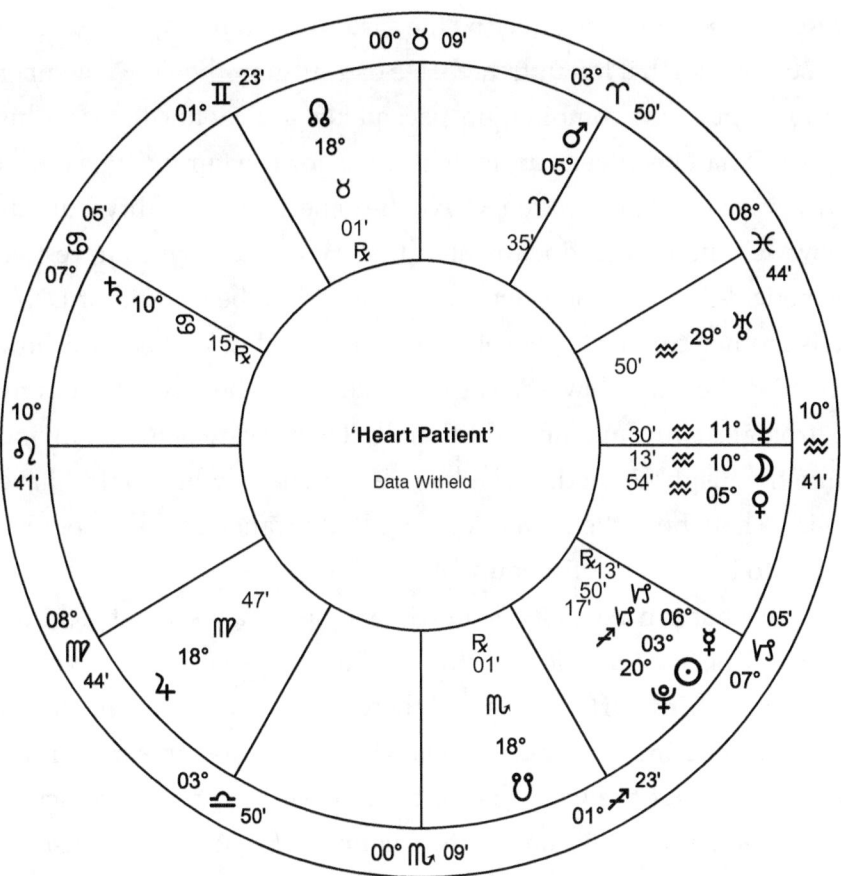

in the context of the transpiring moment to help create meaning and deepen our experience of the present. As I have often said, astrology discloses to us that even though matters may feel out of our control, they are not out of control. There are larger guiding factors at play.

Above is a child born in 2003 (private data). He has Leo rising with the Sun in Capricorn, take note where Pluto is. In October 2009 when Pluto had just entered Capricorn, he complained that his chest hurt. As the months wore on, he was subjected to a number of tests, then in July 2010 with Pluto retro over his Sun and squaring natal Mars, he was given the diagnosis of an extremely rare genetic condition affecting the cardiovascular system resulting in sudden death if left untreated. He had surgery then in September 2010 to put in a combination pacemaker and defibrillator in his chest. It had been very difficult at times for the family. It has been discovered that both parents have the genetic abnormality, but this boy was the first in documented history at the time to have two genetic defects on the same sodium ion chamber strand of DNA. His mother creatively consoled herself by realizing therefore, how priceless he was. Now, she was not a client so she did not seek any astrological information. Additionally, I was aware of Pluto moving into the neighborhood. If she had been a client, what could I have said to her about the then upcoming Pluto transit at the time? He grew to be a wonderful young man.

So, what can astrologers do when a parent asks about a child's chart? One way to address this is simply by having a policy of not doing third party charts and thereby demonstrating an ethical stance. Sometimes these questions arise within the context of future concerns about the welfare of a child. If you are not a predictive astrologer, then it is not within your professional expertise to comment upon the child.

The astrologer might consider asking the parent what makes this question about their child an important concern for them at this time. What lay coiled beneath their query? There is something behind their question. Their response may open a whole new line of inquiry for exploring their chart with them.

Having a somewhat Daoist orientation, I am a person and parent with a *laissez faire* attitude that is mirrored in the ways in which I believe astrology may contribute to parenting. I think by having our child's chart, it can help us cultivate a sense of detachment so we can get out of their way, reducing our interference as they explore their lives, knowing that there is nothing we need to do except to nurture, educate, ward and watch them unfold.

Astrology may help strengthen our faith that Life knows what it is doing, that the chart is perfect just as it is. We don't need to work to turn squares into trines, the squares are our true blessing. We get the children we get and they get us.

Looking at our charts we can see where we may be prone to be overly attached or distancing, dominating or too permissive with our kids and yet oddly enough, these behaviors may contribute to their eventual overcoming of obstacles and meeting success.

Astrology can aid us in contemplating our attitude toward children by examining the fifth house, the Moon, and related matters in our chart. Astrology may help us be supportive of their gifts and perhaps more importantly, accepting of their inferiorities.

Knowing our child's chart may help us come to honor our children as they are (and the choices they make) and not how we wish them to be.

Looking at the synastry between the charts, we may discern areas of consonance and dissonance between us so as to not take inevitable conflict too personally.

These are some of the ways that I find astrology helpful to the process of parenting.

The following are essentially benign exercises for parenting with an astrological mindfulness. They have been adapted from *Everyday Blessings* by Myla and Jon Kabat-Zinn.

Try to imagine the world through your child's point of view. Look through their Ascendant – what kind of world might they see? Wear the mantle of their Sun, apprehend the kind of fuel they need. Allow yourself to sink deeply into their Moon to feel how they may experience self-soothing and emotional connection. In the broadest of brushstrokes, think about earth, air, water, and fire moons.

Imagine how we might appear to our child as a parental figure – their Sun/Saturn and 10th as playmate, disciplinarian and authority, Moon, Venus and 4th as nurturer, comforter, and figure of repose. Might this modify parental behavior?

Contemplate the child's Mars position; try to foster its healthy assertion. Imagine what it's like when it's frustrated.

Practice seeing the child as a shining example of their chart just as he or she is, moment to moment they express its wholeness, complexity, and diversity. Practice this when it's hardest to do so, when we want things to be other than they are.

Be mindful of the elemental distribution in our child's map and in our own, see where the needs clash and stumble and where they dance together. Affirm that there will be periods of conflict and periods of ease.

Engage the Aquarian impulse and practice altruism, putting our child's needs, not wants, above our own whenever possible. Look for common ground so that the needs of both can occasionally be met.

There are very important times when we need to practice Saturn in a strong and unequivocal way with our child. Let this arise out of discernment rather than fear or the desire to control. "Good parenting does not mean being overindulgent, neglectful, or weak; nor does it mean being rigid, domineering, or controlling."

When at a loss about how to respond to our child's troubling behavior, be still. Rather than enact Saturn by being closed, rigid, and cracking down, or engaging Mars by expressing temper and anger, reach into the Moon and listen carefully to the silence. Let the moment speak of its need.

Affirm the difference between the map and the territory. The chart images layers and layers of possible unfolding, but our child is who they are in the immediacy of this moment. Always place children before charts.

Each child is special, each chart sounds a unique tone, holds an image of children as Divine seeds in the great flowering of Life and act accordingly.

Children tend to reawaken much of what is childlike and childish within us. This is important in understanding our cosmic responsibility toward these sacred charges. This awareness can foster compassion for what it's like to be a small person in a big, overwhelming world.

Let me close this chapter with a poem by past American poet laureate Billy Collins to remind us of what it was like.

"On Turning Ten"

The whole idea of it makes me feel
like I'm coming down with something,
something worse than any stomach ache
or the headaches I get from reading in bad light--
a kind of measles of the spirit,
a mumps of the psyche,
a disfiguring chicken pox of the soul.
You tell me it is too early to be looking back,
but that is because you have forgotten
the perfect simplicity of being one
and the beautiful complexity introduced by two.
But I can lie on my bed and remember every digit.
At four I was an Arabian wizard.
I could make myself invisible
by drinking a glass of milk a certain way.

Dark Skies

At seven I was a soldier, at nine a prince.
But now I am mostly at the window
watching the late afternoon light.
Back then it never fell so solemnly
against the side of my tree house,
and my bicycle never leaned against the garage
as it does today,
all the dark blue speed drained out of it.
This is the beginning of sadness, I say to myself,
as I walk through the universe in my sneakers.
It is time to say good-bye to my imaginary friends,
time to turn the first big number.
It seems only yesterday I used to believe
there was nothing under my skin but light.
If you cut me I would shine.
But now when I fall upon the sidewalks of life,
I skin my knees. I bleed.

8

Chiron: Learning to Fall

Chiron was the wisest of centaurs and this was due in large part to his having different parentage and a different upbringing from the rest of the centaurs.

Centaurs were characterized as lustful, violent, barbaric, wild and untamed. Their father was Xion, an ancient king in Thessaly whose father in some stories is Ares. The mother of the centaurs was Nephele, a minor cloud deity disguised by Zeus as Hera to test Xion's integrity. Xion failed, made love to Nephele and fathered the race of centaurs. Other variants suggest he fathered Centaurus who then became the father of the centaurs.

Chiron's father was Cronus, a Titan son of Uranus and Gaia and his mother, Philyra, a water nymph and daughter of two Titans, Oceanus and Tethys. Cronus disguised himself as a horse so that his wife, Rhea wouldn't see him having intercourse with Philyra, then fled. Philyra became pregnant and was so repulsed by Chiron's appearance that she abandoned him (though some variants say she stayed and raised him), so he was raised by Apollo, god of light, reason, healing, art, music, prophecy, medicines, and poetry. Apollo taught Chiron all these skills and in time Chiron himself was known far and wide for being the eldest, wisest and the most just centaur. He was civilized, humane and intellectual. He taught many a Greek hero such as Asclepius, Achilles, Jason, Phoenix (cured him of blindness), Peleus and other scions of ancient kings the use of weapons, hunting, healing, medicine, surgery, music, prophecy, and poetry. Continuing the above episode, Hercules pursued the routed centaurs to Mt. Pelion where they were seeking protection from Hercules' good friend, Chiron. Hercules again fired arrows at the centaurs and one passed through one of the centaurs and struck Chiron in the knee, although other variants suggest the thigh. This situation of the poisoned arrow penetrating an immortal creature results in a Chiron with an incurable wound yet unable to die.

This quote is from *Bibliotheca 2.5.4*, and describes the death of Chiron. "Having an incurable wound, he delivered himself into the cave. Wanting, and being unable, to have an end, because he was immortal, [then with] Prometheus offering himself to Zeus to become immortal for him, thus he died."

There are also variants of the story that have Chiron offering himself to Zeus on Prometheus' behalf. In any case, Chiron preferred the finality of death over the pain of living.

Mythologically, Chiron has to do with being a teacher, healer, surgeon, herbalist, and mentor.

Chiron came into our awareness with its discovery in 1977. One of the early meanings attributed to Chiron is from an early researcher Zane Stein in touch with astronomer Brian Marsden, Ph.D. and was that of 'maverick', a term that Marsden used to describe the orbital history of Chiron, and Stein ran with that, looking into the origin and meaning of the word. A "maverick" is stubbornly independent, not a joiner, here and gone, doesn't take sides.

Stein is also convinced from his early research with charts that one of the primary meanings of Chiron is "key," something which opens doors to new worlds which isn't too far from astrologer Barb Clow's understanding of Chiron as a wounded healer and as a "rainbow bridge" something connecting inner to outer planets (Saturn to Uranus and beyond).

Its orbit reaching from perihelion inside Saturn's orbit to Chiron's position at aphelion near Uranus orbit suggests its function may be that of an integrator weaving the meanings of Saturn/Uranus together, of the traditional and the new, the established and the novel, the norm and the eccentric, between hard work and inspiration.

In her book, *The Continuing Discovery of Chiron*, early researcher Erminie Lantero, primarily thought that Chiron meant healing or wholemaking.

In *A View From Chiron*, Zane Stein offers a number of keywords: The first is maverick, quest, guide, key, healing, doorway, now, learning, healing, loophole, qualifier, tap, mentor and whole host of other words he associates with Chiron.

Melanie Reinhart in *Chiron and the Healing Journey* offers at least 50 themes of Chiron ranging from holistic thinking, shamanism, and wounding to persecutor, violence, futile struggles, and ecology.

Martin Lass in his book, *Chiron: Healing Body and Soul*, describes Chiron in this manner; an innate drive toward connectedness, togetherness, wholeness, belonging, nurturing, being wanted, finding meaning, direction, harmony, inner peace and love.

In Liz Greene's recent work on Chiron titled *Chiron in Love* there is a section on Chiron as Wounded Healer which is well worth a look. She notes that at various times in diverse cultures, different variants of the story come into focus and attention according to the needs of the culture. Since myth is a vibrant entity, it has a livingness that keeps it relevant to its hearers. Greene suggests that we not lock ourselves into one variant but seek out different sources for the telling of the myth for the possibility of seeing Chiron with fresh eyes.

Another angle on Chiron's meanings has to do with its transit activities. Chiron transits are said to reflect turning points in a life, a change of direction or status, a "road to Damascus" event.

Chiron's rulership has been much discussed by astrologers over the years with much disagreement. In my reading of Chiron material, it's been associated with Taurus, Leo, Virgo, Libra, Scorpio, Sagittarius, Capricorn, Aquarius, and Pisces. For me, this reflects some confusion about what Chiron's meaning is and how can it be useful in a chart.

Should there even be a ruler? Centaurs and asteroids may not require that status especially as we discover and name other bodies. Al Morrison did not believe it ruled any sign. I too have difficulty with it. For me signs are compact metaphors for basic human needs and the planets associated with them are agents with the responsibility to satisfy the need of the sign as Glenn Perry noted in his book An Introduction to AstroPsychology. Planets do not rule signs, they work for them. Chiron, however, and the other centaurs and asteroids – how do we make sense of them?

Lantero writes, "[M]uch has been said of Chiron that was previously ascribed to other planets or their Signs. Obviously the meanings of any "new" planet will overlap those of planets already known.... Chiron shares ground in common with almost all other planets."

I'd like to take some time to circle around and amplify some of the images associated with Chiron to see how that may help us. In reflecting upon images, I frequently resort to a text titled *The Book of Symbols* from which I have borrowed liberally and highly recommend.

Centaur – a creature that is half human and half animal. Much of the conventional understanding of this image suggests it is a combination of our higher human nature over our lower animal nature, of the mind ruling over the body, and intellect over instinct. Some people recognize a value bias with these statements. Words like higher, ruling, and over suggest a privileged value given to human, mind, and intellect. This bias reflects the assumption that humanity is the crown of creation, the pinnacle of the evolutionary process, near the top of the Great Chain of Being, and that logic and reason are greater than passion and feeling.

It is also a feature of the fundamental assumption about a universe of dead inert matter in contrast to spirit and rational consciousness. Reaching as far back as Descartes, it is humans who have a soul and a consciousness. Animals, plants, etc., do not have souls. Do you see how this seeps into the image of the centaur? The Greeks pictured the race of centaurs as barbarous brutes, wildly sexual, untamable, and unpredictable (like Freud's Id) with two exceptions, the centaurs Pholus and Chiron, because of their parentage being the issue of deities with different upbringings.

Now if our fundamental assumption is that humanity is not a divinely or a hierarchically related special species but rather part of the web of life, that we come out of this world instead of into it from somewhere else, then higher nature over lower nature is nonsense. The arrival of the centaur into our awareness brings a more ecological awareness and an opportunity to regain our animal wisdom, the intelligence of the body, with reason and emotion being mutually dependent, not hierarchical – that is a unity consciousness, like yin/yang; parity among partners, an integral feature in the more than human world. So, I suspect Chiron echoes a new paradigm of ecological awareness, interdependency and holism.

The environmental movement in its nascent beginnings gathered steam in the early 70s in the U.S. as Chiron was moving toward its Chiron return in the U.S. chart (Sibly).

The American Holistic Medical Association was founded a little after Chiron's discovery.

South African Statesman, Jan Smuts coined the term holism and published *Holism and Evolution* in 1926 and 1927 in its 1st and 2nd editions when transiting Chiron was hovering around his Taurus Ascendant. The book became popular again with new editions in the 60s and 70s. From the Amazon blurb for the book, "After Albert Einstein studied HOLISM AND EVOLUTION, he wrote that two mental constructs will direct human thinking in the next millennium, his own mental construct of relativity and Smuts' of holism."

Personally, I think this was due in no small part to Dane Rudhyar who mentioned it in his writings that also saw resurgence and popularity in the 70s.

Arthur Koestler also published *Janus: A Summing Up* in 1978 when transiting Chiron was in opening square to his natal Chiron. In this text he developed the philosophical idea of holarchy. "The idea of the holarchy is that everything we can think of is composed of holons (simultaneously both part and whole), so that each holon is always a constituent of a larger one and yet also contains other holons that are constituents of a smaller system within. Each whole is a part of something greater, and each part is in turn an organizing whole to the elements that constitute it." This is also the image given to us in Rudhyar's book *The Sun is Also a Star*.

The point so far is that a mind/body or unity consciousness gives equal value and status to heaven/earth, spirit/matter, mind/body, and rational process/ passionate intensity. One is not better than or more important than the other, they are a unity, essentially interdependent. One does not rule the other anymore than the heart rules the stomach.

Joseph Campbell wrote in *The Inner Reaches of Outer Space*,

"In other words, it then occurred to me that outer space is within us inasmuch as the laws of space are within us; outer and inner space are the same. We know, furthermore, that we have actually been born from space, since it was out of primordial space that the galaxy took form, of which our life giving sun is a member. And this earth, of whose material we are made, is a flying satellite of that sun. We are, in fact, productions of this earth. We are, as it were, its organs. Our eyes are the eyes of the earth; our knowledge is the earth's knowledge."

His statement is both humbling and holistic.

I believe Chiron symbolizes the mutuality of human and animal or human and earth. Human beings are not higher, just one variation of a multitudinous diversity. Chiron is an image of consciousness rooted in the body, an ecological identity that can spur us to recognize and correct what author Barbara Kingsolver in her essay "A Good Farmer," that appeared in *The Nation,* notes that all our people and leaders are participating in…

> "a mass hallucinatory fantasy in which the megatons of waste we dump in our rivers and bays are not poisoning the water, the hydrocarbons we pump into the air are not changing the climate, overfishing is not depleting the oceans, fossil fuels will never run out, wars that kill masses of civilians are an appropriate way to keep our hands on what's left, we are not desperately overdrawn at the environmental bank and, really, the kids are all right."

Another image we have is the Cave. Chiron of course lived in a cave on Mt. Pelion. Caves are openings into the underworld. They are also symbols of the womb and the tomb. Orthodox Christian icons have Jesus being born in a cave rather than a stable. They are places of refuge, hibernation, incubation, and withdrawal. We might also see them as an opening into the earth whether an orifice into mother earth or a wound like a mine. There is a scene in the film, *The Treasure of Sierra Madre* toward the end when Bogart, Huston, and Holt are leaving their mine. Walter Huston says something like it would take a week to close up the mine and return the mountain to the way it was. Bogart and Holt are incredulous. Huston says, "We wounded this mountain, it's our duty to close the wounds, the least we can do to show our gratitude for all the wealth she give us." Now isn't that a man who lives in an animate cosmos? It's interesting also because the character goes on to live out his life as a worshipped healer in an indigenous village because of an earlier life-saving event he performed. Another aspect of Chiron's cave is that it is high on a mountain, thus the unity of the upper and lower worlds, the light and the dark, the respected and disrespected, heaven and earth.

The next image we have is of the abandoned or orphaned child. Chiron's father beat it on down the line after his sexual escapade with Philyra, and after she gave birth she was so repulsed by the child's appearance and couldn't bear the shame of having produced such a creature that she left him and asked the gods to transform her into anything other than what she was; they turned her into a linden tree.

Melanie Reinhart believes this is the first wounding, the loss of support of a primary foundation, the abandonment by his mother, the fall from paradise. Literature is replete with orphaned loners; we can say that Adam and Eve were abandoned in the Fall, Moses was orphaned as was Luke Skywalker, Harry Potter, Frodo, Tarzan, Batman, Cinderella, Snow White, Dorothy in Oz, Little Orphan Annie, and the list goes on. The characters mentioned all begin a quest for Home in which a fullness of identity can be found. The journeys roughly follow Joe Campbell's monomyth of the hero's journey which to one degree or another seems to be all of our paths. Separation and departure, initiation through crisis, resolution and return with whatever we have gained.

Another image is the poisoned arrow. Released from Hercules bow and accidentally penetrating Chiron's knee, the arrow was allegedly tipped with the hydra's blood. The underworld dwelling hydra, itself perhaps, is a symbol of crisis and painful transformation.

The phallic arrow is an ascension symbol pointing toward the beyond, the transcendent, and can penetrate to the heart of any matter. Poison can both give and take life: too much is fatal, too little ineffective, but use just the right amount of poison and healing may occur. Poisons have long been investigated for their healing properties: botox is used for migraines, toxin from the yew tree is used in the treatment of cancers, a diabetes drug is synthesized from the poison of the gila monster, derivatives from snake venom are used in the treatment of hypertension, and the list goes on.

The knee is a joint that both lends support and flexibility to the body. Kneeling is often a sign of submission, deference, and vulnerability. Of course, not bending the knee may suggest a lack of humility.

Finally, the wound in the story, the segment of the story that is probably most well- known to astrologers. What is a wound? Glenn Perry (See *Mapping the Landscape of the Soul*) and others have written about wounds.

In the image above, I think of the vaginal opening, the source of life. It is from a medieval illuminated manuscript and it is the wound of Christ. Something that is both a penetration and passage to a new world, the crucifixion as a necessary sacrifice enabling humanity to make its way back to the Divine.

A wound is a breach, a violation, an assault, a rupture in the body. It represents piercings, cuts, lesions, abrasions, tears and rents, and reveals and exposes our vulnerabilities, visible and invisible. Wounds are a discontinuity, a disruption in what otherwise is continuous and ongoing. We must attend to wounds, cleanse, evaluate, probe, and dress, and perhaps suture. I don't have a source for this quote, but I've kept it on a piece of paper for many years, "Wounds are the apertures through which the ambivalent energies of the deep structures surface into conscious awareness."

It could be Joseph Campbell. The unhealed wound demands our attention more constantly than a healed scar. If it scars over or if it forever suppurates and weeps as did Chiron's, it is always a potent memory, a bit of biography, and a reflective depth for us. It connects us to the unseen, the dark, the deep Mystery that is life.

In the context of Chiron being a wounded healer (probably the most well-known meaning for Chiron), it is important to recall that he was unable to heal his wound, just as Christ didn't heal his wound. In the same sense not all our wounds are capable of being healed. They always keep us attentive, restricted, vulnerable, reminding us of our mortality and lack of wholeness and integration. They are the material of a life, grist for the mill, something with which we are endlessly called to affirm and bear. It is almost as if Nature continuously brings us back round to discover new and novel attempts at resolving that which is irresolvable in order to deepen us into life.

Melanie Reinhart also associates the wounded healer with the archetypal shaman. It is interesting to note that the Center for Shamanic Studies was founded in 1979 by anthropologist, Michael Harner. Now the Foundation for Shamanic Studies, it is the self-proclaimed foremost training program in shamanism and shamanic healing. So perhaps this cultural interest in the late 70s through the 90s may indeed be echoed by Chiron. Harner himself had Chiron conjunct the Sun.

There is an association of Chiron with culture creatives, people who have a message that helps us to turn a paradigmatic corner. Dane Rudhyar who moved astrology into the psychological 20th century with *The Astrology of Personality* in 1936 and its resurgence in the 70s is one. Rudhyar's rectified chart has Chiron conjunct the MC from the 9th house.

Another interesting figure was existential psychologist, Rollo May, who in the late 70s and 80s had difficulties with the new transpersonal thrust in psychology feeling that there was too much focus on a self, peak experience, and on transcending the human condition. He recognized the necessity of suffering to be fully human. Since he was a well-respected and highly regarded thinker, his books and opinions served as a counterpoint to transpersonal psychology's reaching and perhaps kept psychology grounded in the anxieties and failings of being human. He had Chiron conjunct the Ascendant.

Let me add one last image and that is the title of this piece, Learning to Fall. *Fall* is an interesting word. It's there in the Beginning with Lucifer, meaning light-bearer, who is cast down from Heaven; then there is The Fall, referring to humanity being exiled from Paradise, falling from grace, we fall away from religion, we fall prey to many maladies, our childhood toys fall by the wayside, things fall between the cracks, we fall in love, we fall out of love, then we fall out of favor, we fall flat, falling down drunk, fall off the wagon, oh, how the mighty have fallen, the bigger they are the harder they fall, pride cometh before the fall, "Help, I've fallen and I can't get up." Spring forward, fall back, the apple doesn't fall far from the tree, Humpty Dumpty had a great fall, When the bough breaks the cradle will fall, Jack fell down and broke his crown, London Bridge is falling down, Ashes, ashes, we all fall down. Things fall apart; the centre cannot hold.

Perhaps words fall on deaf ears. Fall is a word that we use for autumn, the dissipation of green at it falls into its seasonal sleep, it's a word for water's love affair with gravity. It's a word we use for a sudden disequilibrium, for a radical change in position and often results in a struggle to regain or reorient ourselves to life.

Chiron: Learning to Fall

Falling implies being out of control and results in a new state. Falling is not part of the fantasy of growth; it is a change of heart, of direction, of status, and habit akin perhaps to walking into a different room in your house. I think Chiron is an image of how we learn to fall in life. In the book, *Learning to Fall* by Phil Simmons, he describes his struggle with ALS. Phil Simmons was a professor of English Literature engaged in a promising career with a wife and two children when he was diagnosed at the age of 35 with ALS.

He had natal Chiron at 16 Aquarius and when he received his diagnosis, transiting Chiron was a few degrees past exact opposition to his natal Chiron. As you might suspect, his life took a sudden and strong turn in a new direction. He wrote that the central theme of his book is that when we learn to fall, "[W]e learn that only by letting go our grip on all that we ordinarily find most precious – our achievements, our plans, our loved ones, our very selves – can we find, ultimately, the most profound freedom. In the act of letting go of our lives, we return more fully to them."

Learning to Fall is a story of apparent tragedy transformed. Simmons writes, "through loss to a wholeness, richness, and depth we had never before envisioned."

This book was part of a larger theme in publishing at the time about how wounding is actually blessing. Books like Thomas Moore's *Dark Nights of the Soul*, numerous other titles hinting at their content, *Sacred Sorrows, Close to the Bone, The Alchemy of Illness, Being With Dying, Living in the Light of Death, The Illness Narratives, The Five Things We Cannot Change, Healing Through the Dark Emotions, The Gifts of Suffering, All Sickness is Homesickness, The Mercy of Eternity, Against Happiness* and on and on. I think these titles can be read as echoes of Chironic themes and meanings.

Several other people I'd like to touch upon include actor Michael J. Fox, whose life took a serious turn after his diagnosis of

Parkinson's in 1991. He has since shared through two of his books, *Lucky Man* and *Always Looking Up*, his struggles and triumphs with his condition, his personal appearances, and his Foundation for Parkinson's research. What I perceive here is someone with an unhealable wound who offers hope and healing to others who hear or read his words. His Chiron is stationary in the first opposing Uranus, significator of the first.

He writes, "In fact, Parkinson's has made me a better person. A better husband, father and overall human being." And "I see possibilities in everything. For everything that's taken away, something of greater value has been given."

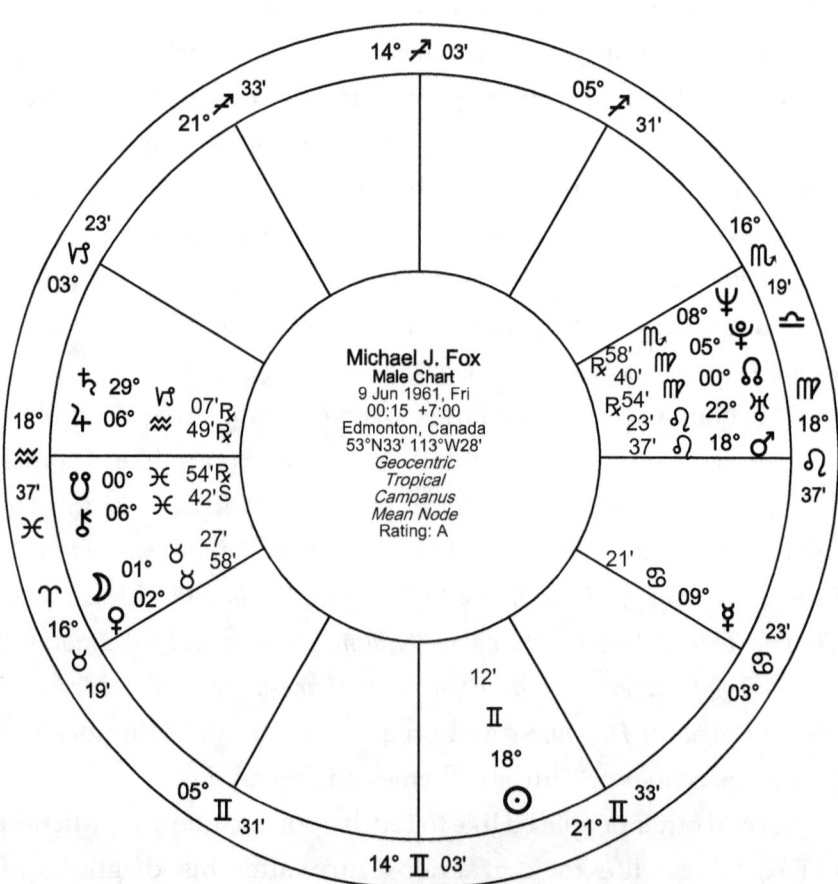

Chiron: Learning to Fall

And, the late actor Christopher Reeve, whose life also took a serious and sudden change in direction through a riding accident on May 27, 1995 that left him quadriplegic. Yet he was still able to produce two books, *Still Me* and *Nothing is Impossible*, which detail that life continues to be worth living even when debilitated by a spinal cord injury. As with Fox, Reeve's books have inspired the people who have read them.

He writes, "I am a very lucky guy. I can testify before Congress. I can raise funds. I can raise awareness." And "I'm not living the life I thought I would lead, but it does have meaning, purpose. There is love... there is joy... there is laughter."

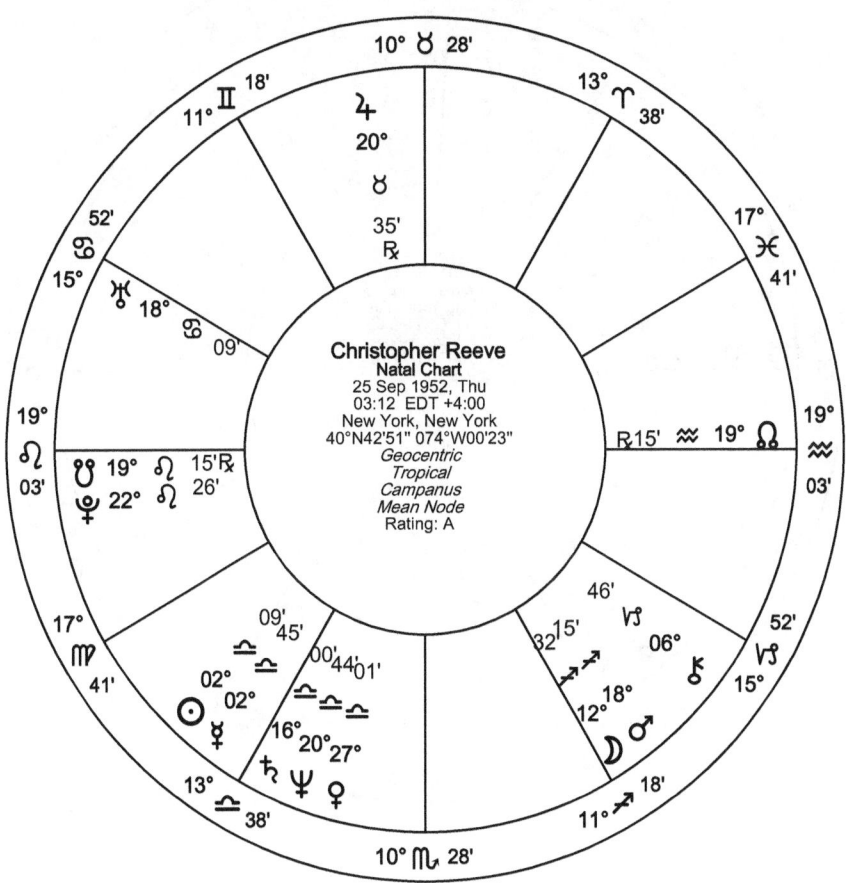

Dark Skies

Last, is Sam Baker, a Texas singer/songwriter. I highly recommend you google his interview with Terry Gross on Fresh Air, that can be listened to or read or a much shorter and different interview on YouTube.

I had the opportunity to see Sam in concert some years back and was able to spend a little time backstage with him after the concert. Here is his noon chart. As you can see, Chiron is busy. It is quincunx the Sun, opposing Jupiter and Uranus, square Neptune, and quincunx Pluto.

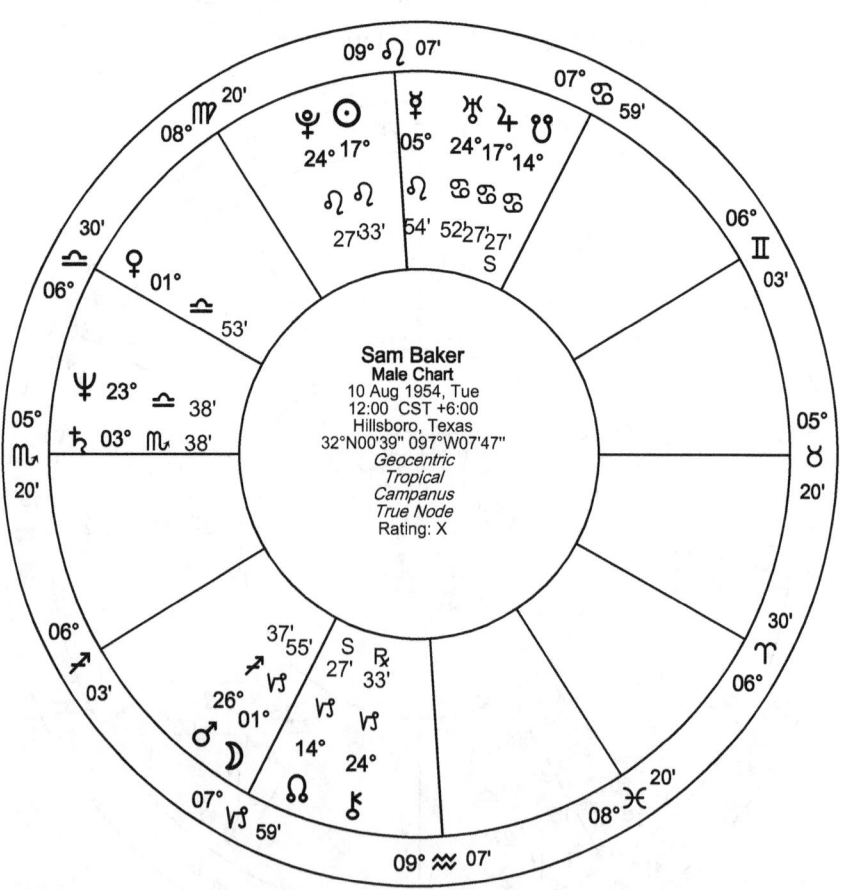

Chiron: Learning to Fall

Below are the transits on the day that he was in Peru, on a train, sitting next to a family and below a bomb that had been placed on a luggage rack above by Shining Path insurgents. It was a fateful day. Transiting Pluto and Mars were quite active that day. Do you see how his wounding awakened him and drove him forward to spread his message about the beauty and fragility of life and paraphrasing Sam, how we are all at the mercy of another one's dreams?

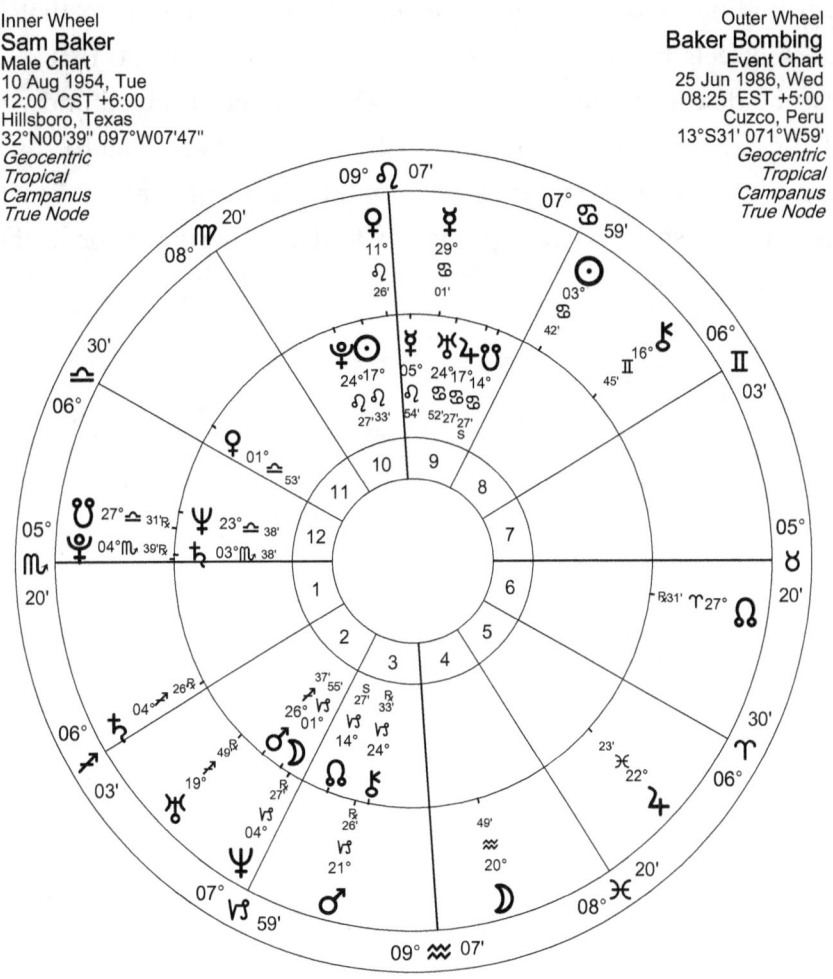

He says, "Gratitude for what remains is more helpful than resentment for what was lost. Ultimately, I came to understand that these days are wicked short and terribly beautiful. All I've got is this one breath, and if I'm lucky, I get another."

Each of these men, having conditions that no one would actively choose, arrived at a place filled with so much hope, joy, and gratitude, are perhaps the finest expressions of what it means to be human. Is the unhealable wound that which keeps us in the body and grounded? My sense is that Chiron has to do with being an image of the affirmation of polarity and the deepening of paradox so that a person feels a truth that doesn't make logical sense. So that one can be diseased and yet hopeful and confident, disabled and yet dedicated and compassionate, disfigured and yet grateful and committed. Chiron suggests the wound and the gift are at heart, one and the same. It gives legitimacy to the notion of Chiron as the wounded healer.

9

Born Under a Bad Sign?

Many astrologers believe that there are no bad signs, malefic planets, or dreadful aspects. If this is so, and the birth chart is a true reflection of the person, then how do we account for the existence of human aberration and evil? Aren't there bad, malicious, dreadful people in the world? Are there bad charts or is every chart as Richard Idemon once noted, the perfect chart? What insights can astrology offer to deepen our understanding of our own capacity for immoral, conflicted, harmful, and ruinous behavior? What are some of the ways bad behavior has been accounted for in the past?

One of the most ancient accountings for evil is cosmological or astrological; the stars can be evil and there are indeed malicious planets. There are religious explanations; possession by devils, demons, or spirits. It could be punishment by the gods/goddesses or sinfulness as symbolized by the Fall. There could be ignorance of the true nature of Reality, i.e., Buddhist thinking suggests that seeing things as separate and disconnected is an error that leads to suffering. Hindu thought understands evil as arising from the consequences of past deeds (karma). It might be a more Gnostic view; the world itself (matter) is evil or biblically, evil as the harvest of our original sinfulness.

We could account for it medically. During the Middle Ages, evil could be accounted for by an imbalance of the four humours – yellow bile, black bile, phlegm, blood, lending a particular temperament: choleric, melancholic, phlegmatic, and sanguineous to the person.

More modern renderings for evil include the philosophical/theological; a misuse of the terrible gift of freedom as Dostoyevsky wrote about it in *The Brothers Karamazov*. Genetic explanations flourish in the bad seed hypothesis; some people are just born evil as the 1956 film *The Bad Seed* depicted. There may be socioeconomic reasons such as conditions of impoverishment, diminished opportunities, lack of education, poverty, lack of cohesive family system. We have contemporary cognitive psychological explanations in terms of schemas; extremely enduring and stable patterns of belief that develop during childhood in response to experience and are elaborated throughout a life. If these schemas are unworkable in satisfying needs, they may lead to antisocial behaviors.

What I would like to point out is that all these explanations are pseudo-explanations. Each has its own merit, pick your poison. There is no method to definitively identify the real cause, nor is it necessary that there be a single cause. We all believe what we need to believe in order to make it through the Night.

Astrology also has a role to play here as we will see. There are many ways of understanding and using astrology, and my own stance is that the dynamic triads, sign/planet/house, symbolize twelve archetypal principles that can manifest in unlimited ways. One of the many ways of understanding the signs is as twelve basic needs common to all people, as Glenn Perry elaborated in *An Introduction to Astro-Psychology*.

The planets, rather than being the rulers of the signs, are the agents of the signs, charged with the responsibility of acting in ways that the sign's needs, to which the planets are conventionally associated as rulers, may be satisfied. The houses mirror twelve archetypal contexts or fields of lived experience in which the action occurs.

Planets can sit comfortably in a chart or be stressed by a variety of other factors being present, the aspect dialogues in which they are engaged, their singleton status, their sign or house position, etc. Consequently, in a planet's attempt to satisfy the needs of the sign for which it is the responsible agent, it may be helped or hindered by other factors in the chart. So rather than function purely and untrammeled, it may reflect an individual who is either out of control (out of touch) with the planetary function or over-controlling that function in their lives leading to problematic attitudes, feelings, and behaviors. The challenge for the person then is to figure out over time ways in which to integrate that function more optimally into their life. For example, when a teen is first learning to drive a car, they sit behind the wheel, ramrod straight, tension in their posture, fully attentive, scanning the view, both hands on the steering wheel, and they are concerned about making an error. Six months down the road however, you may see them drive by, slouched in their seat, one hand on the wheel, sipping a soda with the other, relaxed in mind, and believing they have integrated this skill set sufficiently. It is the same in charts; square aspects often are a reflection of early difficulties. To the extent that the person is able to successfully meet the challenges of the situation symbolized by the square is the degree to which they have smoothed out the functional operation of the conflicting dynamics.

What I'd like to start with then is to examine each of the twelve sign/planet/house triads to see how these archetypal dynamics are reflections of concrete lived experience. I have forgone parading out a large number of charts. The majority are easily available with a Google search. I use the Campanus house system.

Let's begin at the beginning...

Aries/Mars/1ˢᵗ - self-presenting. Aries images the need for survival, the unabashed exuberance to be, the need to assert at all cost, to boldly thrust oneself into Life, action on its own behalf, spontaneous, courageous, birthing, independent, separation from the containing matrix.

But when this archetypal function is excessive, dominant, disturbed or repressed we get problematic expressions of this dynamic, the person may appear impulsive, argumentative, insincere, rash, reckless, arrogant, provocative, inconsiderate, manipulative, impatient, rude, easily bored, shallow affect, a thrill junkie. This may echo combative, oppositional features, aggressiveness, impulse control problems, low frustration tolerance, problems delaying gratification, and being exploitive of others. We

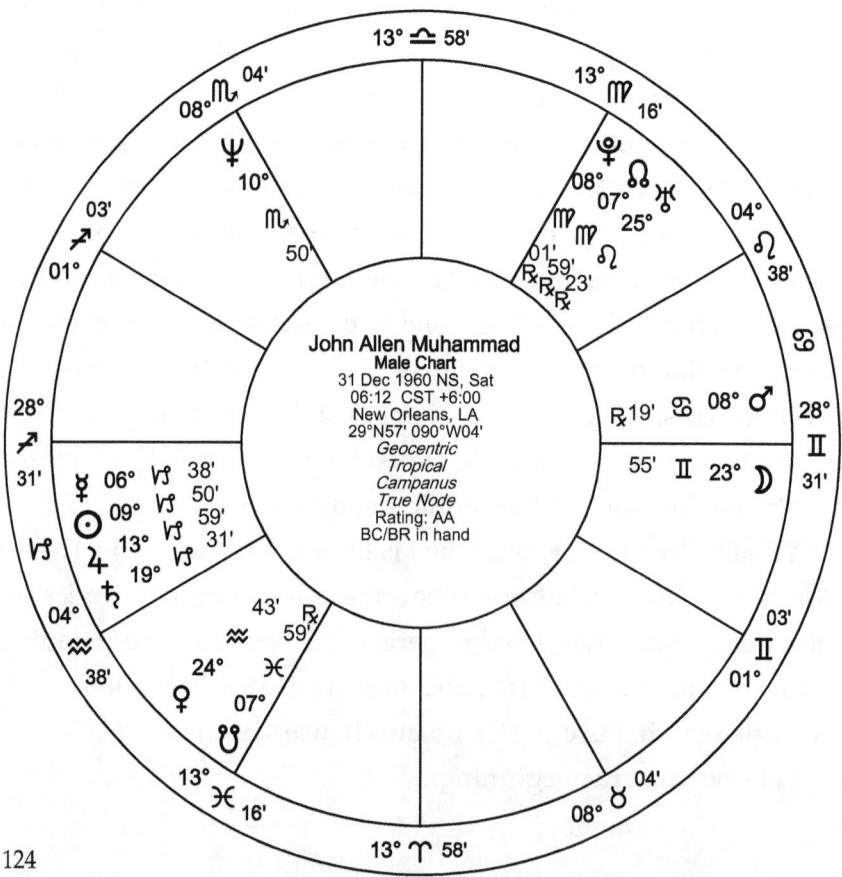

can recall the characters of mob boss, Tony Soprano, actor, Edward G. Robinson in *Little Caesar*, Jimmy Cagney in *Public Enemy*, James Caan's character, Sonny Corleone in *The Godfather*, and the characters in the film, *Goodfellas*.

In actual life, we have John Allen Muhammad, the Washington DC sniper responsible for killing 10 people in 20 days in 2002; the ruler of his chart, Jupiter, unsettled in Capricorn, is involved in a 1st house stellium with Saturn all opposing a stressed Mars, and quincunx Uranus and the Moon. The Aries/Mars/1st dynamic is very dominant.

Another example is Clifford Olson (1 January 1940, 10pm, Vancouver, Canada), a Canadian serial killer responsible for the deaths of 11 teens in 10 months in late 1980-81. The ruler of the chart, Mercury, is the apex of a T-square that is agitated by a Mars/Jupiter square. He also has a very wide square from Mars to the Sun. Additionally Neptune in the 1st house diminishes a strong self-image.

Taurus/Venus/2nd - self-preserving. It images the need for safety and security, motivation toward pleasure, comfort, the sensuous, and the desire to feel permanent and solid, reliable, attached, steadfast, conservative.

When excessive this may reflect problems with embodiment i.e., a history of self-harm or mutilation, eating disorders, obesity, drug abuse, sexual difficulties, hoarding, and money management problems. The person may appear insecure with unstable affect and mood, greedy, cloying, fixated, possessive, desperate, determined, intense and inappropriate anger, manipulative, emotional over reactivity, easily offended, suspicious of your motives, touchy, seductive. Film examples would be the character Alex played by

Glenn Close in *Fatal Attraction* and Jennifer Jason Leigh as Hedra Carlson in *Single White Female*.

In actual life we have Princess Diana (1 July 1961, 7:45 PM, Sandringham, England). She has Venus in Taurus as the apex of a T-square that includes Mars/Pluto/Uranus in the 8th opposing a very unsteady Moon in the 2nd whose cusp in the erratic Aquarius does not reflect safety and comforting security. She had difficulty with bulimia and self-harming behavior.

I also had a client (data private) diagnosed with Borderline Personality disorder who has Sun conjunct Venus in Taurus on the 12th house side conjunct the Taurus Ascendant. This is all opposed by confusing Neptune. Also the 2nd house ruler Mercury in Aries

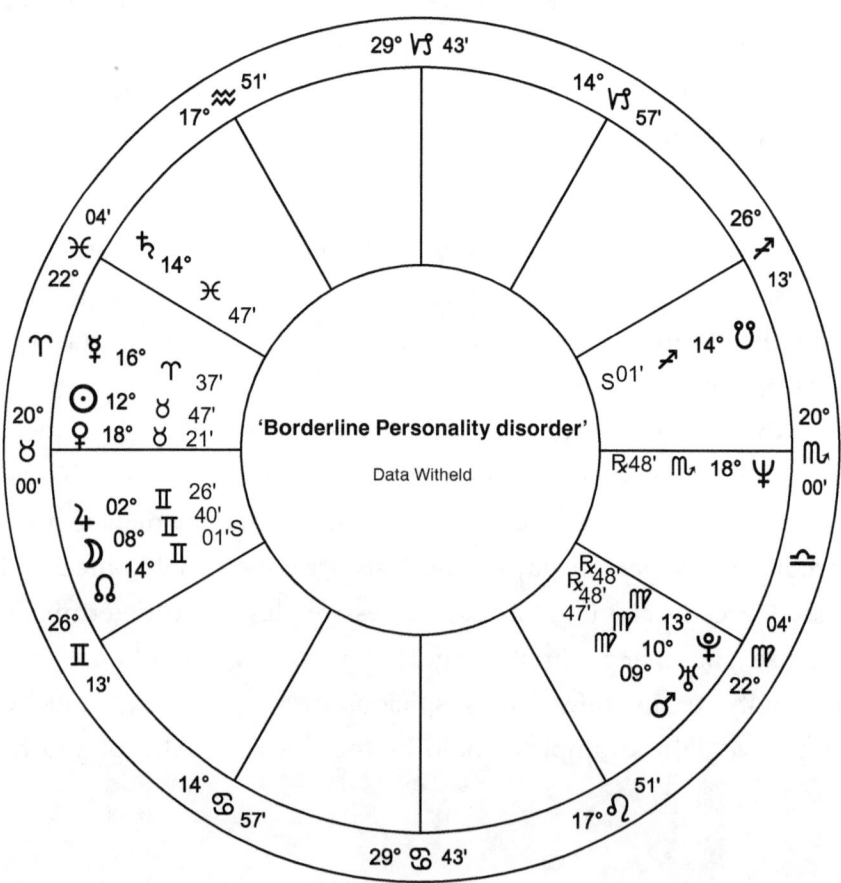

is in the 12th house. Not much identity stability, reliability and permanence is imaged here. This client did a lot of cutting on himself.

Gemini/Mercury/3rd - self-extending. It images the need for learning, adaptability, communication, mental stimulation, curiosity, motivated toward acquiring knowledge, toward exchanging information with the immediate environment.

When in excess the person may appear scattered, flighty, restless, nervous, highly strung, confused, have difficulty being understood or understanding what is being communicated, may be hard to pin down, tentative or evasive in their thinking. This may reflect nervous personalities or persons with learning disabilities, attention deficits, communication disorders, speech problems, and language processing difficulties. Examples are the character Barney Fife from the Andy Griffith Show and "Rain Man" Raymond Babbitt.

In actual life we have the late comedian Joan Rivers (8 June 1933 2:00 AM EDT, Brooklyn, NY), her chart has an emphasis on the third principle, Sun in Gemini conjunct the 3rd house cusp being distressed by the apex Mars/Jupiter/Neptune as part of a T-square with Mercury/Venus in Gemini on the unstable 29th degree. This principle is also enhanced by Mercury being the final dispositor. Joan was quite the talker with a vicious tongue. Her catch phrase was "Can we talk?"

An ex-client (private data) has an elevated Sun/Mercury in Gemini conjunct the MC. Mercury conjunct Saturn and Venus opposing Jupiter/Neptune/Moon. Additionally, there is a Grand Trine in air and Scorpio on the cusp of the 3rd suggesting a wounding and need for healing of that arena of experience somehow. This client was an incessant talker and eternal student, always reading, reading, reading, always learning.

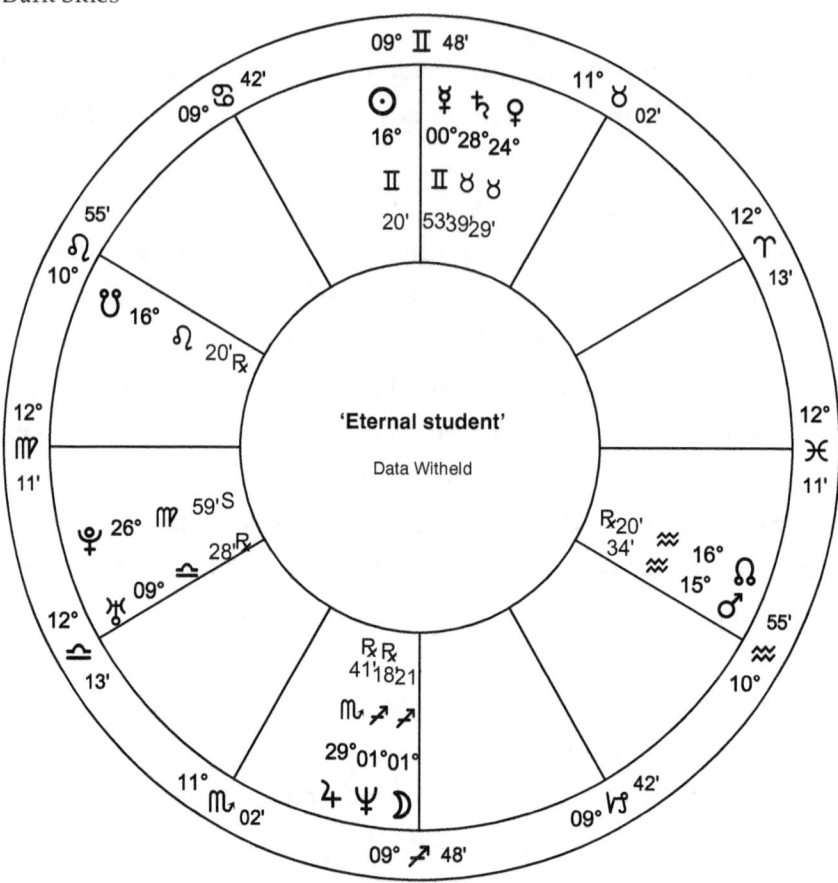

Cancer/Moon/4th - self-containing. This images the need for belonging and acceptance, for emotional connection, for giving and receiving nurturing, for unconditional closeness and protective embrace.

When in excess, the person may appear needy, whiny, childish, dependent, over reactive, watery, sentimental, moody or withdrawn, easily embarrassed, vigilant for signs of rejection, guarded, shy, lonely, passive, guidance seeking. This may reflect problems with dependency, emotional belonging, clinginess, help-seeking behaviors, or conversely be smothering, or overbearing. There can be features of social avoidance with strong fears of rejection and disapproval despite longing for belonging and acceptance.

Born Under a Bad Sign?

Examples would be the childlike dependent partner or the smothering mother character, Marie the mother on the TV series *Everybody Loves Raymond*, Barbara Streisand as Joyce Brewster in the film *The Guilt Trip*, and the character, Ida Morgenstern in the old TV series, *Rhoda*, as the stereotype of a mother who is endlessly caretaking and boundlessly self-sacrificing, overprotective, doting, controlling, guilt inducing, unwilling to let her children emancipate.

Also, a dependent ex-client (private data) who is a triple Cancer, has Venus/Sun/Saturn/ASC in Cancer in a tight square to Neptune suggesting issues around women, the maternal, and love. The Moon in Cancer is in the 1st with the ruler of the 4th, Mercury,

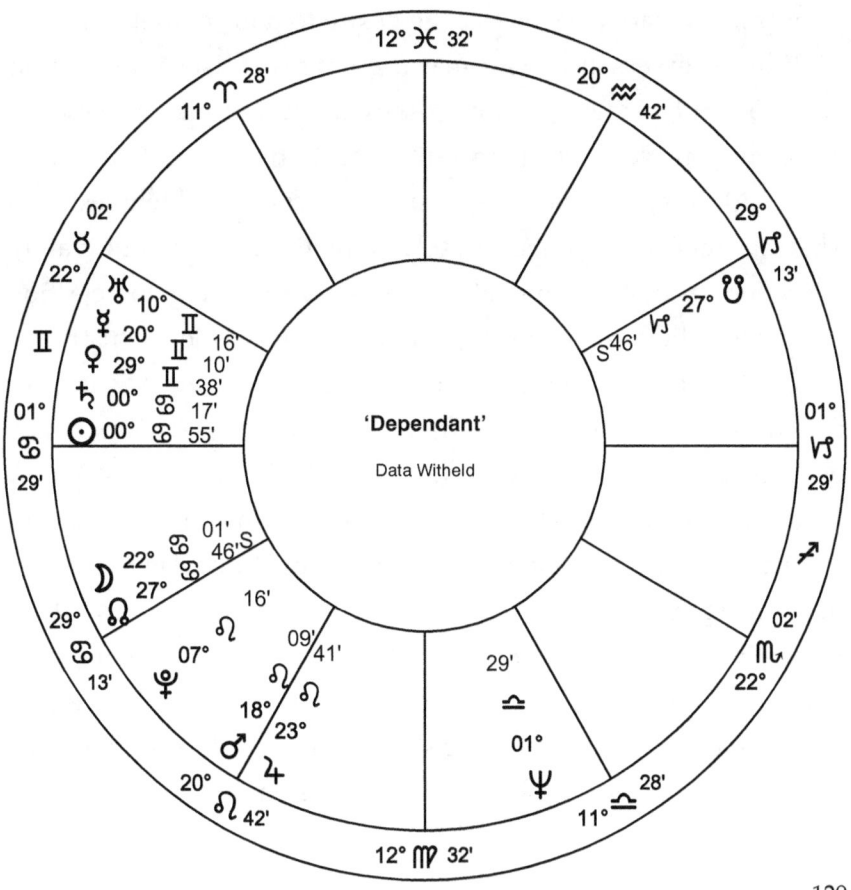

intercepted in the 12th. This client was the most passive person with whom I've worked. He was somewhat of a sad-sack, inept and blundering, wanting someone to love him, to take care of him, to meet his emotional and physical needs.

Nadya Suleman (11 July 1975, 9:29 PM PDT, Fullerton, CA), also infamously known as Octomom, has stress on the sign of mothering, Cancer. The Sun/Saturn in Cancer as the apex of a T-square - suggesting fears and a sense of inadequacy about being a mother - squaring Uranus and Jupiter. Ruler of the 4th Mercury, unstable at 29, is squaring Pluto in the 8th house.

Moving to Leo, Leo/Sun/5th - self-displaying. This images the need for validation, esteem, and approval, to shine, to be seen, to perform, to creatively express, the desire to pour oneself out.

When in excess the person may present as egotistical, exhibitionistic, boastful, prideful, attention-seeking, well protected, envious, a showoff, entitled, self-important, special, theatrical, flamboyant, vain, faith in superiority, gregarious, vivacious, and tempestuous. This may reflect problems with self-dramatizing behaviors, craving adoration, adulation, and affirmation, overreacting to rejection, requiring others to bolster their image, narcissistic, or histrionic. We can think of the character, Ron Burgundy from *Anchorman*, and the character of Hank Moody from the cable series *Californication*.

In actual life, Peter O'Toole (2 August 1932, 12:15 AM, Wicklow, Ireland), has the Sun/Moon in Leo in the 5th in fearful opposition to Saturn. He becomes a professional (Saturn) Leo. He has played many aristocratic, royal, autocratic, celebrity, heroic roles – King Henry in *The Lion in Winter*, a British nobleman in *The Ruling Class*, autocratic director in *The Stunt Man*, the aged and vain celebrity in *Venus*, the washed-up movie star in *My Favorite Year*, the heroic Lawrence of Arabia in the film of the same name.

Donald Trump (14 June 1946, 10:54 AM, Jamaica, NY), has Leo rising intensified by Mars and Pluto bookending it. He has the Moon in the 5th house in expansive Sagittarius. And the Sun electrified by Uranus and easily inflated by a trine from Jupiter. This is a lot of Leo.

Virgo/Mercury/6th - self-denying (extreme expression of differentiation). This symbolizes the need for competency, efficiency, and self-efficacy, wishes to be of use, to be of service, to thoroughly analyze and to assess toward more efficient functioning.

When in excess the person may present as critical, fault finding, carping, picky, correcting, overly conscientious, extremely fearful of self-error, afraid of disarray or disorder, fastidious, ritualistic, and excessive concerns about cleanliness. This likely reflects obsessive, compulsive issues with the person being preoccupied with seeking correction, seeing the trees and not the forest, missing the larger picture due to sidetracking on smaller and distracting details, overly analytical to the point of paralysis.

We have TV characters like "Monk" in the series of the same name, "Niles Crane" in the original "Frasier," and the character Felix Unger in Neil Simon's *The Odd Couple* – fussy, conscientious, fastidious, organized, nit-picky, clean freak, annoyingly critical and intrusive.

On television Felix Unger was portrayed by the late actor Tony Randall (26 February 1920, 9:00 PM, Tulsa, Oklahoma), known for his fussy roles, who had Sun conjunct the 6th house cusp in Pisces distressed by the singleton Saturn in Virgo, the only Earth sign and as part of a T-square. There is a lot of energy pouring toward that 6th house cusp.

Howie Mandel (29 November 1955, 10:00 AM, Toronto, Canada), who not only identifies himself as having ADHD but also as a germophobe with OCD. He has Sun/Mercury conjunct in Sagittarius, the dispositor being Jupiter in Virgo, a singleton as the only Earth sign, intensified by a conjunction with Pluto. All of this is entangled with a T-square to the Moon conjunct the 6th house cusp.

Libra/Venus/7th - self-equilibrating. This is the need for Other, for relatedness, partnership, companionship, for cooperation, balance, and harmony, and the aesthetic function.

When excessive, the person may present as very agreeable, placating, and conciliatory. They may be complementary towards you, giving all the right responses, deferring to you in conversation, not wanting to express an opinion or behave decisively. They may be docile, compliant, often concealing hidden anger and depression. There may also be an inability to appreciate or identify beauty in the world, an aesthetic hyposensitivity. It may reflect problems with assertiveness, autonomy, codependency, being overly ingratiating, or submissive. It can image neglect or abuse in all situations, subordination of their own needs to protect relationship which is prioritized, indecision, self-sacrifice, and self-undervaluing. Perhaps the character Edith from the TV series *All in the Family*, also the women in the film *The Stepford Wives* would make good examples.

One ex-client (private data) has five planets in the 7th house with Libra on the cusp. Mars/Venus/Uranus/Pluto are all in Libra in the 7th or widely conjunct the Descendant, the Sun and Mercury are in Scorpio also in the 7th house. He never really expressed his own opinions and perhaps had none, fearing upsetting anyone. Consequently, he was very complacent and diplomatic.

Another ex-client (private data) has Sun conjunct Venus in the 7th house opposing Saturn and squaring Neptune in a T-square

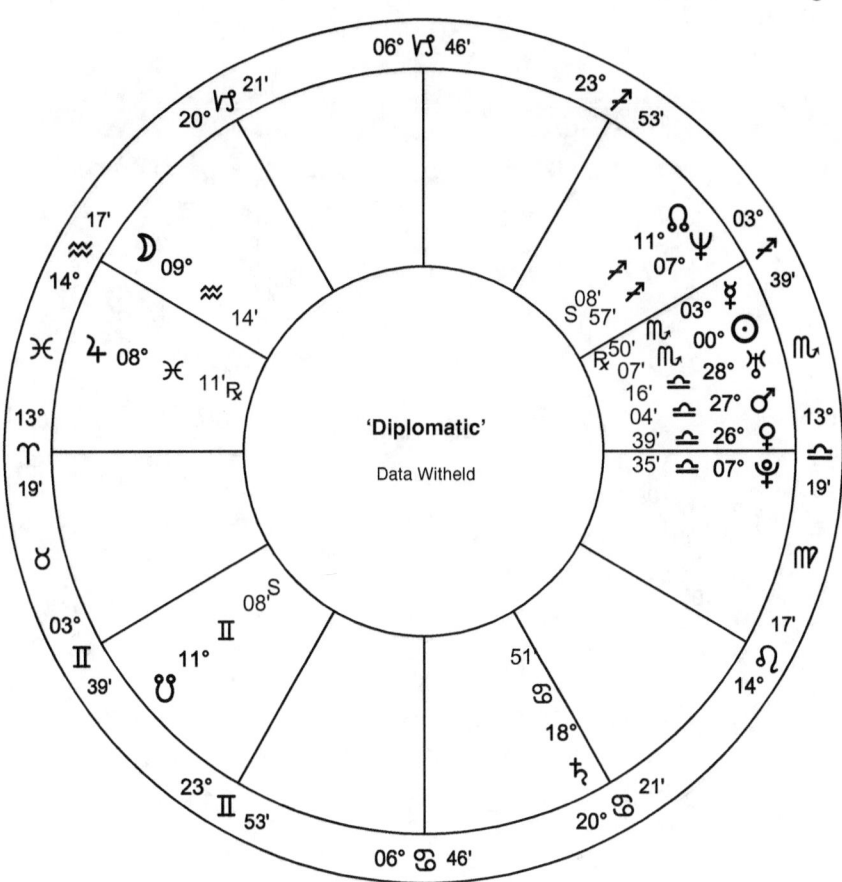

configuration. The Moon, ruler of the 7th, is very uncomfortable at 29 Aries with a wide quincunx to Mars. He couldn't imagine upsetting anyone, being very compliant, appeasing, and conciliatory. He just abhorred interpersonal discord.

Scorpio/Pluto/8th - self-concealing. Images the need for transformation, wounding, healing and regeneration, catharsis, and renewal. The archetypal image of the cycle of life (birthing/dying/rebirthing), Eros, the motive force which draws and holds all things together, the urge to merge, to go beyond our selves reflecting power, depth, intensity, and integration.

Dark Skies

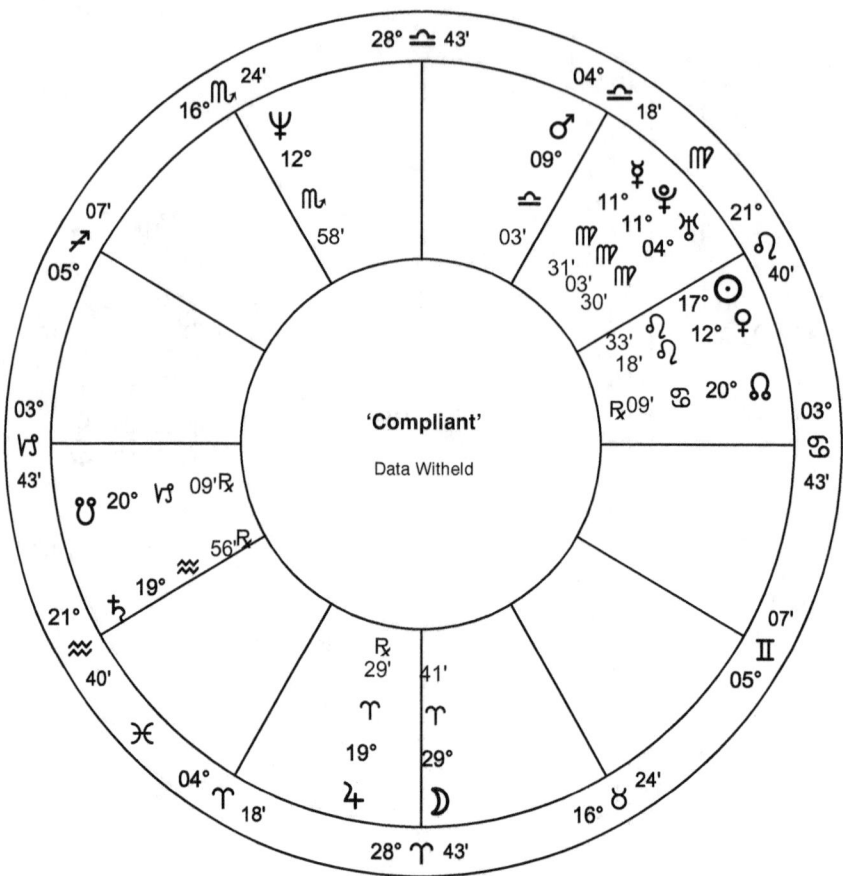

When in excess the person may present as shadowy, guarded, wary, suspicious, tense, not very open, unemotional, controlled, secretive, touchy, envious, jealous, sensitive to deception, insult, depreciative comments, clue seeking, reluctant to offer any self-disclosures, oriented to power and one-upmanship. This may reflect severe issues around trust and betrayal, boundary violations as found in histories of abuse, sexual or otherwise, conspiratorial world views, and paranoid perspectives stemming from unacknowledged and unexplored shadow issues. The characters of the paranoid Lt. Commander Queeg in *The Caine Mutiny* played by Bogart, and of course Don Corleone as "The Godfather."

Born Under a Bad Sign?

In actual life, we have Al Pacino (25 April 1940, 11:02 AM EST, Manhattan, NY), in just about any of the dark roles he's played, from Michael Corleone, the Luciferian character in *The Devil's Advocate*, to the excessively violent gangster in *Scarface* and the criminal attempting redemption in *Carlito's Way*. He has Pluto on the Leo Ascendant squaring the Sun/Saturn conjunction in the 10th house. His Neptune, ruler of the 8th is distressed as the apex of a T-square.

The actor, Jodie Foster (19 November 1962, 8:14 AM PST, Los Angeles, CA) has 4 planets in Scorpio conjunct the 12th house cusp acting as the apex of a T-square. Mars is distressed in the 8th and

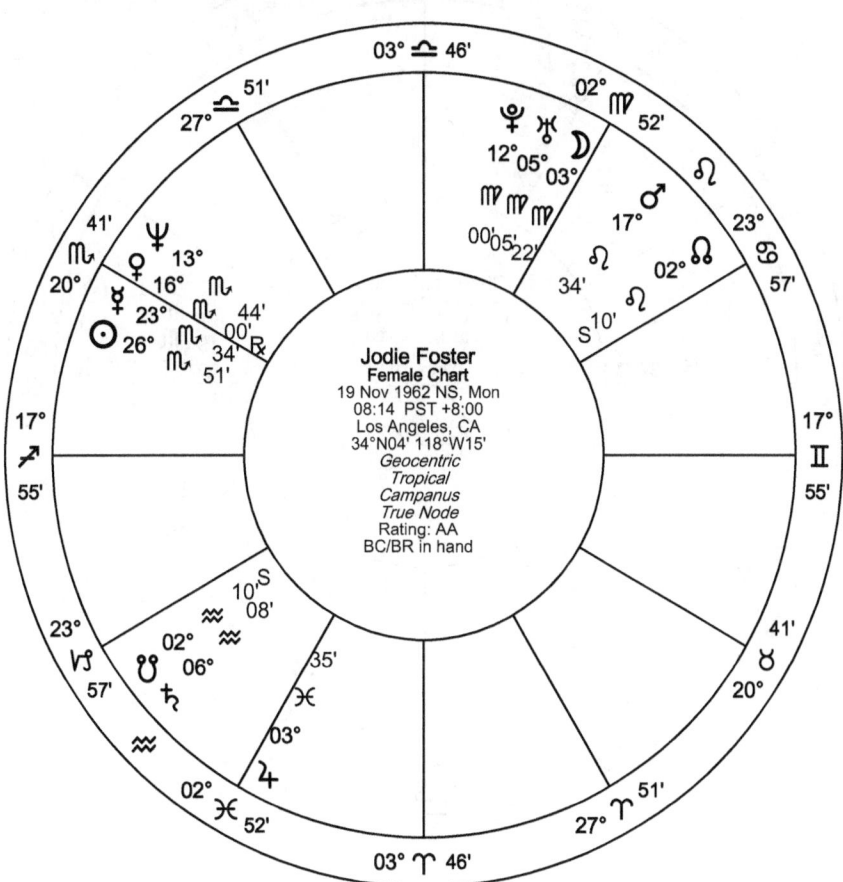

Dark Skies

the ruler of the 8th, the Moon is conjunct Pluto/Uranus. Her underworld roles have included the 13-year-old prostitute in *Taxi Driver*, to FBI trainee, Clarice, in *Silence of the Lambs*, home invasion victim, Meg Altman in *Panic Room*, to Erica Bain in the violent vengeance soaked *The Brave One*.

Charles Manson has 4 planets in Scorpio, ruler of the 8th, Jupiter is involved in a Grand Cross with Pluto, agent of Scorpio. Need more be said? It is a strong reflection of a troubled man.

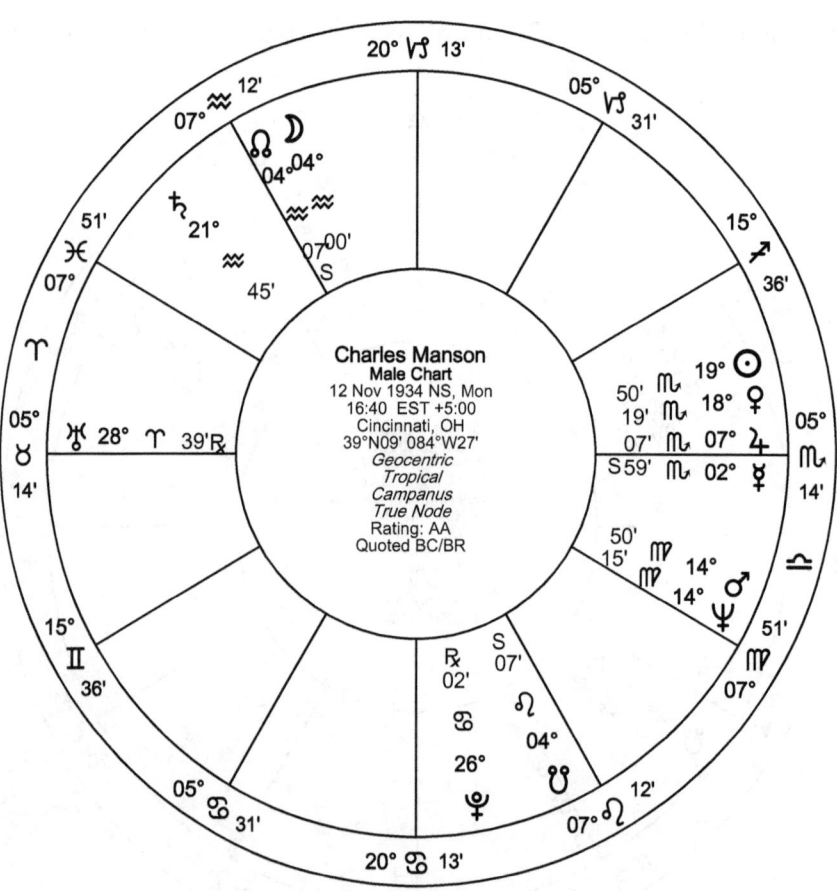

Sagittarius/Jupiter/9th - self-promoting. Images the need to broaden oneself, to expand horizons, go beyond the facts, to seek meaning, purpose, truth, justice, virtue, and morality.

When excessive, the person presents with a sense of grandiosity, extravagant enthusiasm, unrealistic optimism, an inflated sense of self, exaggerated sense of abilities and achievements. They can be overly talkative with pressured speech, irritability, easily angered, illogical thinking, impatient, interruptive, and perhaps with religious or sexual preoccupation. This may reflect mood difficulties known as mania where the person experiences essentially too much of a good thing. The expansive mood can be out of control, affecting thinking, behavior, and social facets of a person's life. In America, we have the cartoon character Foghorn Leghorn and the quintessential blustering Senator Claghorn from the old Fred Allen radio show upon whom Foghorn is based.

In actual life there was Senator Strom Thurmond (5 December 1902, noon chart, Edgefield, SC) the real-life filibustering, long-winded, long-lasting Senator with Sun, Mercury, Venus, Uranus conjunct in Sagittarius opposing Pluto amplifying the Sagittarian character.

The late actor and mental health advocate, Patty Duke, had the Sun conjunct Mars in Sagittarius in the 4th house square the Moon and opposing Uranus as part of a T-square. Jupiter/Venus in Scorpio suggesting some woundedness, square Saturn/Pluto – Venus being ruler of the 9th. And Mercury, ruler of the chart, located in Sagittarius conjunct the IC. This is a lot of distressed Sagittarius energy.

Dark Skies

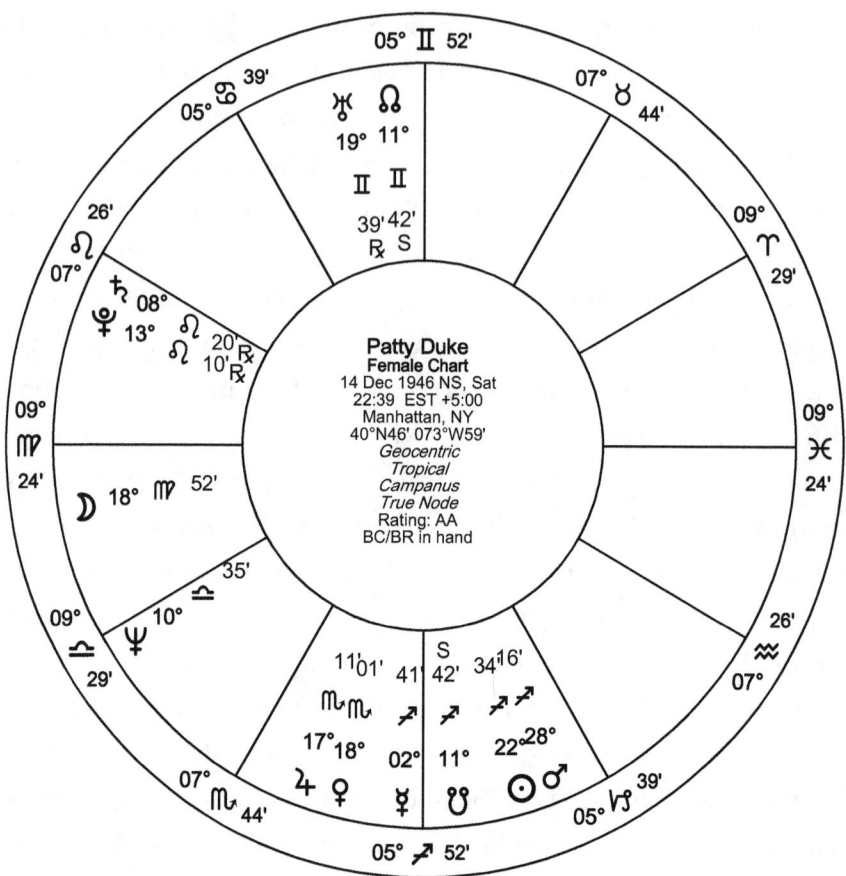

An ex-client (data private) with Bipolar Disorder has a Sagittarius Ascendant. Its agent, Jupiter, is conjunct Saturn, quincunx Uranus and opposing Moon in Cancer in the 8th house. The Sun, ruler of the 9th house of expansion, is square Neptune, softening and confusing the sense of identity, and quincunx Pluto.

Born Under a Bad Sign?

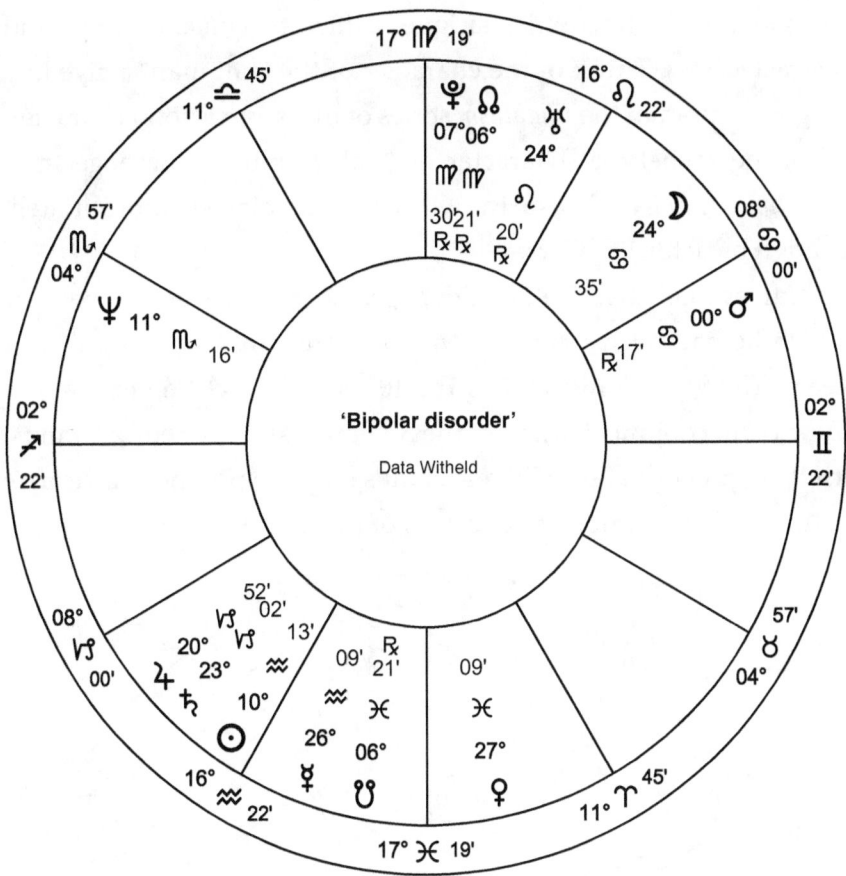

Capricorn/Saturn/10th - self-restraining. This images the need for structure, order, position, orientation, place, clarity, authority, and being motivated toward perfection, achievement, and control.

When in excess, the person may present as melancholic, gloomy, dejected, despondent, forlorn, bitter, sad, tearful, glum, miserable, pessimistic, driven, burdened, workaholic, beaten down, suffering, worn out, drained, exhausted, troubled, dispirited, morose or tense and wrapped too tightly. This presentation would suggest significant depressive qualities with disturbances in appetite and sleep, feelings of helplessness, hopelessness about the future, lack of motivation, anhedonia, fatigue, difficulty concentrating, and distractedness. Think of the character of the "tall man" played by Angus Scrimm in the *Phantasm* series of films, or cartoon character. Also, the archetypal character of "Bah humbug!" Scrooge in *A Christmas Carol* and also the Grinch both played appropriately enough by actor Jim Carrey.

Carrey has disclosed lifelong problems with depression for which he had been treated with antidepressants for a number of years. The Sun, significator of the 10th, is conjunct Venus/Mars in Capricorn, conjunct Saturn in the 3rd house and quincunx Uranus, itself conjunct the Leo Midheaven. It's easy to spot the Capricorn/Saturn/10th dynamic as a reflection of his life.

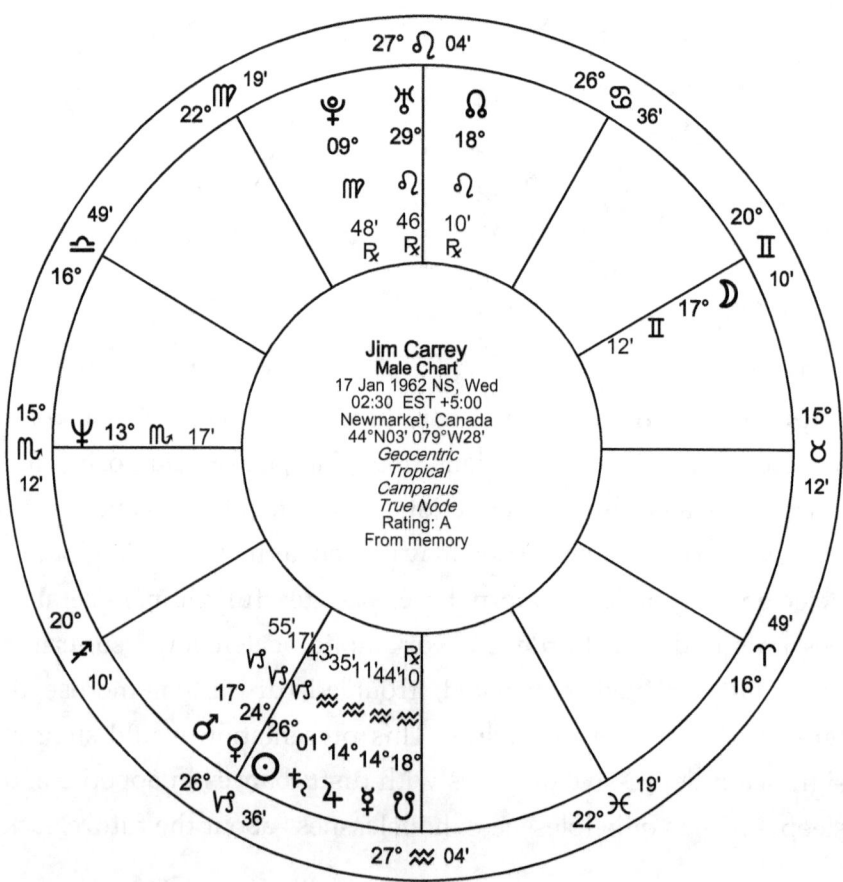

Mary Tyler Moore (29 December 1936, 10:45 AM EST, Brooklyn, NY), who played the highly competent but overly burdened Mary Richards and the tightly wrapped, highly controlling, heavily denying mother in the film, *Ordinary People*, for which she received an Oscar nomination is another example. She had Sagittarius on the Midheaven; its agent Jupiter is conjunct the Sun in Capricorn and quincunx the Moon/Pluto conjunction in Cancer. Mercury, ruler of the 4th house, images her early roots in Capricorn opposing Moon/Pluto in Cancer. And Saturn itself is conjunct the Ascendant distressed by an opposition to Neptune. Here also we see the strong presence of the Capricorn/Saturn/10th archetypal dynamic.

Robert Burton (18 February 1577 8:55AM LMT, Lindley, England), is the author of a book published in 1621 and which has never been out of print as far as I know, titled *The Anatomy of Melancholy*, a massive tome on all facets of melancholy as was known in the history of his day. It is believed that he ended his own life after being a lifelong sufferer of depression. His book was and is extremely well regarded. He had Saturn conjunct the Midheaven in Capricorn.

Arthur Schopenhaur (22 February 1788, Noon -1:15 PM LMT, Danzig, Germany), was the 19th century philosopher of all-encompassing gloom and pessimism who elaborated the fatality of existence. We only have a noon chart for him. He has Sun/Saturn conjunct in Pisces.

Aquarius/Uranus/11th - self-objectifying. This images the need for change, deviation, progression, advancement, revelation, awakening, breakthrough, emancipation, wide perspective, impartiality, group consciousness, motivation toward being a cultural creative, humanitarianism, and being a trickster figure.

When excessive, the person may present as eccentric, bizarre, off the wall, strange, odd, detached, revolutionary, rebellious, radical, shocking, remote, aloof, withdrawn, indifferent, emotionally flat, unfeeling, impassive, overly intellectual, living in their head, mechanical, absent minded. This may reflect a person with schizoid features who can be emotionally constricted, socially isolated, self-absorbed in their own interests, broad without depth, lacking deep feelings for others, loving ideological abstractions, like truth with a capital 'T', utopian societies, humanity in general but not interested in the nitty gritty of relationship or pragmatic living. They can love Humanity but dislike people. In its extremity, we find characters with a bit of genius and madness, the absent-minded professors, the eccentric geniuses, ones we've all seen in films. The character, Doc Brown in *Back to the Future*, the eccentric genius Laslo in the film, *Real Genius*.

In actual life we have talk show host, Howard Stern (12 January 1954, 1:15 PM EST, NY, NY), the shock jock with a tight Sun/Merc/Venus conjunct tightly opposing Uranus.

The Unabomber, Ted Kaczynski (22 May 1942, 10:45 AM CWT, Chicago, IL) has the Sun, ruler of his Ascendant conjunct Uranus on the 11th house cusp squaring the Moon.

Salvador Dali (11 May 1904, 8:45 AM GMT, Figueras, Spain), the thoroughly original, eccentric, one of a kind, has Sun/Mercury/Mars in 11th house quincunx Uranus, the most heavily aspected planet. There is also Saturn in Aquarius squaring those 11th house planets, and Venus in the 11th.

Another ex-client (data private) who carried a Schizoid diagnosis has the Sun/Venus in Aquarius conjunct the Ascendant from the 12th and Uranus squaring the Moon. He was in his mid-20s and misread a relationship with a fourteen year-old girl. He thought she loved him as he loved her and then spotted her with

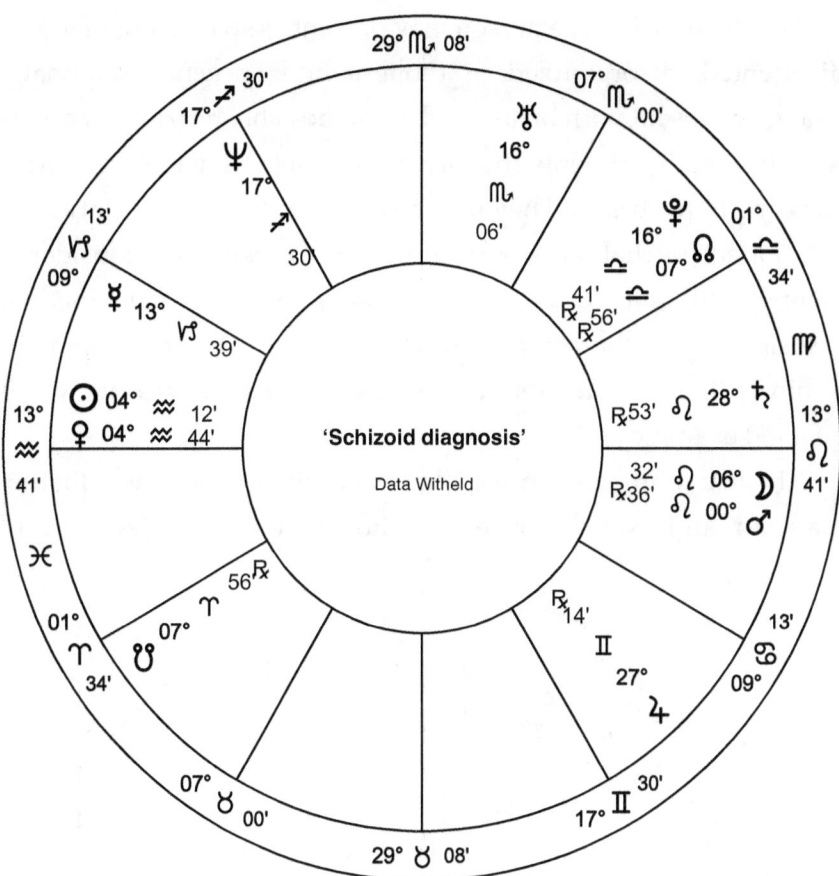

another fellow more appropriate to her age. One day he walked up behind her as she was waiting for the school bus and shot her in the head, killing her. In his telling of this event and its aftermath, he was very dispassionate and detached in that odd Aquarian way.

Pisces/Neptune/12th - self-releasing (extreme expression of non-differentiation). Images the need for total transcendence or surrendering identity. It images obliteration, an oceanic consciousness, a boundless undifferentiated unity, a return to the womb, a nostalgia for paradise, a 'God' experience of infinite and ideal love, beauty, and compassion.

When excessive, the person may present as spacey, out of touch, disoriented, disorganized in thought and speech, emotionally strange or absent with bizarre behavior, possibly hearing voices, or reporting body ailments that are not possible (like feeling worms crawling in his brain). They may also appear 'high' or ecstatic.

Characters that we see in film that are generally considered mentally ill, out of touch with reality, bizarre, hallucinating, delusional. The character Birdy in the film of the same name or Robin Williams' character Perry in the film, *The Fisher King* would be good examples.

The late John Nash in the film, *A Beautiful Mind* was a mathematician and Nobel Laureate, who carried the diagnosis of

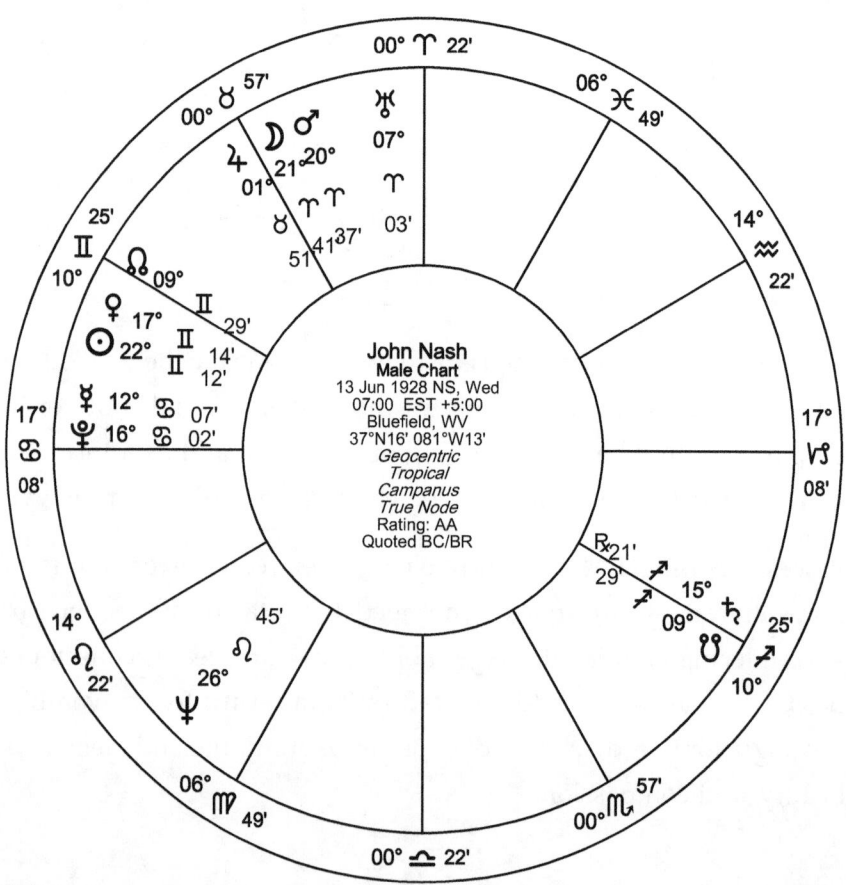

schizophrenia. He had 4 planets in the 12th house opposing and quincunx Saturn, and Neptune sextile Sun and trine Moon/Mars/Jupiter softening and diffusing those planetary functions.

Antonin Artaud, the famously imaginative early 20th century French playwright, poet, actor, and theater director had lifelong opiate addictions, various delusions, and physical tics. Current psychiatric thinking would diagnose him with a delusional disorder or schizophrenia. He was involved with automatic writing, dreamwork, crafting magic spells, creating astrology charts, leading the surrealist movement in the 1920s, and developing what he called the Theatre of Cruelty. He had a walking stick that he believed belonged to St. Patrick, Jesus, and Lucifer. He

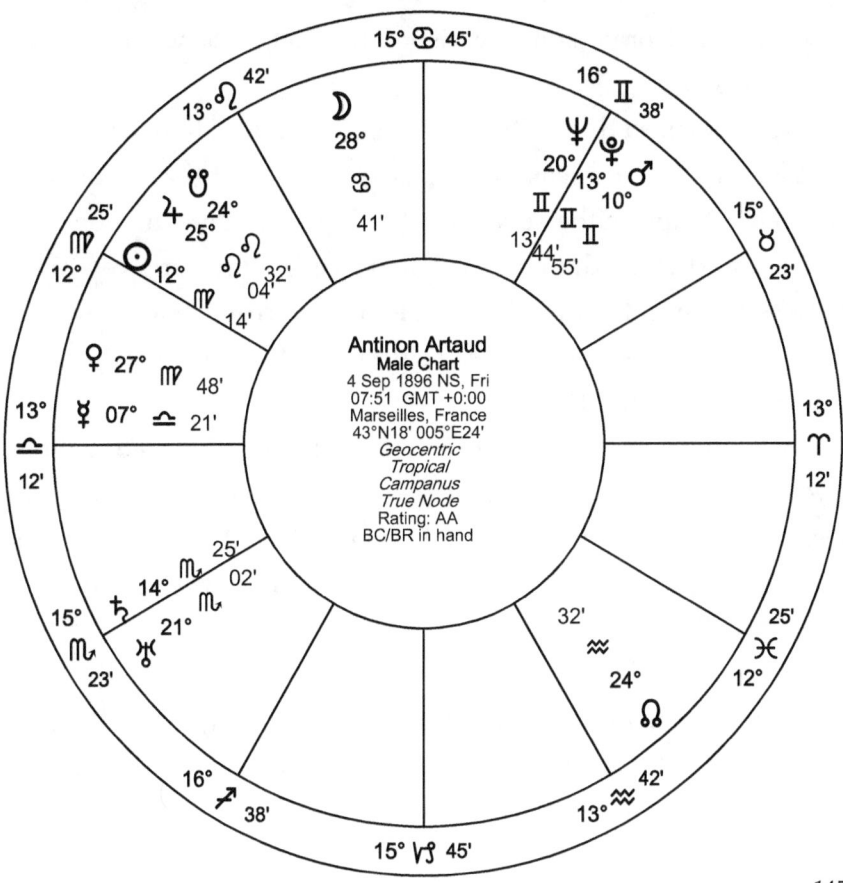

went to Ireland to return the stick but was unsuccessful. He has the Sun conjunct 12th house cusp in wide square to Neptune/Pluto/Mars conjunction in Gemini. His Venus, ruler of the chart, and Mercury are in the 12th.

We've spent time examining the extreme expressions of archetypal needs and functions of the famous and infamous. In psychology these extreme expressions are termed psychopathology, a word deriving from the Greek; *psyche*, *pathos*, and *logos*. We can understand this as the speech or speaking of the suffering soul. These symptoms and behaviors can be viewed as a crying out from some deep inner part of us. When people express certain complexes or symptoms, they get labeled with terms such as depressive disorders, anxiety disorders, mood disorders, psychotic disorders, and/or personality disorders, though the value of this is controversial.

Now, I suspect that each of us has suffered. And I further believe that we each have at least one planet in our chart that tends to be problematic, and either over-functioning or under-functioning it mirrors particular difficulties that we've had in our lives. What I'd like to do is to turn the astrological mirror toward my own chart and use it as an example of a problematic planetary dynamic: Capricorn/Saturn/10th.

We're not looking for quick fixes here but rather contemplative engagements. In my own case, I have Saturn in Virgo on the Descendant, Capricorn is on the cusp of the 12th house, and the significator of the 10th is posited in the 12th. The suggestion is that I may have difficulties in my life that are echoed by the 10th dynamic. Saturn is not only angular but a singleton, being the only planet in an earth sign. Earth is an inferior function in my chart. Being in the 7th house it has been easy to disencumber myself of it, to just toss it to my partner to carry for me.

For example, I have terrible difficulty with the practical necessities in life. Balancing a checkbook, paying the bills, doing the taxes, taking care of insurance and mortgages, making home improvements, any sort of handyman endeavors, paying attention to the required details of living, even the idea of practicing a skill; all are uncomfortable for me. Additionally, I've had lifelong problems with Saturnian authority and the status quo, having little respect for it in almost all situations. Unfortunately, this also reflects the awkwardness of becoming an authority in any meaningful sense or having any sense of expertise and competence in matters. I don't care much for effort, ambition, or achievement, all Saturn reflections.

This placement also images the perplexity of maturity for me, the arduousness of endings, the never having the sense of being grown up, i.e. mature. There are occasions of feeling like an imposter, and I have a lack of seriousness about most matters. At its worst, it will erupt out of my inattentiveness as cynicism, faultfinding, being judgmental, cantankerous, irritable, and inadequate.

One of the unfolding outcomes is that in wrestling the Saturn of interior spaces I have difficulty being the author of my own story, I recognize and share authorship now with an appreciation for the Other. There is also an enlightened capacity for embracing melancholy, and to stand with humility rather than hubris in the presence of the Fates.

What are we to make of these sentiments? Don't most of us seek out happiness, pleasure, sanity, wellness, peace, and life while trying to avoid sadness, suffering, craziness, illness, conflict, and death? Don't we talk about trying to live a balanced life believing this to be the intended outcome of a spiritual path? Yet wishing to be rid of troubles in favor of consistently enjoying balance is to deny the realities of existence. Ongoing wellness without illness is an absurdity. Equilibrium without ever being thrown off kilter is an impossibility. To attempt to be rid of imbalance, uncertainty, ambiguity, strife, upset, dissonance, or discord is to deny half of human reality. We perhaps need to remind ourselves that half of the planet at any one moment is in darkness. When we try to identify exclusively with the light, it results in our leading lives of partiality instead of wholeness. It makes as much sense as keeping the North Pole and eliminating the South Pole, keeping our fronts while removing our backs, or preserving the mountains while eradicating the valleys. These are not possible and any attempt to do so will fail as it destroys the entire system of which these polarities are integral properties.

Happiness is not a reward for a good life nor is suffering the return on a poorly lived life. Pain and pleasure are simply features of the human landscape. Our problems and pathologies are not to be resolved any more than the goal of life is to be had in the end of the journey. The journey itself is the meaning of life. This very moment in which we are immersed is its own significance. Our quirks, oddities, symptoms, perversions are the hidden blessings in life intended to be worked, simmered, fermented, and massaged in ways that enrich our beings.

Often, I will refer to signs and planets as being either yin or yang. From a Daoist perspective the universe is processual; a word meaning always flowing, always dynamic, always impermanent. This means that movement is really movement toward stillness, and stillness is stillness pregnant with movement. Homeostasis or balance is inherently unstable, moving toward disequilibrium and not intended to be maintained or lived in. Our own discipline of astrology tells us this in the stillness of the solstices and the dynamism of the equinoxes. Think of the movement of a pendulum, the outer edges of its swing are the momentary solstices. The quickest momentum is to be had at the base of the arc, the equinoxes. Balance is always precarious and dynamic; not quite one terminus of the polarity (solstice) yet not quite the other either.

In closing, it must be said that this is an evolving work initiated by Richard Idemon in the mid-1980s and given greater substance by Glenn Perry and Greg Bogart in this century. My intent has been to show that any of the twelve archetypal principles under duress, functioning excessively (or repressed), parallel certain structures of challenge in a life. To answer the question posed in the title, our charts and by this I mean our planets, signs, aspects, and houses are not inherently bad.

Everything has value within a particular context. The aspect dialogues in which the planets are engaged such as oppositions that bring the potential for awareness and illumination, and the squares and quincunxes better considered as growth-inducing aspects, rather than evil, do not cause our problems but rather it's the beliefs that we hold about the world and ourselves. The real cause of our suffering is the belief we hold about it. To blame anything for our troubles is to relinquish choice, agency, and creativity.

Our fate appears as the "given" in each situation in which we find ourselves. Our freedom is in our chosen responses to the challenges life offers us. The emphasis that many of us take on potentially problematic concerns mirrored in our charts allows us to escape responsibility for our lives and blame it on our stars. This, in John Paul Sartre's language, is "bad faith," the refusal to accept the freedom and responsibility that is ours alone. It takes the "courage to be" as existential theologian Paul Tillich noted, and "the courage to create" as psychologist Rollo May espoused, to give life meaning, relevance, and power. The chart is a bottomless well from which we may constantly draw new insights into the structure of our beliefs and how they help or hinder us in our efforts to create a satisfying narrative about our lives.

Take these challenging ingredients in your chart; massage and knead them, allow for leavening, fermenting, mulling, simmering, and then heating it all with reflective attention. This process will deepen and enrich us and in so doing will disclose the great value that we sense in astrology.

10

Astrology as Spiritual Path

Astrology is in essence not a belief, a method, a science or pseudo-science, or even an art. At base it is a form of relationship between human life and the world, a relationship in which we learn about ourselves by observing the sky. The idea that we have a sky within allows us to imagine the heavens as our interiority turned inside out. In the mysterious dynamics of macrocosm/microcosm, the *anima mundi* infuses both as the interiority of all things.

In communicating what follows, I think it is necessary to define the terms 'astrology', 'spiritual', and 'path' since these terms can have many meanings and I'd like to avoid any misunderstandings. Let me begin with 'astrology'. Because of our literalistic perspective and our scientific prejudice, many people believe that astrology is a hodgepodge of superstitious star lore filled with fatalistic pronouncements about ourselves and our futures. But in a more imaginative time in Western history, astrology held legitimacy. It infused art, medicine, literature, drama, philosophy, architecture and social institutions during the Middle Ages and Renaissance. In fact, every major culture of which I'm aware in the last 5000 years has had a form of astrology. I contend that this did not so much represent a nascent and primitive science in its attempt to understand the natural world as much as it reflected the ontological recognition of the interdependent unity of humanity and cosmos.

Among the many types and approaches to astrology, I wish here to write about natal astrology. This is the definition I'd like to work with; astrology is an archaic wisdom tradition similar to the Kabbalah, the Tarot, and alchemy, that holds as its fundamental assumption, the tenet that the positions of the sun, moon, and planets at the time of a person's birth are related in a significant and discernible manner to the intrinsic character and development of that person. There is no causality associated in any manner with this statement.

This definition implies an ecological model of humanity, viewing people as interdependent expressions of a living cosmos, an integral part of a larger cosmic community, the Great Net of Being (wholes within wholes within wholes) where all the various nodal links resonate with one another in ways about which we have little or no understanding. This is not hard to entertain when we realize that each and every atom in our bodies was formed in the fiery heart of a star. In other words, as Joni Mitchell proclaimed in the 70s, we are stardust. She wasn't kiddin'.

In *Astrology's Truth* found in Thomas Moore's *The Re-Enchantment of Everyday Life*:

> "Astrology is a form of imagination emerging from nature and having direct relevance for everyday life. It's an applied poetics, a vision of life on earth stimulated by movements in the heavens, which can take us into areas of self-reflection as no other system of symbols and images can."

The same structuring principles and processes at work in the world are also at work within us. This suggests that the form and movement in our lives is reflected in the movements in the sky.

As readers know, the primary tool an astrologer uses is the natal or birth chart which is literally a stylized map of the solar system as seen from the particular place and moment of a person's birth. More imaginatively however, it is an image of psyche or soul, a mapping of the topography of our inner landscape. As a map, it is used for purposes of orientation, helping us fathom where we are in life, sounding out our centers, and getting our bearings.

The chart provides a framework for imagining a profound intimacy between ourselves and our world. We hear this deep intimacy echoed by Moore in the same essay in quoting the words of early Church Father, Origen when he stated, "Know that you are another world in miniature and have in you Sun and Moon and even stars."

But for our charts to say anything to us, astrology must hinge on the fantasy that our world is a living being capable of speaking to those who have the ears to hear and the eyes to see. Historically we find this thinking in the Old Testament in Psalm 19,

> "The heavens declare the glory of God; the skies proclaim the work of his hands. Day after day they pour forth speech; night after night they display knowledge. There is no speech or language where their voice is not heard. Their voice goes out into all the earth, their words to the end of the world."

What is this psalm but a faith statement about the world's capacity to speak with us, to communicate with us, whether it's the birds singing their message, the wind in the trees, the clouds on the horizon conveying the weather, the days becoming shorter, or the dance of the planets, the world affords us the opportunity to understand our situations. The world discloses itself to us and also reveals us to ourselves.

There is no Muslim moon or Catholic sun, no Buddhist season or sign, the heavens do not play favorites. The sky is all inclusive, it speaks to everyone. It's the perfect container for a global spirituality for it is something under which we all gather and share in common.

Even Martin Luther in a more provincial tone wrote, "The gospel is written not in the Bible alone, but on trees and flowers and clouds and stars." Luther recognizes that the "good news" is spoken throughout nature.

Philosopher, Vincent Vycinas in <u>Earth and Gods</u> suggests, "Truth as revelation is not located in the mind,...but in the world itself. Since the world is the interrelation of earth, sky, gods, and mortals, this interrelation, this mirror-play is the primary revelation, the primary truth."

Additionally, philosopher Paul Ricoeur as presented in Richard Kearney's *Poetics of Imagining* notes,

> "To manifest the 'sacred' <u>on</u> the 'cosmos' and to manifest it <u>in</u> the 'psyche' are the same thing.... Cosmos and Psyche are two poles of the same 'expressivity'; I express myself in expressing the world; I explore my own sacrality in deciphering that of the world." Here we can see the interface of cosmos with psyche as mirroring each other and are essentially two sides of that coin we call "Reality."

Let me slip more toward the direction of the spiritual. I use this word when I'm engaged in thinking and conversation about Ultimacy, about the Sacred, about Holy Imagination, or Divine Mystery. I'm somewhat at odds with the word, God, as it has so many meanings. The popular image of God as a benevolent being, expressly anthropomorphic, and lodged somewhere off in the distance is fairly meaningless to me though I admit having a cosmic parent to take care of me and grant my wishes is a comforting thought. This image of God became empty for many Jews after the holocaust as well established by theologian, Richard Rubenstein in *After Auschwitz*. For Christians in the 1960s, theology encountered the Death of God movement which effectively killed God as papa for me and many of my contemporaries. The image of God as cosmic parent began to dissolve as a satisfying truth for many, and new images of Divinity arose. Several theologians like Sallie McFague in her *Body of God* and Grace Jantzen in *God's World, God's Body* imaged the world as God's body thus reclaiming an archaic idea of the world itself as sacred and others like Rosemary Radford Reuther feminized the Divine in *Sexism and God-Talk* granting it greater maternal over paternal attributes, less hierarchical and more relational in our fantasies of the Divine.

The image of God as panentheistic, meaning that God is in All and All is in God, was reawakened by Charles Hartshorne in process theology and Matthew Fox and others in the creation-centered tradition, lending divinity to the cosmos (see the writings of Matthew Fox, Thomas Berry, Brian Swimme and Ursula Goodenough). Their ecological perspective also harmonizes with indigenous writers like Vine Deloria, E. F. Cordova, Gregory Cajete, and Brian Burkhart). This eco-spirituality is quite attractive and consonant with astrological thinking since much of astrology depends on the natural world for its meaning. The signs of the zodiac for instance derive their meanings from the rhythms and seasons of the earth in its orbit around the sun. This structure of the natural yearly cycle in terms of birth, growth, culmination, decline, and demise lends significant meaning to the zodiac and all cycles of activity.

A creation-centered spirituality (including astrology) is inclusive and does not have the lopsidedness of traditional fall-redemptive spirituality where we're all hoping to catch the elevator up to God in his azure Heaven. Typically, the focus is on illumination/ascension imagery with little mention of darkness and descent imagery.

A creation-centered spirituality as its name implies recognizes the sacredness of Creation which includes not only the fire/air imagery but perhaps even more importantly, earth/water imagery that takes us into the depths of our being even when we wince, tremble, shudder and shake. It gives us the experience of Persephone and Inanna in their descents into the heart of darkness in which much was suffered, and much was gained.

Sometimes a person's spirituality can include prayer, i.e. petitions to the Divine for intervention. Oftentimes I think this kind of prayer shows a lack of trust in life; it tends to express our longing and personal desires for matters to be different. It suggests that the universe is not conspiring for our benefit. I think rather than petitionary prayer, a prayerful attitude is best, a deep sense of reverence, gratitude, and a willingness to be open to awe, both awesome and awful, to find the dark seed of the Sacred buried in the most ordinary and difficult events. It's a willingness to say yes to life.

Saying yes to life includes honoring the claims the soul makes upon us as envisioned in the image of our natal chart. As James Hillman points out, the planetary gods, Mars, Venus, Jupiter, etc. are not so much to be believed in as to be imagined, to see their presence in our styles of consciousness, attitudes, affective states, and archetypal behaviors.

I come at last to the word 'path.' I follow Fox's thinking here. A path is not necessarily a way to get from point A to point B, moving from spiritual novice to spiritual master for example. Sometimes a path is not goal oriented but rather, it is the way itself, a meandering of sacred moments and holy interludes. In other words, we are blessed with the revelation that it is not the destination but the journey. It doesn't matter if we wander in well-worn ruts, onto side trails, or trackless lands. It all counts, and it's all reflected in the birth chart.

We can explore the features in our birth map in order to deepen our understanding of our experience and situation. People often come to astrologers to seek answers to their problems. I gently frustrate these efforts. As I do with my own practice, I try to help them find the questions. I rely on Rilke here, that apostle of Trust in *Letters to a Young Poet*.

He encourages us to

> "Have patience with everything unresolved in your heart and to try to love the questions themselves...don't search for the answers which could not be given to you now, because you would not be able to live them. And the point is to live everything. Live the questions now. Perhaps then, someday far in the future, you will gradually, without even noticing it, live your way into the answer."

When we believe we have found our answer, it closes off the imaginative flow and extinguishes the very exploration that sinks us more deeply into the ground of our being. It is important to cultivate imagination by engaging the natal chart as a catalyst for generating questions that lead the person onward.

One fantasy about the horoscope consistent with this approach is attributed to psychotherapist, Charles Ponce, "The horoscope is a field of imagination and reflection not only through which we see ourselves but by which we see through ourselves to the archetypal ground that has created this dance called life."

We can explore these astrological images without having to resort to a literal belief in the influence of the physical planets upon us, or as simply, mere metaphor, but rather as a way according to Thomas Moore to be "connected to the mystery in the world around us by means of a vivid, concrete, trusting imagination."

Imagination, then, provides the opportunity to construct a worldview that takes the world into account as the source and ground of our being. The astrological images remind us of this fundamental connection to the world. Moore writes, When I "place my birth in relation to the planets out there, am I not also establishing a connection with the planets within and with the vast universe of my interior life?" After all, where is it that I begin and end? In a college lecture in 1971, Alan Watts said, "Trying to define yourself is like trying to bite your own teeth." What are the boundaries of my being? We are creatures of such depth and mystery that we never come to the end of exploring our charts. This form of thinking suggests an ecological soul, a boundless energy spinning variety and novelty into being.

Let me end where I began with Thomas Moore writing in *Astrology's Truth*. Our paths can be re-enchanted "by a fresh appraisal of astrology, moving away from any hint of superstition toward an intelligent, sensitive, poetic, and existential intimacy with nature, who shows herself in the enchanting light display of the night sky. We can look deeply into that night sky and see ourselves."

11

Without Shadow, There is No Substance

This phrase sounds a bit the wrong way round, doesn't it? I am writing this on behalf of shadow, to take a stand for darkness, to champion inferiority, to honor the black nights of the soul. I hope to persuade you to reimagine its necessity and the blessing of shadow in our lives.

Here is our itinerary for the trip. And I hope you'll bear with my rather lengthy expository comments about shadow before we get to its astrology.

Night, Nyx, Shadow, Hades, Pluto, Hecate, Kali, the Grim Reaper, the Big Bad Wolf, the Vampire, the bogeyman, the monster under the bed, the creature in the closet, the nightmare on Elm St., the Hellraiser, ghoulies, ghosties, and long-legged beasties, things that go bump in the night.

It is the realm of shadow and darkness, of shades, underworld, etc., is all our woundedness, inferiority, and blind spots, all referencing the more distasteful elements of human experience. In the shadows, in the darkness in our lives dwell the thief in the alley, the rapist in the shadows, the murderer in your heart, ex-spouses, and innumerable others. It is peopled with shades.

There are some people of North Asia who believe that in the underworld everything is topsy-turvy, an inverted image of this world, up is down, right is left, day is night, summer is winter, etc. This notion of inversion is not all that uncommon.

We find this contemporary underworld in our nation's prisons. In our conventional day world, kindness, hospitality, honesty, patience, generosity, and compassion are regarded as character strengths and virtues to be practiced, but in the underworld of prison, there is an inversion of values and these virtues are held as weaknesses and are viewed as undesirable. This is a world of deep shadow.

Many years back, I read that in some indigenous cultures when walking by a river or stream, a person takes care not to let their shadow fall on the water for fear that a crocodile might rise up and seize it, thereby killing the person.

Other tribes loathe stepping on a person's shadow so as not to bring harm. Shadow for some indigenous peoples seems to have a meaning close to our words, soul, image, double, and reflection. Perhaps we've seen films where the tribal peoples did not want their pictures taken as it seemed a means whereby their soul would be captured. There are folkloric tales of people who have made a pact with the Devil and consequently no longer cast a shadow. So, we can see that for some human societies, shadows have had a sort of supernatural, numinous, archetypal quality attached to them.

Now shades and shadows are very curious. They seem to be an instance of nothingness implying somethingness, of Non-being intimately entwined with Being. Some shadows are very dark as when we view them within the solar, heroic, egoic, yang perspective of the day world and at other times, when we engage the more receptive, yin, soft, lunar perspective of the night world, shadows are barely discernible from the surrounding environs.

Seeing shadow implies substance. Substance without shadow is almost nothing at all; transparent, sheer, diaphanous, gossamer, wispy, and indefinite. It's thin and insubstantial, spirit blown every which way.

Without Shadow, There is No Substance

Substance implies something solid, reliable, and dependable; it persists. When you Google the phrase "a person of substance" you find a person of strong character, a person with true grit, a person of honor and trustworthiness, of depth, not vacuous or shallow. A person of substance carries weight, has presence, and therefore casts a shadow. This should be a hint of the importance of shadow in our lives.

Respecting shadow means to re-spect, to look at it again. Jung has supposedly written, "The brighter the light the darker the shadow." We can just as easily turn that around to say "the darker the shadow, the brighter the light." We tend not to think of it in that manner, however. In the same habit, astrologers like to say, "As above, so below" and leave it at that, ignoring the rest of the quote which inverts the first and states with equal power, "As below, so above."

This is important because in our cultural imagination we tend to think causally, that this causes that and we give *apriori* status and higher value to the categories of 'above' and 'light,' completely ignoring the equality and necessity of both 'lower' and 'shadow'. We suppress the interdependency of shadow and substance, light and dark, upper and lower. We forget that they arise mutually and then we tilt our astrology toward the light and upward movement thinking that 'light' is better than 'dark' and that ascending toward the light is better than descending into darkness. And finally, we believe that dayworld consciousness is to be preferred over the depths of the underworld.

This lopsidedness has been problematic evoking an astrology that is biased toward spirit at the expense of soul, biased toward progress, avoiding regress, preferring linearity over circularity, and hierarchy over democracy, growth instead of stasis, and enlightenment while avoiding endarkenment. We prefer a spirituality that allows us to climb to the mountaintop where the goodies are rather than to live in the valley of the shadow of death.

Now if your astrology carries a spiritual cast and rather than being substantial you believe a realized person is one who has become transparent to others, whose motivations are clearly seen, and who attempts to illuminate his shadow bringing it to the light, integrating it, if you will, then perhaps you will disagree with what is written here. Astrology as it is commonly practiced is used to bolster and strengthen the heroic ego, to give us a sense of control over our lives, pointing us toward personal growth and progress. Astrology can also be used however to cultivate imagination or in the terms of poet, John Keats and psychologist, James Hillman, "soul-making" which I believe has much to do with working with shadow.

Jung used the word shadow to denote the darker characteristics of our personalities constituted by our inferiorities, having autonomy, an emotional charge, and an obsessive/possessive quality. Because we are not prone to affirming these unacceptable impulses, thoughts, wishes, and shameful, under socialized behaviors, they have a tendency to fall into shadow and likely to be carried by others in our lives. Jung believed that shadow could only be realized through relationship. This can refer to individual relationships and also to relationships with groups, communities, and nations. Shadow according to Jung is "the thing a person has no wish to be" so all that is disgusting, perverse, and twisted within us lodges there. Evil gets located here as do devils and demons. Additionally, these primitive, awkward, and unpleasant features are carried by each and every one of us. It is what our ego casts behind it. Recall one of the foundational documents of western culture, the New Testament, "Get thee behind me Satan." It's important to remember however, to not reify this term, shadow, as if it were a thing, like a table or a tree. Shadow is metaphor, a useful fiction, like the planets, like the ego or the archetypes, and not a literal thing. Shadow is imaginal.

The cure or care for shadow has little to do with transforming it or bringing it into the light. Despite Alice Bailey's Labors of Hercules where Hercules wrestles with the Hydra, bringing the darkness to Light by lifting the Hydra into the light, this is the opposite strategy of what we wish to do. In his selected poems, Wendell Berry writes, "To Know the Dark,"

> *"To go in the dark with a light, is to know the light.*
> *To know the dark, go dark. Go without sight,*
> *and find that the dark, too, blooms and sings,*
> *and is traveled by dark feet and dark wings."*

Berry issues an express caution here if we wish to truly know the Dark. It is not about transforming it into the visible but to immerse ourselves in the invisible.

Now shadow for Jung is primarily a moral problem. For Hillman however, shadow is also a dilemma for love; how do we come about to affirm and give place to these ruined, deformed, loathsome aspects of our being without demanding they transform? There is a clue here, "without demanding they transform." In Hillman's thinking, loving shadow begins with carrying it even as it is a burden. It adds weight and gives substance to our character.

When we try to muzzle, control, or incarcerate our undesirable and less attractive features we face the moral dilemma and archetypal split of Dr. Jekyll and Mr. Hyde, Bruce Banner and the Hulk, Beauty and the Beast, and Dorian Gray with his ever-shifting shadowed portrait.

Much of life happens in darkness and shadow. Without the vast black matrix of space, we would not ever experience the stars. As the length of our days shortens, the beauty of the night sky opens to us. Seeds germinate in the dark soil, babies come to fruition in the darkness of the womb, and the body's organs operate in harmonic resonance without ever seeing how to do so or knowing the light. Injured creatures retire to dark out of the way places to recuperate, our own wounds cloaked in the darkness of the bandage allows the healing process to invisibly occur.

Working with shadow wounds cannot be done by facing the light because shadow remains unseen behind us. Befriending shadow requires turning away from the light, not toward, turning our backs to the light of spirit, ego, power, control, heroics, and facing our darkness without being overcome by it.

Keeping Chiron in mind here, the great healer who was unable to heal himself, the heroic ego is wounded and in order to move toward healing process, there needs be a surrendering of our sense of invulnerability and personal agency. There is a question here of faith; can I allow myself to relinquish control, to let go, to trust the process of my life as reflected in the dynamics of the natal chart?

The wound is an opening by which we are penetrated by Life, through which the Other may enter bringing us the experience of nascent wholeness. Keeping our wound, if only as scarring, reminds us of the burden we bear. This is the image of the wounded healer. The wounded healer is just that; wounded, not healed. It joins healer and patient in compassion. These dark elements of psyche, these negative qualities are discovered to be what make us human, unfolding our perfection (and by perfection I don't mean Virgoan flawlessness, which is an ego desire, but rather Piscean completeness or wholeness, wounds and all). As we learn to welcome our failures and shortcomings as best we are able, we find a welcome home for them in our lives.

Without Shadow, There is No Substance

Shadow as an archetypal image is not actually a problem to be solved but rather a mystery into which we are initiated; it can be experienced, explored, and affirmed as part of who we are. It is the Other calling to awaken us to the wholeness of experience. Its care requires the paradoxical acknowledgement, as Hillman notes in *Insearch* of "the moral recognition that these parts of me are burdensome and intolerable and must change" with "the loving laughing acceptance which takes them just as they are, joyfully, forever."

As is often the case, there is great truth in paradox. Living with that tension is the key to shadow work or soul making. Affirming shadow lends a certain liveliness, lustiness, and rascality to our lives. We see this in the figures of Zorba the Greek, Cool Hand Luke, Randall P. McMurphy from *One Flew Over the Cuckoo's Nest*, in the behaviors of Gurdjieff and Alan Watts. Psychologist, David Richo writes in *Shadow Dance*, "befriending the shadow is where good is worked with by bringing it out, evil is worked with by facing it and refusing to act it out." Notice he is not saying transform it into light.

In *Dark Nights of the Soul*, Thomas Moore writes, "Many people claim to have integrated their shadow sides, but that effort is itself a work against the dark. To integrate it is to co-opt it into the light. The real task is to live in, and with, the darkness, appreciating its unredeemed value and loving its irreversible qualities."

The work of integration is a heroic task of the ego as a way to strengthen and bolster it. Accepting shadow as it is denies this act of hubris and engenders humility, helping to keep us human and in our places rather than attempting to usurp planetary powers for our own purposes.

We fall into shadow or the daimonic, as the late Rollo May termed it in *Love and Will*, when any natural function with the power to take over the whole personality, overwhelm it, and behave in possessed compulsive ways, does so.

We become more aware of its features through suffering and dis-ease and we are deepened by this uncomfortable recognition.

Additionally, however, Jung and other analysts believe that shadow also carries positive qualities, creative impulses, normal instincts, and unrealized potential that for one reason or another we wish to keep hidden, something humanistic psychologist, Abraham Maslow, termed the "Jonah complex."

Where are we to find shadow in the chart? Almost anywhere! Inferior functions - elemental, modal, orientation, the 7th for unrecognized or disowned material, the 4th, 8th, and 12th houses for matters left out of awareness, hard aspects from the outer planets perhaps especially Saturn and Pluto.

Many assume that we know that when an element has a large presence in our chart it is likely a reflection of a familiarity and a flowing with that element. Fire as passionate, vital, alive, magnanimous, enthusiastic, creative action flowing easily. Earth has a good grounding in body, in the physical, the practical, the utilitarian. Air has an easygoing sociality, relational dexterity, and intellectual proficiency with a keen interest in a wide ranging field of topics. Water flows smoothly and without impediment expressing emotional congruity and situational sensitivity.

When an element has no planets or just one we think of that element as missing or inferior. Lacking Fire may erupt with heated intensity as rage, inappropriate anger, have incendiary temper tantrums, and be self-consuming. Inferior Earth may have difficulties with embodiment in general; it may erupt in illness, eating disorders, sexual disorders, substance abuse, depression, withholding, miserliness, criticism, and rigidity. Air can erupt with anxiety, panic, can't breathe, not enough air, too much spaciousness, agoraphobia, frightful clarity with a fear of going crazy, misjudging relational space being too close or too distant. Water may erupt with emotional flooding, feelings of being overwhelmed, fear of drowning in chaos, identity dissolution, or escapist behavior.

Lacking planets in Cardinal signs may burst out in impulsivity, sudden and unexpected starts and stops, explosive spontaneity. Lacking Fixity can erupt in irrational resistance to change, stubbornness, fixation or obsession upon someone or something, unhealthy attachments, difficulties letting go and moving on. Mutability can shadow forth as a coming apart at the seams, a falling to pieces, physical and emotional collapse, indecisiveness, and paralysis of will.

Lacking planets in Personal signs may erupt as irrational selfishness and self-centeredness. Lacking Interpersonal signs may burst with social neediness, may not wish to be alone, anxiousness in solitude. Lacking Transpersonal signs can emerge with a sudden zealousness or fanaticism for causes or movements.

My imagining of the chart is that it is an image of psyche or soul. We do not have a chart, we *are* a chart. We belong to it as cell to tissue, not it to us. It is not to be overcome or mastered, actualized or fulfilled, the chart is to be plumbed, fathomed, and entered into as one would a river. One can always revisit and draw deeply from the chart; it is a bottomless river of ever-fresh insighting.

The chart is a configural totality that includes both our inscape and our landscape. We experience life both from the inside and the outside. The 7th house paradoxically configures both us and Other. That which we dislike the most in others and triggers a strong affective reaction within us is likely to be a shadow quality. With the 7th house, we can look at the qualities of the sign on the cusp and any planets domiciled there.

It is likely that the more strongly we identify with our Ascendant, the more easily we meet and are drawn to the qualities of the DESC in the Otherness of the world in order to close or complete the gestalt, the unity of organism/environment. We may both disdain and desire these qualities and functions in an ever-shifting figure/ground relationship. Of course, any planets in the 7th can have a sense of otherness and autonomy about them. We recognize them in others yet occasionally their expressiveness can erupt out of our own unsettled ground frequently in the context of relationships. To the degree that we are unable to embrace these shadow qualities and functions is the degree to which we may find suffering and discomfort.

What's so special about the 12th, 4th, and 8th houses? One way of considering these houses as potential carriers of shadow is by recognizing that the houses that follow these are the houses of identity, the 1st, 5th, and 9th according to Arroyo in *Astrology, Psychology, and the Four Elements*. Awareness is inherent in these houses of identity, so what is left behind (out of awareness, if you will) resides in the preceding houses; 12th, 4th, and 8th, the qualities that go unrecognized or rejected in the larger matrix of our being. So we may wish to examine the signs on the cusp and the planets held within. I think the 8th house planets may be the most obvious because they express themselves within the context of our deepening of relationship, so reflection is more easily available via the mirror of the Other.

Lastly, think of the outer planets as trying to break us out of our lives and into our deeper layers. Are we finding ourselves obsessed and focused, becoming rigid and brittle perhaps under Saturn or fractured by Uranus, or feeling Neptune's dissolutive process, or Pluto flaying us alive, then dismembering or crucifying us?

Let us look at some examples. Chart data is generally from AstroDatabank (www.astro.com) and biographical information has been supplied by Google searches. First we have the chart of Dennis Wilson, the late drummer and founding brother of the Beach Boys.

Sun/Mars sextile Neptune trine Moon/Pluto and a Leo Ascendant - We can see a lot of energy in the chart and in fact Dennis was the only surfer in the Beach Boys. Besides being described as reckless, risk-taking, and living the fast life, he was also considered generous and overly sensitive. He had a lot of physical energy and was seen as combative.

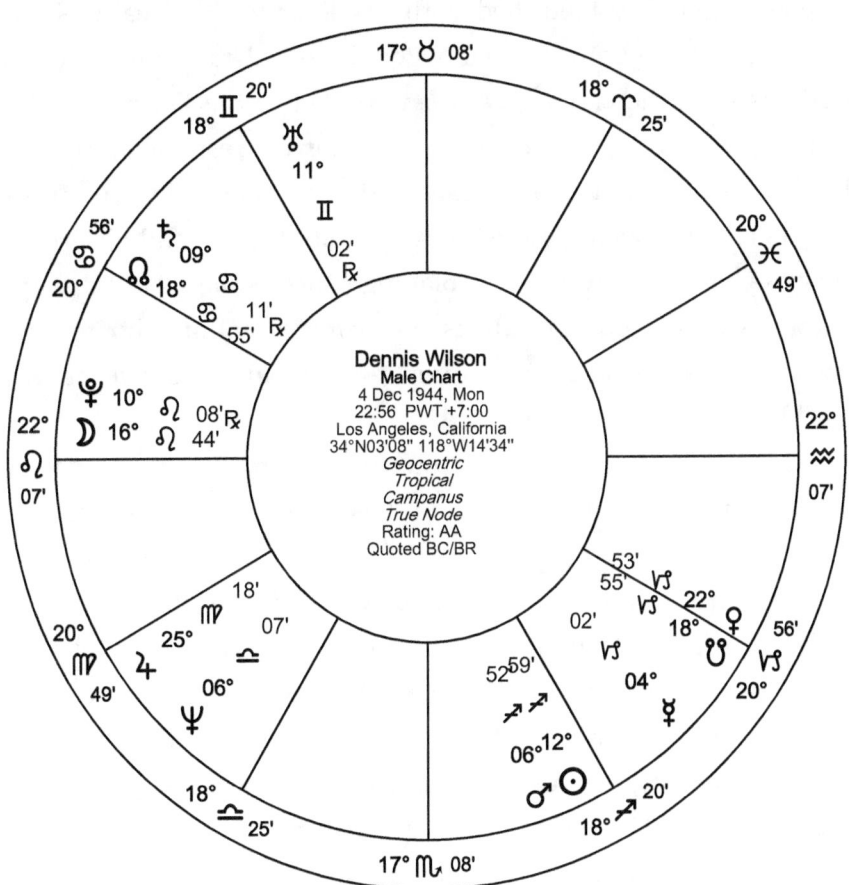

Saturn in Cancer - What intrigues me about shadow is this is the only planet in a water sign, so it would seem the feeling life would be an inferior function. There may have been fear of not having a sense of belonging to family. Additionally, we see Pluto possibly abducting the Moon in its placement in the 12th house. When the feeling function is in the underworld, there can be a deep emotionality that needs to be held in check, a fear of being flooded with feelings, fears of drowning in chaos, of being overwhelmed and loss of control and emotional balance. He refused to participate in family sing-alongs.

With Sun/Mars opposing Uranus and also quincunx Saturn, I believe he easily identified with his solar/martial features but had trouble with both the shadow qualities of Uranus and Saturn, perhaps even the classic *puer/senex* conflict of the Peter Pan who doesn't want to grow up. Dennis abhorred responsibility and battled the authority of an abusive father and authority structures in general. He was notorious for his rebelliousness, and his erratic reckless behavior. Even while playing concerts, he would disrupt shows with his onstage antics including streaking during one show while the band played. Anxiety-filled and aggressive, he was the black sheep of the family.

The possibly disowned Uranus in Gemini was the agent of his Aquarius 7th house cusp and this echoed in his 4 troubled marriages.

Neptune is the apex of a T-square and one of the ways it reflected the reality of Wilson's life was in his drug and alcohol abuse. It was reported that he was intoxicated when he died and his inferior function was literalized in his death from drowning. Oddly, transiting Uranus was conjunct the natal package of Sun/Mars opposing Uranus and quincunx Saturn.

Next, we have the chart of David Bowie.

Without Shadow, There is No Substance

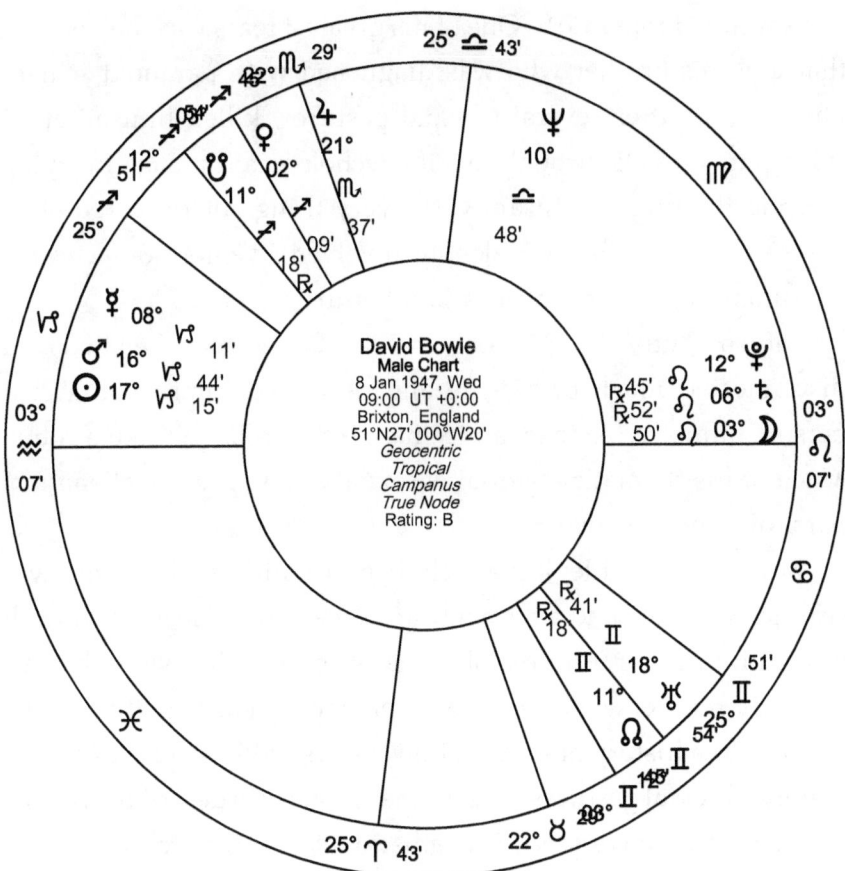

Aquarius Ascendant with Uranus in Gemini in 5th house - Career marked by continuous reinvention, innovation, and visual presentation. He changed his name, adopted personas, promoted an image of androgyny & bisexuality, wore dresses in public, was flamboyant, and flaunted sexual conventions and mores. Bowie was considered a musical chameleon. His desire was to shock the world; he initiated glam rock. Bowie permeated and altered more lives than any other pop culture figure at the time.

Sun/Mars/Mercury square Neptune can represent living in a fantasy world, identity confusion, deluded thinking, addiction problems, and softened masculinity.

Neptune Libra in 7th – One of his greatest fears was the insanity that took his brother who was diagnosed with paranoid schizophrenia and after several suicidal gestures, killed himself at 47. "One puts oneself through much psychological damage in trying to avoid the threat of insanity, the very thing you're scared of..." For several years he was deeply involved in enormous cocaine consumption, alcohol abuse, and other drugs.

Saturn/Pluto/Moon in Leo in 7th – Bowie felt alienated and disconnected much of his life and described himself as a cold person, numb to feelings, an iceman; offstage he felt like a robot. Much of his thematic material is sexual and expresses alienation, paranoia, and survival.

Bowie was an illegitimate child in a family where there was ceaseless harping and a tormenting atmosphere. The most warmth toward him came from his older half-brother with whom he was close. His mother was described as someone out of a nightmare. His family had a history of suicide. Bowie's first wife was a bit volatile, making suicidal gestures, and dramatic. She was described as "like living with a blowtorch." Bowie had fabled ability to cut off and sever relationships. Interestingly he ended up marrying a black Somalian supermodel in 1992, a combination of literal darkness (Pluto), and the perfection (Saturn) of the female form (Moon) who happened to have her Sun in Leo.

Jupiter in Scorpio in 8th – the wound. He was overindulging in problematic beliefs. He had fears of being possessed by a fiend, believed Satan was living in his indoor swimming pool, had an exorcism performed and thought witches wanted him to impregnate them. He believed in the occult, explored fascism, was intrigued by the Third Reich and Nazi mythology, and owned Nazi memorabilia. It is said much of this immersion in the darkness was related to excessive and extreme drug use.

Without Shadow, There is No Substance

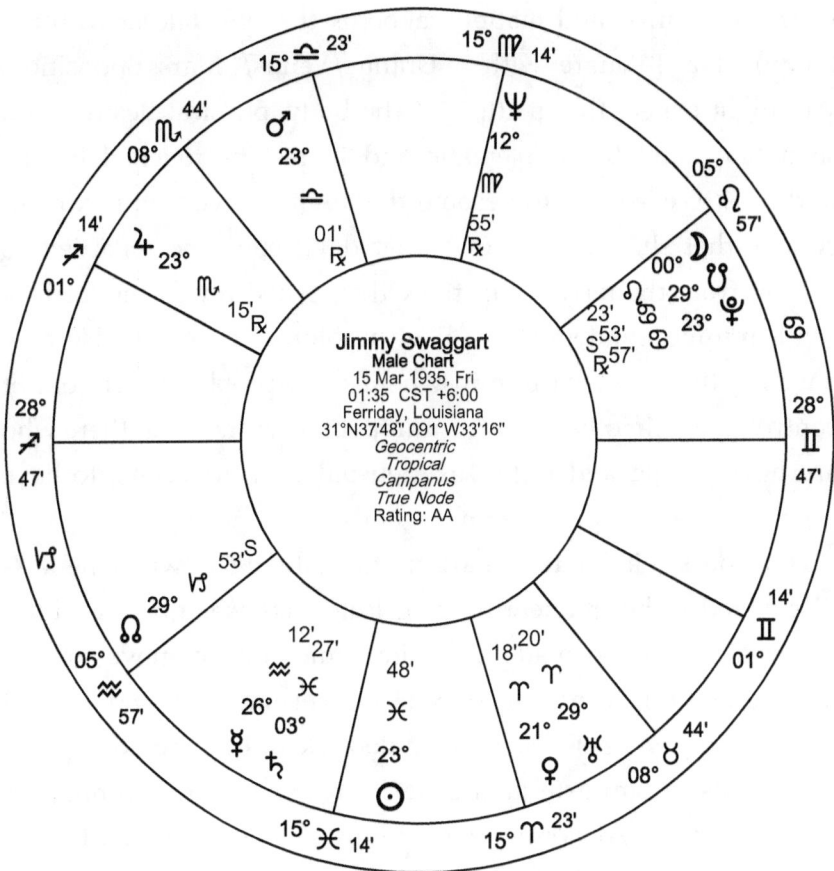

Next, the defrocked televangelist, Jimmy Swaggart.

I am indebted to psychotherapist/astrologer, Glenn Perry (www.aaperry.com), for much of my thinking in this chapter. Jimmy Swaggart was one America's great hellfire televangelists, the bastion of holiness and moral authority for thousands of believers in a world oozing with corruption and degradation. Through the 1980s he was at the top of his game with more than 3000 television stations and cable systems broadcasting his message about a sinful humanity and the need for redemption on a weekly basis.

Please note that Pluto in the 7th, the image of death and resurrection, crisis and transformation, wounding and healing, intensity, control, and matters taboo, is the apex (along with the Moon) of a T-square with a Uranus/Venus/ Mars opposition. We might expect that matters of the body, physical desires, and sexuality could be problematic and in fact be touched by the darkness of existence to become the devil's playground. Now of course, that shadow, that evil, that devil could be regarded as arising from the territory of the Other, especially in the form of the Feminine, the temptress, Eve the Mother of all ills. He may have felt that it wasn't him in whom these problems were out of control, it was in others, all the unrepentant sinners out there who are having wild and filthy sex. Sensual pleasure seems to have been a primary target for him.

Of course, it all fell apart in the late 1980s when he was discovered to be frequenting prostitutes. He was given a pulpit suspension and he made a public confession to move toward healing and forgiveness in 1988. His governing body did not feel him to be genuinely repentant, defrocked him, removing his credentials and ministerial license. He responded by becoming an independent non-denominational minister. Two years later he was again discovered to be in the company of a prostitute. It was then announced that he would temporarily step down for a "time of healing and counseling." I believe he missed his opportunity for healing if it is true that he believed that his indiscretions were due to demons trying to possess his soul. This is simply a continuation of casting his shadow behind him rather than turning to embrace it.

Another interesting feature of Swaggart's chart is the singleton Neptune in Virgo in the 8th, suggesting a wounded Neptune. It is in the only earth sign and is unaspected by major aspects. One of the ways of imagining this is as the suffering servant who seduces or is seduced, someone perhaps who has an idealized image of sexual intimacy; clean and pure. There can be a strong fascination with an idealized, perhaps disembodied sexuality, preferring watching to nitty-gritty involvement. Real sexual intimacy may be sacrificed in favor of a fantasy world of sex. With Neptune also conjunct the 9th house cusp we might expect his religious message to orient around the necessity to clean up sex, purify it, make it hygienic.

Let's take a look at the late right wing American radio host, Rush Limbaugh's chart.

One of the ways of reading Limbaugh's chart is to examine the western planets in their shadow functions. Limbaugh emerges out of a Capricorn matrix with a number of attorneys and judges in the

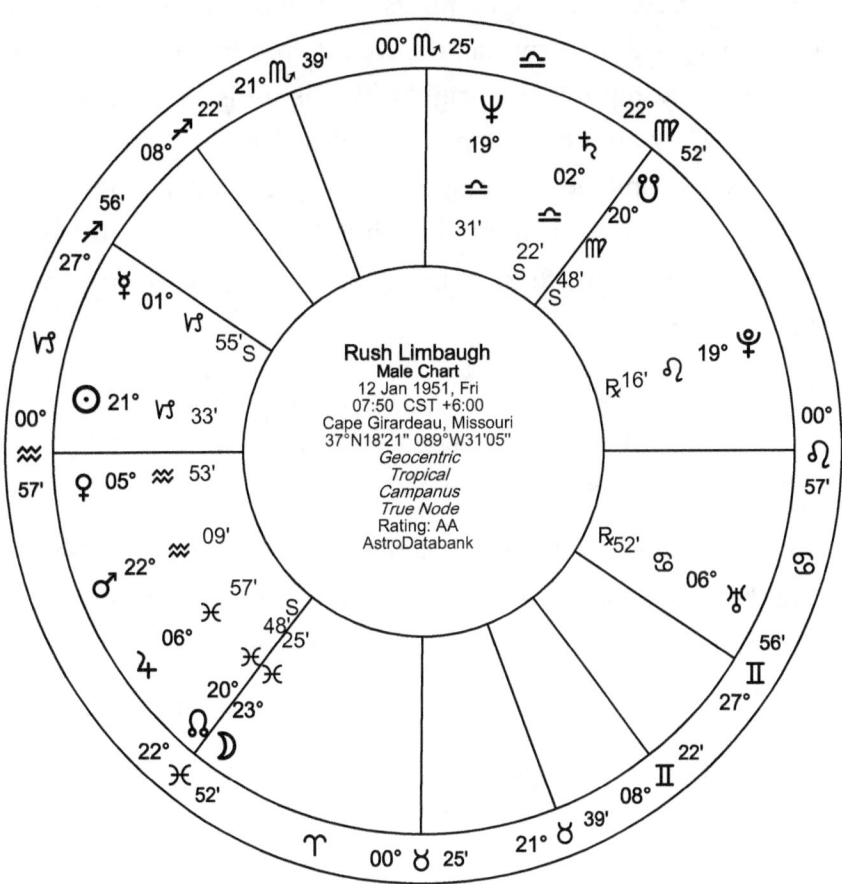

family including his grandfather, father, uncle, and brother and I believe he has an easy time identifying with the Saturn/Capricorn dynamic in his chart. I do imagine his Saturn to be wounded as he expresses his rigid authoritarianism.

Mercury opposing Uranus can image his use of communication technology to express his views and it can also be read as someone who tends to identify more with the conservative Mercury/Capricorn end of the aspect while disidentifying with the more progressive/liberal Uranus in 6th house attitudes especially around health and environment. A shadow Uranus can function as a provocateur and agitator, serving principles rather than people.

Themes associated with Uranus/Neptune such as liberalism, social progress, affirmative action, welfare programs, the feminist movement and reproductive rights stir his ire in ways that seem excessive. They are hot buttons for him and reflective of shadow issues as exemplified by his near relentless attack upon the reputation of law student Sandra Fluke for her testimony about health care and contraception. Limbaugh said of her testimony in 2012,

> "What does it say about the college co-ed Susan [sic] Fluke who goes before a congressional committee and essentially says that she must be paid to have sex," he said.

> "It makes her a slut, right? It makes her a prostitute. She wants to be paid to have sex. She's having so much sex she can't afford the contraception. She wants you and me and the taxpayers to pay her to have sex."

Additionally, the Sun square Neptune suggests once again identification with his Sun/Capricorn while his Neptune is shadowed in the 8th house. He has for many years attacked drug use in this nation (Quotes) yet he himself had to admit an addiction to prescription drugs, alleged doctor shopping, and was also found to be in possession of a quantity of Viagra that had someone else's name on the script.

It would appear that his identification with conservatism and sometimes the judgmentalism of Saturn/Capricorn leaves no room for honoring the compassion and acceptance of Moon/Pisces. His comments about Michael J. Fox lack common decency and sensitivity. Limbaugh said in 2021,

> "In this commercial, he [Fox] is exaggerating the effects of the disease," Rush said in the 2006 broadcast, while mocking Michael's tremors. "He is moving all around and shaking and this is purely an act. I have never seen Michael J. Fox display any of these symptoms of the disease."

Limbaugh has been married four times, none of which were long lasting. I think of Pluto in Leo in the 7th here opposing Mars and quincunx Sun and Moon.

He has been called vain and self-absorbed, referring to himself as the "epitome of morality and virtue, with talent on loan from God." We certainly hear some grandiosity here. He has also been accused by observers of misstating facts for his own purposes, engaging in deception, fraud, and outright lying on his show. This can be echoed by the shadow Neptune and Jupiter in Pisces in the 1st.

Lastly, the late singer, Whitney Houston.

In 2009, Whitney Houston was acclaimed as the most awarded female artist of all time by the Guinness World Record organization. She had been raised in an environment saturated with successful and independent women involved in gospel, R&B, soul, and pop music (Cissy Houston, Dionne Warwick, Darlene Love, Aretha Franklin). She was also raised in the Baptist church and exposed

Dark Skies

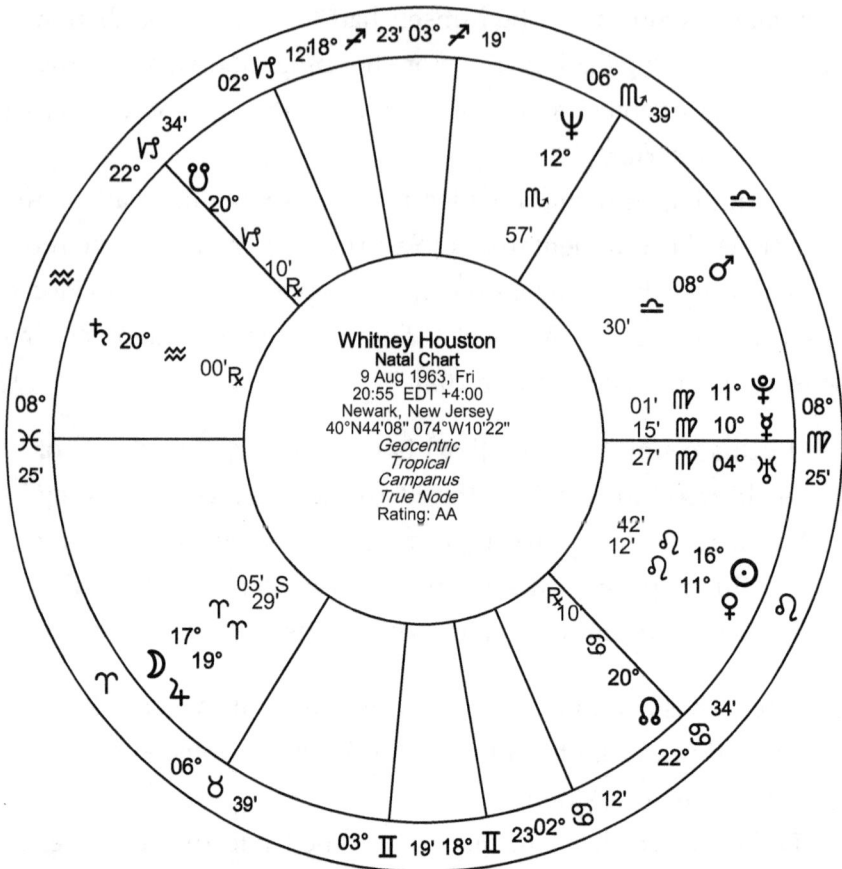

to the Pentecostal faith and went to Catholic girl's high school. She was very involved in the anti-apartheid movement and a variety of charitable organizations including her own Whitney Houston Foundation for Children.

I think we can agree that Pisces rising and the Moon/Jupiter conjunct in the first house image this quite nicely along with her own life-long performing activities echoed by the Sun/Venus conjunct in Leo in 6th trining that Moon/Jupiter. She was already working as a backup singer, developing her skills, at ages 14 and 15.

Without Shadow, There is No Substance

To the casual observer, she had it all. She was living the American dream, a glamorously beautiful model, famous, artistically successful, wealthy, immensely charitable, loved by many, and had solid religious values. She was popularly described as angelic, having divine talent, a national treasure, a singer's singer, a talent beyond compare, an amazing inspiration, the greatest singer ever heard, and a paradigmatic life for others to admire and emulate. Reading about her life up to a certain point is like reading a fairy tale. This, of course, is a terribly lopsided image to have to live up to for anyone. Where is the shadow out of which we're all woven?

Unfortunately, apex Neptune in Scorpio (singleton water) in the 8th and its significator, Pluto in the 7th suggest problems in those areas. I do not think it a stretch to suggest that her ex-husband, Bobby Brown, whom she met in 1989 and married in '92 (divorced '07) is Pluto walking into her life and accompanying her descent into the Underworld. As it turns out, he was abusive to her and together they were deeply involved in drugs on at least a daily basis by 1996. She had a significant history of alcohol, marijuana, crack, and cocaine use. She had on several occasions been to rehab but as her death indicates these substances continued as her unclaimed demons. I might also suggest that her earth planets hovering around her Descendant reflected the possibility of others carrying her earth for her and suggested embodiment issues. I find it interesting that both Wilson and Houston with singleton water planets died by drowning.

Much of the time we have protected ourselves well against Shadow not capitalized elsewhere, against the Night, girding our loins, tightening our belts, honing our weapons, and only occasionally getting a glimpse of something dangerous through the chinks in our armor. We try to keep a fairly tight rein on our little world, shoring up our walls, reinforcing our beliefs, traversing only narrow passageways to the outer world.

We have fantasies of confronting the guardian at the threshold, the sentinel at the bridge, the sentry at the checkpoint, the cherubim with the flaming sword at the gates of Eden and we get anxious, worried, and depressed to the point of scaring ourselves silly; becoming fearful of fear, anxious about anxiety, and sad about being depressed. We rarely take the step necessary to yank the mask from this foreboding figure to discover our original face. This move is paradoxical in that it is actually an instance of finding the courage to surrender our invulnerability and personal agency by stepping through the gate, over the bridge, across the threshold, into the underworld as the Sumerian myth of Inanna demonstrates. Like the later tale of Jesus, these are foundational narratives of Western culture, the notion of the necessary and willing sacrifice.

Befriending shadow is an opportunity for choice. We can make it an ego project and try to see what we can get out of it or how we might profit from it, making it an attempt at transforming dark into light, trash into treasure, or squares into trines. Or we can surrender to it; discover its claims upon us, moments when we are suffering and matters feel out of control, allowing our boundaries to disintegrate in order that we may truly meet Otherness in the forms of the daimonic, or genius, or soul.

The care that we offer the orphaned aspects of our selves is the cure that we seek. These are alchemical transformations that enrich us, deepen us, and initiate us into life's deep mysteries. These occasions reopen channels that allow the flowing of life to move less impeded through us. Thomas Moore, like Dante, cautions us to give up all hope; for growth, success, progress, or enlightenment and encourages us to be present to the world as it displays itself to us and perhaps discover what our service to the world may be.

These occasions do not necessarily require action or doing, they may simply require witnessing, being there in the midst of life swirling around and moving through us. This is not so much a resigned passivity or an impotent spectating as it is what Robert Romanyshyn in *Ways of the Heart* calls an archetypal activism. It is an intentional openness to the immediacy of existence, a willingness to be face to face with reality. It is taking a stance for what is; life inclusive of the neglected, the despised, the repulsive, the marginalized, and the forgotten. The energies that shape the cosmos, inform nature, and are personified as planetary gods, are the self-same energies that inform and comprise our deepest becoming in all its manifesting process. Shadow is who we are, as we are light also. Affirming dark elements is saying "Yes" to life in the midst of chaos, suffering, and death. Find that dark god in your chart and embrace it. Everything will change.

Let me close with a poem, "The Guest House" by Rumi.

This being human is a guest house.
Every morning a new arrival.
A joy, a depression, a meanness,
some momentary awareness comes
As an unexpected visitor.
Welcome and entertain them all!
Even if they're a crowd of sorrows,
who violently sweep your house
empty of its furniture,
still treat each guest honorably.
He may be clearing you out
for some new delight.
The dark thought, the shame, the malice,
meet them at the door laughing,

and invite them in.
Be grateful for whoever comes,
because each has been sent
as a guide from beyond.

12

Astrology and the Unseen Side of Relationship

Many of us have junk drawers at home with forgotten bits and bobs jumbled inside or closets where too much stuff is stored. Some of us have rooms or basements that we prefer company not see. We all have secrets, sometimes embarrassing and dark secrets that we don't easily share with others, not just about stuff in our rooms that we don't want people to see but also about people in our lives.

Classically it's been said that women love the bad boys. How many are willing to acknowledge this kind of relationship? Some of these relationships carry a strong hint of foreboding or a whiff of danger. Some can leave us feeling ripped off, perhaps feeling stalked by an ex, and/or emotionally torn apart.

For men, we sometimes answer the seductive song of the sultry siren and abandon our established life, everything that has anchored us, and pursue this goddess embodied to who knows where.

And I assume that these relational difficulties also apply in the LGBTQ+ community as this is a human problem. Perhaps there is a deeper understanding of these attractions and their hidden blessing despite their having been problematic in our experience.

The birth chart is not only a literal map of the sky showing where the planets in the solar system were at the originating moment when we emerged out of the world but is also, an image disclosing the hidden architecture of a temporary moment that echoes throughout a life. One of the things that a chart reflects is our likely attitudes about relationships, the kinds of people we are drawn to, and what is it that we are seeking in relationship? Plato thought we were seeking completion. In his Symposium, he tells the story of the original humans who were joined back to back as round beings. Because of human strength and rebelliousness, Zeus cut them in two and so they eternally seek for their other half, their original wholeness.

Relationship, especially marriage, is a minefield; we are pushed and pulled in so many directions, so many fantasies, so many sudden attractions and stressful demands, so much boredom, the occasional excitements, the chase for security, romance, disappointments, and triumphs. Marriage can be a chalice of transformation that challenges us to hone our skills for interacting with others in truly authentic and intimate ways and helps us recognize parts of experience that we normally ignore or keep out of view.

Carl Jung (CW 9, para. 126), noted that for him, "The psychological rule is that when an inner situation is not made conscious, it happens outside as fate." In other words, we can say that our relationships manifest the unacknowledged business within ourselves. Jung also gave us the word, 'shadow' to denote the unwanted baggage constituted by our inferiorities, carrying an emotional charge, having an obsessive-possessive quality, and possessing autonomy. I'm not fond of the word shadow as it's overused and seems to have taken an exclusively negative cast in our culture. You've used it a lot in other chapters Perhaps we can refer to this darkness as our shade, a word carrying a more neutral connotation. Shade can be something protective, cooling, and beneficial as well as referring to the wandering denizens of Hades.

Because we are not prone to affirming impulses, thoughts, wishes, and shameful, under-socialized behaviors that we find undesirable, this baggage tends to fall into the shade and is likely to be carried by others in our lives. Say for instance that we are the kind of person who abhors aggressive, pushy people and prefers to act in a cooperative and diplomatic fashion. We may find that we frequently attract the kind of people that we dislike. This is shade material which Jung believed could only be realized through relationship. One classic example of this is the play *The Odd Couple* by Neil Simon.

These unwanted qualities that are all disliked, repulsive, and twisted within us lodge in this Otherworld. Evil gets located there as do devils and demons.

When we try to muzzle, control, or incarcerate our undesirable and less attractive features we face the moral dilemma and archetypal split of Dr. Jekyll and Mr. Hyde, Bruce Banner and the Hulk, Beauty and the Beast, and Dorian Gray with his ever-shifting, darkening portrait.

My imagining of the chart is that it is an image of psyche or soul. We do not have a chart, we are a chart, the chart is a reflection, an image that mirrors our interiority, while at the same time expressing that we are images of a larger cosmos. Though many astrologers believe the chart is to be overcome, mastered, or fulfilled, my own point of view is that the chart is to be plumbed, fathomed, imagined, and entered into as one would a sacred pool. One can always revisit and draw deeply from the chart; it is a bottomless well of ever fresh insighting. The chart is a gestalt; a configural totality so unified as a whole that its properties cannot be derived from a simple summation of its parts.

Similarly, our lives appear to be wholes within wholes, within wholes though often we feel alone, alienated, and fractured within our relations. Bringing awareness to these distinct areas of our lives, by discerning these figures in the Otherworld, is part of the role of astrology.

We can find shade in any number of places in the chart but the focus here is upon the 7th house, the planets within the 7th house, and planets challenging Venus, planet of Love. Additionally, what are the 1st and 7th houses referencing? The chart includes both our inscape and our landscape. We experience life both from the inside (experience) and the outside (events). The 7th house paradoxically configures both us and Other. We are drawn to certain people who express our longing, and we are drawn to that of which we are unaware and often dislike most in others. This triggers a strong affective reaction within us and is likely to be a disidentified quality. With the 7th house, we can look at the qualities of the sign on the cusp and any planets domiciled there.

The Self/Other polarity is a yin and yang dynamic or magnetic north and south, it is the wholeness of which we are part. Self is in the foreground and Other is generally in the background. It is likely that the more strongly we identify with our Ascendant, the more easily we meet and are drawn or repulsed by the qualities of the Descendant in the Otherness of the world. In order to close or complete this gestalt, the unity of organism/environment, it does not require that we master the planets or the sign on the cusp of the 7th. Others may always express those factors of which we are disidentified or unskilled in managing. What may be important is that we becomes aware of, affirm, and learn to appreciate those qualities and functions that we may both disdain and desire and are in a dynamic ever shifting figure/ground relationship.

Let us look at the 6 pairs of signs imagining each dyad on the Self/Other axis.

Aries/Libra - Aries rising with its orientation toward being assertive, competitive, direct, impulsive, spontaneous, decisive, fearless, and impatient. Aries can have difficulty claiming the

Libran qualities of being relational, cooperative, compliant, collaborative, diplomatic, tactful, considerate, fair and balanced that are in the background i.e., to be found in others.

Taurus/Scorpio - Taurus rising with its orientation toward being calm, placid, stable, reliable, conservative, patient, steadfast, comfortable and pleasure-seeking has difficulty admitting the Scorpionic qualities of being intensely passionate, provocative, erotic, penetrating, deep, destabilizing, transformative, dramatic, and power-oriented.

Gemini/Sagittarius - Gemini rising is oriented toward curiosity, immediacy, amorality, restlessness, versatility, superficiality, scatteredness, clever, witty, endless fact-gathering and studiousness. Finding a place for the Sagittarian qualities that establish frameworks of meaning for the facts, (morals and philosophy) for being visionary, for planning ahead, seeing the big picture, knowing when to stop and teach, preach, promote, and disseminate is the challenge.

Cancer/Capricorn - Cancer rising is oriented around being tender, emotionally warm, nourishing, caring, gentle, protective, nurturing, sensitive, responsive, and unconditionally accepting. It has difficulty owning the Capricornian qualities of conditional acceptance, being judgmental, setting standards, being exacting, disciplined, reserved, rigid, perfectionistic, ambitious, and prudent.

Leo/Aquarius - A Leo Ascendant is oriented toward being special, creative, expressive, fiery, showy, egocentric, boastful, dramatic, prideful, confident, and playful. There may be difficulty honoring the Aquarian qualities of just being a face in the crowd, part of the group, democratic, freedom-loving, aloof, detached, unusual, impersonal, and shocking.

Virgo/Pisces - Virgo rising is oriented toward precision, competence, discrimination, improvement, utility, and looks at the world as needing to run more efficiently, to be made better through critical assessment, and detailed analysis. It finds it hard to imagine Piscean inclusiveness, compassion, mushiness, complacency, vacillation, laissez faire, and go with the flow, escapist attitudes.

We can also reverse these to examine Aries on the 7th, then Taurus, Gemini, etc.

Libra rising with Aries on the 7th exemplifies the qualities of being relational, cooperative, compliant, collaborative, diplomatic, tactful, considerate, deferential, fair and balanced. It may have difficulty affirming being assertive, possessing a me-first attitude, competitive, direct, impulsive, decisive, spontaneous, and impatient.

Scorpio reflects being passionate, intense, provocative, penetrating, deep, transformative, dramatic, and power-oriented. There may be a problem incorporating a sense of calm, stability, reliability, patience, steadfastness, and just being placid.

Sagittarius wants wanderlust, travel, teaching, preaching, making meaning (morals and philosophy), being visionary, making pronouncements, grand plans, seeing the big picture, finding that the grass is greener elsewhere. It may have a problem owning the trivial, superficial, restlessness, scatteredness, endless curiosity, fact-gathering, and cataloguing.

Capricorn wants to organize, structure, give form to, and control. It is exacting, ambitious, and seeking perfection. It is disciplined, reserved, formal, and prudent. It has great difficulty with unconditional, non-judgmental, acceptance of others and doesn't grasp wanting to nourish, express caring, nurturing, sensitivity, and responsiveness.

Aquarius wants to be part of the group, democratic, freedom-loving, easily gathering perspectives, innovative, progressive, and liberal. It may have problems with the Leo qualities of wanting to feel special, showy, egocentric, dramatic, being in the spotlight, and entitled.

Pisces rising is sensitive, delicate, compassionate, romantic, poetic, imaginative, and retiring. It has trouble with Virgo's dynamic to involve itself and serve in a pragmatic fashion, seeking self-improvement to function competently, efficiently, and able to manage the world.

Of course, any planet in the 7th can have a sense of Otherness and autonomy about them. We recognize them in others yet occasionally their expressiveness can erupt out of our own unsettled ground frequently in the context of complaints about the relationship. The degree to which we are unable to embrace these Otherworld figures indicates the point where we may find stress and discomfort.

Those with the Sun in the 7th may be challenged to feel like an independent whole person without a partner in their life. The partner may carry all the shine in the relationship and stand in the spotlight for the couple. Shade becomes visible when the person accuses the partner of being too self-centered, too childish, always demanding attention, clamoring for praise.

The Moon may have problems being in touch with their feeling life without a partner. They seek emotional security and nurturing, wanting to be cared for by their partner. The dark side appears when the person accuses the partner of being too dependent, too clinging, insecure and moody, always needing the person to lead the way.

Mercury in the 7th will find themselves attracted to partners who may be witty, clever, curious, and intelligent. Sometimes a partner who can handle everyday problems with competence, efficiency and with a keen eye for what needs to be done. Tiny devils gather when this person starts to complain about the partner being too critical or intrusive, or a know it all who just chatters on all the time about trivial matters.

A 7th house Venus will be attracted to a partner who exhibits beauty, sensuousness, and social desirability, someone who expresses social graces, mannerly and tuned in to other's needs. Disappointment arises when the person charges the partner with being flirtatious, a people pleaser, not standing up for oneself, overly accommodating and too conciliatory.

Mars may seek a partner who comes across as confident, bold, decisive, assertive, energetic, heroic, and dynamic. Difficulties can be found when the person complains to the partner of insensitivity, impatience, touchiness, selfishness, domineering, being pushy, hot-headed, and always on the go.

Jupiter may be attracted to partners who seem wise and cultured, philosophical and/or religious, a morally upright partner who is optimistic and enthusiastic, perhaps an outdoors person or someone who loves to travel. The underside is revealed when the person complains that the partner is too preachy, pompous, dogmatic, hypocritical, restless, or given to exaggeration, with commitment difficulties.

Saturn suggests that the person will be attracted to someone with status and authority, who is responsible, well organized, serious, disciplined, reliable, hardworking, punctual, goal oriented, and manages life well. The scene darkens when the person complains that the partner is an old stick in the mud, lacking excitement and playfulness, never wanting to have fun, perhaps too demanding, critical, miserly, and frequently becomes an obstacle.

Uranus may be drawn to the liberal, humanitarian, inventive, avant-garde, socially involved, cutting-edge partner who will carry these progressive qualities for the person. The Otherworld begins to peek out when the person complains that the partner is detached and distant, more involved with causes than intimacy, always agitating, inconstant in affection, and undermining the relationship.

Neptune may be drawn to the romantic, the poet, the musician, the monk, the dreamer, the visionary - compassionate, empathic, imaginative, devoted, and forgiving. Darkness seeps in when the person starts to complain about the big dreams and no results of the partner, of passivity, apathy, being unrealistic, impractical, drinking too much, and/or other escapist behaviors.

When found in the 7th, Pluto becomes the classic bad boy attraction - someone who is slightly dangerous, mysterious, out of the ordinary, reckless, powerful, lives by their own rules, lives on the wild side. Shadow erupts when the person complains that the partner is dominating, possessive, jealous, and controlling, perhaps uncaring, untrusting, and overly suspicious.

Now I also mentioned that we might want to pay attention to challenging aspects to the planet of love, sex, and relatedness, Venus.

Venus in challenging aspect to Saturn may seek partners with status and authority who are emotionally restrained.

With Uranus, they may draw partners who are erratic in giving affection, detached or poorly committed.

Neptune may be drawn to dysfunctional partners whom they can rescue or save.

Pluto seeking drama, excitement, passion, and may wish to remake their partners.

Houses (4/8/12) preceding those of Identity (5/9/1) may be looked at for qualities left out of our awareness. These would include missing or few elements in the chart, modalities, and orientation. Outer planet transits may provide meaningful opportunities for contemplation of relational problems.

It is not easy working with these Invisibles. It is apparent because they sit outside of our awareness and are as complicated as the chart is deep and as complex as a person. We are enigmatic creatures and relationships are one of the deep mysteries of being human.

Here is an exercise for engaging relationships through the interpersonal signs, Leo, Virgo, Libra, and Scorpio.

Begin with Leo; which can be imagined as our own sense of enclosed identity in relation to a social community.

Virgo - Then, focus upon three things about your partner that are either strongly disliked or drive you crazy. List them; write about each one in exquisite detail. What is bothersome about them, how is it troubling, what would it be like if they disappeared or conversely, became a constant companion?

Libra - Further engage this shade material by making it a partner, personifying it in a way that makes sense, maybe it's a critical parent, or a dark stranger, or a controlling lover, or a needy child or a smothering spouse; whatever personification works. Have an imaginary dialogue with it, write down or record the conversations, what does it want? How may it help?

Last, Scorpio, after engagement, we want intimacy, to deepen the relationship, to affirm it, to honor it. Do not try to change it, bring it into awareness. If it's an angry darkness, get closer to the anger, into feeling angry without endangering anyone. If it's childish, be childish for a short period of time. If it is very formal and uptight, experiment with being formal and uptight, if it's free spirited, be free spirited for a half hour. The point is to experience those qualities which we disdain, become familiar with them without having to act them out unawares. Choose one, try on its awareness, its style, attitude, and feeling tone, hold the tension of this uncomfortable stance and allow it to blossom within and then recede.

Last, as we finish the exercise with the interpersonal signs, we move to Sagittarius, fire at a different developmental level (transpersonal); reflect upon this experience and discover if it has meaning. Do matters make a bit more sense now, is there an intuition that some understanding has been gained? My thinking is that if it works, a complex of feelings may appear, including a sense of being slightly humbled, less self-important than Leo, and more accepting of others.

Shade material is often like a small child tugging at our pant leg. It will continue to tug on our leg until we address its concern. Once attending to its need, it has no reason to continue to be a bother and we have no need to pass this baggage off to our partners to carry for us.

We'll get a better sense of how we're doing when someone enacts our hidden figures and immediately after our emotional response, we chuckle, recognizing what happened. Later on down the road when shade or shadow is enacted again by someone, rather than emotional upset, we will smile to ourselves in familial recognition.

We can run from Otherworld elements and still encounter them over and over again in our relationships, we can make working with dark matters an ego project and try to see what we can get out of it or how we might profit from it, making it an attempt at transforming dark into light. Or we can surrender to them; discover their claims upon us, honor them and have no need for this shadowed manifestation of seeming fate.

Affirming our rejected or unacknowledged aspects is a saying "Yes" to life in the midst of discomfort, disappointment, and failure. Find the dark gods in life and engage them. Everything may change.

13

Belonging to Nature: As Below, So Above

The following comments are directed toward the field of psychological astrology and working with clients. My contention is that our practice of astrology is lopsided, tilted toward fire and air, too spacey and so out there that it tends to overlook the client's situated presence by ignoring the more earthy/watery elements. This diminishes the power of this wisdom tradition. I will suggest that there are ways to give astrology greater groundedness, bringing out its ecological undercurrent. The subtext here is exploring how our beliefs impact our conception and practice of astrology.

I begin by asking, "Am I a body (1st house) or do I have a body (2nd house)? The implication of how one answers this question is profound as it discloses one's fundamental orientation to life. A phrase attributed to Jesuit priest, Pierre Teilhard de Chardin, makes the claim, "We are not human beings having a spiritual experience. We are spiritual beings having a human experience." I suspect that many readers have heard this before and many no doubt hold this position. But is there another way of viewing our situation?

Having a body (2nd house of possessions) implies a dualism between self and its possessions, between spirit and matter, an idea that asserts we are something different and separable from our physicality, a kind of ghost in the machine, an idea that gained major footing from philosopher Rene Descartes (whose only certainty was, "I think, therefore I am.") in the 17th century and essentially launched the 'objectivist' point of view that allowed science to detach from an animated world and begin a centuries-long interaction with a humanity seeking control, predictability, and mastery of nature. The 'ghost in the machine' is the metaphor associated with the mind/body dualism that Descartes firmly established. It is the idea that some discarnate something – spirit, soul, self, mind incarnates at birth and then leaves upon death. It has been historically considered to be the eternal aspect of a person, i.e., who a person truly is. Accompanying this belief is the notion for some that we are here for learning lessons, that human life is a testing ground of some sort after which we expire and then travel on to another existence. It is clear from this perspective that earth is not our origin and is not our true home.

To say that I am a body (1st house) suggests that identity and existence are seamless, whole cloth, non-dual, a whirling expression of an intelligent, vital, flowing, living cosmic network of which humans are integral and inseparable wholes within wholes within wholes. This line of thinking was initially introduced to astrology by Rudhyar in 1936 when he wrote about the concept of holism. His book, *The Astrology of Personality*, though strongly colored by Theosophy, is still a must read for serious astrological thinkers.

The idea to consider is that we don't come into this world from somewhere but rather are born out of it, our becoming is a material event, we body forth headfirst from a great feminine mystery at a specific moment, not some other moment, and in a specific place, not some other place. It is through us that nature becomes aware of itself within a never to be repeated, unique and particular perspective which is hinted at by the axes in a chart. In a sense the axes which are the most individualized feature in the chart denote our unique perspective through which we experience the phenomenal world. In a lecture delivered by cultural historian and astrologer, Patrick Curry titled, "Enchantment, Embodiment, and Ecology," he states,

> "First, you are not merely 'in' a body, nor do you merely 'have' one, as if you were essentially unaffected by it. Your body is what makes it possible to be a person at all: not only to live, but to know and feel anything whatsoever, and to be apprehended in turn."

From this point of view, one could no more separate spirit from body than we could separate north from south, foreground from background, or organism from environment. Each partner within a polarity implicates the existence of the other, provides contextual meaning whether its 1st house/7th house or Cancer/Capricorn. These partners are eternally dancing with one another and are inseparable, like the dynamism of the tai chi symbol or Pisces.

Though we can't know with certainty when and where astrology first originated, what we do know is nearly every major culture had some practice of observing the heavens, its movements and turnings, and creating meaning from this. These civilizations tended to be patriarchal, having a king, emperor, pharaoh, or crowned sovereigns of some sort who were regarded as ruling by divine right or were believed to be divine in themselves. These were solar cultures whose focus quite naturally was in the sky, the realm of the gods. It is easy to imagine the dominance of the Sun in these cultures with the social structures being patriarchal, monarchial, and hierarchical. Already we are looking up and away from the earth. (Now is that to say there were no female deities or rulers? Of course not, but these would be the exception rather than the rule.)

The sky is traditionally associated with masculine and paternal and the earth is traditionally associated with the feminine and maternal; Father Sky/Mother Earth. These metaphors were developing long before the beginnings of western civilization. As it happens the foundational orientation of the west developed within the metaphors of fire and air, as did our social structures, educational systems, religious traditions, and our astrology.

When a civilization has a solar or sky god orientation, then fire and air which rise and move freely about, tend to be the dominant metaphors for all that is deemed good, powerful, and carries value. Spirit is up, the sacred appears or lives on the high mountain peaks - on Mt. Olympus, Mt. Arafat, Mt. Sinai, Mt. Fuji, Mt. Kalish, Mt. Etna, and the list goes on. Mountains are holier than swamps and afford a great view and therefore a wider perspective available from on high. You can more easily see trouble approaching from a distance. The Christian god resides in a heavenly abode but also appears as a burning bush or in a whirlwind, Jesus ascends to Heaven, angels abide in starry realms, near death experiences move us up toward the Light, answers are to be found in the planets and other heavenly significators, etc.

Height opens the possibility of moving away from the depths of life, the nitty gritty messiness of living. There is no mud and stink in the sky or on the mountain where it is sunny, dry and the air is fresh. Malevolent angels and immoral people are cast down to where we find the hot, fetid, and stagnant places. Earth itself is soiled, stained, and dirty. Historically, nature, the body, and woman have been repudiated and devalued in western civilization as simply objects and commodities for use in any way that we please. Of course, the masculine world made the rules and constructed the game plan.

So as a culture, we tend to privilege metaphors of up over down, height over depth, raising over lowering, ascent over descent, spiritual over material, light over dark, masculine over feminine, expanding over contracting, superior over inferior, and growth over stasis to offer more metaphors. Contemplating the vast heavens opens us to the possibility of unlimited expansion stirring fantasies of being the biggest and the best, to be on top, to be #1 to enact the Doctrine of Discovery which allowed European explorers to claim and colonize all lands "discovered." This colonizing settler attitude promulgated the idea of Manifest Destiny of America's expansion, in the 19th century. The West had carved up the world as it pleased and brought civilization, religion and science to every people in every land, leaving carcasses and indigenous culture behind.

We like to fantasize that our thinking and rationality, located in the head, are superior to feelings and intuitions located lower down in the heart and gut. We consider our cognitive skills to be civilized higher functions and our feelings primitive and lower. Men are designated as rational beings and women as emotional beings. It is easy to see how the deck is stacked against earth and water.

My contention is that our astrology with its fire/air emphasis contributes little or nothing toward the benefit of a planet in peril. To borrow from the late Thomas Berry, we are not the crown of creation, the human species is derivative, it is the earth that is primary and revelatory of the sacred. It's impossible to achieve or maintain human flourishing within an environment that is severely damaged. We are consuming our planet and ourselves and our astrology may contribute to this. I do have a sliver of hope that our culture may be recovering this ancient direction judging by the publishing world. So many books are being released that reanimate the world bringing our attention to the place of our species on the planet; books about re-enchantment, eco-philosophy, deep ecology, indigenous writings, erotic biology, environmental psychology are burgeoning but I have not discovered anything in astrology.

When our astrology aligns with fire/air metaphors orienting us skyward, the chart and what it signifies provides a shift in perspective away from our grounded existence, our lived experience. When we look upward, we pay more attention to the planets than to people. For instance, when we hear of a tragedy occurring, rather than absorbing the emotional jolt of the experience, we quickly move toward abstracting a chart for the event seeking astrological reasons and conditions. Concrete tragedy (earth/water) becomes intellectual exercise (air/fire). How many of us do this I wonder. The mass shootings, the collapse of a building, the structural failure of a bridge, the sudden death of a person, the kidnapping of a child, the earthquake that destroys a town, the sinking of a ship, etc., are all reported by a 24/7 media that saturates us with an endless flow of human suffering. It is not surprising then that we may move toward astrology as a strategy for detaching and defending ourselves from pain and discomfort. We distance ourselves by looking to the heavens.

We also move away from the untidiness of living by empowering the planets up there over the people right here. The language we use betrays us. When I learned astrology, the chart assumed the metaphor of a timepiece, a clock by which we could measure our lives and activities. The chart was also understood by the metaphor of a mirror reflecting our Life-world. We may still give lip service to those metaphors but pick up almost any dictionary or astrology text and you'll see the language used often suggests that planets have agency and serve to explain how you are as a person. And yet, a timepiece showing noon does not explain my hunger nor does a mirror produce the age spots I see on my face. The metaphors that

Belonging to Nature: As Below, So Above

I learned for understanding astrology are invalidated by common definitions of astrology.

> From the *Oxford Dictionary* – "the study of the positions of the stars and the movements of the planets in the belief that they **influence** human affairs."

> From the *Free Dictionary* – "The study of the positions and motions of celestial bodies in the belief that they have an **influence** on the course of natural earthly occurrences and human affairs."

> *Merriam-Webster Dictionary* – "the divination of the supposed **influences** of the stars and planets on human affairs and terrestrial events by their positions and aspects."

> *American Heritage Dictionary* – "The study of the positions and motions of celestial bodies in the belief that they have an **influence** on the course of natural earthly occurrences and human affairs."

> *The Collins English Dictionary* – "the study of the movements of the planets, sun, moon, and stars in the belief that these movements can have an **influence** on people's lives."

If the above are what the general public has access to for understanding astrology, I can understand why the majority of people give it little credence. But it's not just dictionaries that locate agency in the heavens, astrologers do also. Some examples from popular authors (words in **bold** are my emphasis):

"Saturn **teaches** one virtue above all others…. Saturn **seeks** to focus the will…" (Forrest, *The Inner Sky*, p.123)

"This Mars **wants to penetrate** into …." (Hillman, *Planets in Play*, p.178)

"The **energies of the planet** that Pluto is transiting…." (Hand, *Planets in Transit,* p.477)

"Transiting **planets…tend** to awaken new awareness of the issues related to that house." (Bogart, *Planets in Therapy*, p.300)

"**Saturn's ambitions** are magnified and vitalized by Leo." (Tierney, *Twelve Faces of Saturn*, p.119)

"Mars square Jupiter – **This makes you** want to experience everything you can." (Van Toen, *The Mars Book*, p.79)

I do not mean to imply that these noted astrologers believe the planets have actual agency and influence our lives but rather that our language maintains the dualism that keeps us separate from a grounded life.

I am not asking any astrologer to change their language but rather asking that we be aware of how we use language in ways that may be disempowering to clients while trying to empower clients at the same time. Personal agency seeps away from the person.

I believe this is more of a problem with the structure of our language than it is a true belief in the power of planets. Language and reality mutually shape and reflect each other and consequently how we use it in astrology matters if we wish to empower people rather than planets, to ground a person in their own personal agency. With the Romance languages, there is the idea of nouns (subjects) performing actions (verbs) on the world (objects), it entirely separates humans from the cosmos to the extent that we are somehow alienated from nature and cosmos. So when we suggest a planet (noun) influencing, impelling, causing, making (verb) me (as the object) do something, it diminishes my own power to act in ways that I can own. It's a nice way to victimize ourselves and conveniently escape responsibility by saying, transiting Pluto was behind it, the devil made me do it, a chemical imbalance made me this way, or my rotten childhood is responsible, etc., etc., etc.

As I've mentioned numerous times in lectures, the maxim, "as above, so below," is dangerous because it suggests a subtle causal emphasis from on high (active fire/air over receiving earth/water). It privileges above over below. The phrase is from *The Emerald Tablet of Hermes* (Merchant Books, 2013), a hermetic document first appearing in Arabic about 1400 years ago. In full translations of this opening line, there is no suggestion of *apriori* value of higher over lower; each is mutually dependent upon the other in the manner of yin/yang, front/back, and foreground/background.

Some translations of this first line:

"That which is above is from that which is below, and that which is below is from that which is above, working the miracles of one."

"The above from the below, and the below from the above, the work of the miracle of the One."

"As below, so above, and as above so below. With this knowledge alone you may work miracles."

"What is above is like what is below. What is below is like what is above. The miracle of unity is to be attained."

"See, the highest is from the lowest, and the lowest from the highest, indeed, marvelous work of the Tao."

These are all statements of mutuality, of interdependence and reliance upon one another, neither having "power over" the other, but rather "power with". In the same manner, the planets above do not have power over us, they mirror our agency. We mutually reflect each other and therefore what the heavens reflect is the vast sky within us. The planets that we see are ciphers for a deeper solar system within. Bring the planets out of the sky and into the person. According to author, Thomas Moore, one of the images of our interiority during the Renaissance was the night sky (*The Re-enchantment of Everyday Life*: ch. "Astrology's Truth").

Patrick Curry, who I quoted earlier notes in an article from the *Journal for the Study of Religion, Nature, and Culture* titled, "Grounding the Stars: Toward an Ecological Astrology" that astrology is something "human beings do, and something in which the Earth – where we have evolved, of which we are made, and which makes everything we are, do, and know, possible – is restored to its rightful place at the centre."

A revaluation of earth/water gives us an ecological astrology and helps return us to this grounded center, this rightful home, recall that ecology originates in the Greek word, *'oikos'* meaning 'home' and 'household.' We originate here in a specific moment and place.

What I believe Curry is alluding to is that there is no separation between humans and cosmos, people are expressions of the earth and by extension, the solar system and on and on. So, planets do not do things to us, planets, earth, and humans are all temporary features of a cosmos come to life. The chart is us, a condensation of a moment, a particular perspective of the cosmos looking at itself.

In one sense grounding astrology has to do with engaging earth/water thinking as much as we dwell in fire/air. We descend from the crisp, clean air of the mountains with its themes of bright futures, optimism, clarity, idealism, spiritual growth, expanded consciousness, and the sun coming out tomorrow and wander down deep into the valleys where shadows are long and the air humid and heavy.

I think that a more grounded astrology from the perspective of earth/water would focus upon bringing heaven to earth, of empowering people, not planets, of locating personal agency within the person and not attributing events in our lives to the action of the planetary alignments. Perhaps first and foremost, we need to be client-centered in our work and not chart-centered, of recognizing there is no escaping our freedom by giving our responsibility to the heavens. The chart is a mirror of our interior structure and dynamics, not the immediate cause. It may be necessary to shift the language we use with clients to reflect this.

Ground the client by first being present to them, giving our full attention, establishing good eye contact, maintaining an open posture, explore why they came, get them to ground by identifying their specific concern, what expectations do they have about outcomes, how will they know if these expectations are met. We may spend 20-30 minutes without even bringing up the chart but just allowing them to tell their story – maybe family of origin, relational status, education, religious orientation, work history, health history – whatever seems relevant and important. Some clients claim they've come out of curiosity; others want to know about the future. These airy abstractions move the client away from the grounded moment. Perhaps explore what's going on now that triggered them to take action on this curiosity about astrology or what is it about the present that makes the future important to them?

Regarding our own status in the relationship, lose the idea that we are a cosmic pipeline or that we speak truth for the planets. Share appropriate feelings with the person. Consultations are two people meeting on level ground, not opportunities for satisfying our own needs, be there for the client. Sit in the consultation space with the recognition that we are not separate from our environments, the astrologer is not some objective reporter but an intimate part of the client's chart either natally or by transit and is fulfilling a role. The client might perceive us as an authority or as an obstacle, or perhaps they view us as someone who is encouraging them to try something novel or innovative, or perhaps urging them to consider taking action or to pull back and rest. Maybe we want to explore this with the client with the chart in mind to keep things clean between both of us. Avoid advice giving as much as possible and join the client in shared problem solving. When a client views us as the expert, as someone who can convey answers to them, or make them better, or as someone who can save them from their dilemma, guide them to their own autonomy. We may be skillful in astrology, but the person is the expert in their own life because they have the inside view. They can have much to say and this is where our patience and listening skills come in. The astrologer sits listening without judgment, open to the unfolding of the client's story and difficulties.

Help is most effective when the participants are focused on mutual enhancement rather than the astrologer telling the client what they need, attempting to remedy concerns, correct the person, or fix them according to some preconceived notion. How can one person possibly know what another person needs?

In a loose translation of chapter 3, verse 35 of the Hindu sacred text, the Bhagavad Gita reads, "It is better to die doing your own dharma poorly, than doing another's well." Or at the pearly gates, perhaps St. Peter does not ask why weren't you more like Christ but rather why did you not become who you are? We are each a unique particularity, a quantum of experience originating in a moment and place that is tied into every other place.

It is also presumptuous to reassure clients that all will be okay, everything is contingent upon something else in the weave of nature, pulling in one direction, pushes something in the other.

Remember that the moment and place of birthing is crucial. Imagine a picture puzzle; it's all of a piece with one part of it missing, that's us. We can still say something about the form and pattern of this particular organism born in this specific moment and place by looking at what surrounds it, in the case of astrology, the pattern and rhythms of the planets. Rudhyar would say this organism fills a specific need of the whole. The landscape or place of our birth is important because following poet/philosopher, John O'Donohue in his book, *The Four Elements* (p.143), "Landscape is then a condition of the possibility of everything. Without landscape there would be no where. Without a where there could be no thing." Earth is fundamental to our astrology and recognizing that we are expressions of this ancient landscape. It is our source, our substance, and destiny, everything issues from place.

Another strategy alluded to earlier is to be aware of when we're using language that disempowers the client giving it to the planets. Instead of Saturn conjoining the Moon being the cause of and explanation for low mood, or sadness, or chronic depression for example, let the client unfold this concern and then explore the astrological meanings of the natal aspect. Rather than thinking of planets as influencing, causing, explaining, making, producing, triggering, or instigating situations or conditions, consider them as reflecting, imaging, echoing, mirroring, paralleling, resonating with, etc.

Another matter to consider is to notice the kind of metaphors we use in describing this person as a manifestation of a birth moment.

Are we using mostly techno-mechanistic metaphors for describing people as machines or computers, reducing them to parts that can be replaced or amped up? Are people running on empty, or out of gas, or needing to defuse their situation, or their memory needs more RAM, or they are spinning their wheels, or they should put the brakes on, or they need a tune up, or a reboot or reset in their lives? The idea is not to dispense with all of these but to notice how often we're distancing an immensely complex human presence from the natural world by reducing them to machines or technology. Remember organisms originate from the inside out, machines from the outside in. Organisms grow, machines are constructed with replaceable parts.

Seek out more natural metaphors and descriptions – she has a sunny disposition, he has a stony countenance, when upset, he retreats into this icy stare, having a monkey mind, tears streaming down his face, he becomes a raging bull, feeling at the edge of a cliff, blooming where you're planted, a human tumbleweed, blossoming, rooting, branching out, drifting, floating, snowed under, strutting like a peacock, stormy relationships, lightning quick, etc. Be creative, looking for anything that connects the client to the natural world when dialoguing their chart. For anyone conversant with the language of Tai Chi and Chi Gung – phrases like "Snake tosses aside fear," "Sparrow flies through forest and disperses anger," "Bear guards his honey," all describe healing movements in Chi Gung. Tai Chi movements keep us in nature as well with names such as "High pat on horse," "White crane spreads wings," and "Grasp sparrow's tail." These imagistic phrases connect us to the natural world rather than the mechanistic one.

Bringing more earth into our astrology is to recognize that often astrology simply blusters with words of inspiration talking about topics like karma, past lives, soul purposes, expanding consciousness, personal growth, peak experiences, evolution, the future, destiny, etc., all abstractions that move away from the "concrete magic" (earth/water) of the moment in which two people present and engaged in mutual dialogue that is astrology. Additionally, if the client doesn't believe in these concepts, they may lose interest in what we're saying.

Of course, much depends on how we want to practice astrology, whether we are simply trying to help in a topical way by providing answers, remedies, or assistance to a client by giving them what they want and feeding them for a day and that's okay, it provides immediate though temporary aid. If we are drawn toward helping the client in developing a fuller sense of richness and depth, initiating a process oriented toward increasing openness, acceptance and self-supports, loosening a need for control and birthing a greater sense of at-homeness in the world, then we may want to consider bringing the starry heavens to earth in our practice. Ground the consultation in the present moment of engagement, attending to the here and now.

If we can help our clients come alive to the richness of this very moment the future will take care of itself. A grounded astrology (includes all the elements) and helps in healing the split between person and planet, between matter and spirit, of dualistic thinking where we cast ourselves as spiritual beings encapsulated in bags of flesh. An ecological astrology is a grounded astrology, one that cherishes the things of the world, where we feel kinship, comfort, and deeply at home on this beautiful planet, recognizing the sacredness of a living cosmos. When we are planted firmly in the present, with the client situated in the given, accepting that the future arrives in its proper time, then we are more in tune with the rhythms of sky, sea, and soil. We become cognizant of the circulating heavens, the seasonal cycles, the dance of moon and sun, our inner tides, and the arising, maturing, and dispersing of the ten thousand things that are impermanent, imperfect, and unfinished.

Poet, Nancy Wood (*Spirit Walker*, p.53) writes….

All is a circle within me.
I am ten thousand winters old.
I am as young as a newborn flower.
I am a buffalo in its grave.
I am a tree in bloom.
All is a circle within me.
I have seen the world through an eagle's eyes.
I have seen it from a gopher's hole.
I have seen the world on fire
And the sky without a moon.
All is a circle within me.
I have gone into the earth and out again.
I have gone to the edge of the sky.
Now all is at peace within me.
Now all has a place to come home.

14

Watering Our Field: Imagination in Astrology

The point of view shared here is neither correct, right, nor better than any other informed view. It is simply viewing astrology through a different lens, a lens that might alter or deepen our thinking about astrology and find that a moister astrology has certain advantages within certain contexts.

This view aligns itself more with the humanities (religion, history, philosophy, literary criticism) than with the sciences. It is not so much related to the science of the stars as it is a tradition of the heart, being closer to poetry, story, and myth than to methodology, testing, and rational review. This view places high value on Imagination; regarding astrology as a meaning-bearing language allowing users to assign meaning to patterns forming and unforming in the sky.

The following has two entwined currents flowing through it. The first is a demonstration of the presence of Imagination in the very structures of astrology, the second, the awareness and use of Imagination in the consultation itself to move it toward depth.

The act of imagining is frequently devalued or entirely dismissed in our culture. People who rely on imagining are said to be woolly-headed, dreamers, space cadets, drifty, having a few screws loose, fantasists, romantics, idealists, mediums, psychics, visionaries, crazies, artists, psychotics, etc. Not always a desirable picture for those who are immersed in Imagination.

So, I think perhaps we need to define Imagination if I'm going to write about its presence in astrology.

Here are a variety of definitions....

Cambridge Dictionary – "The ability to form pictures in the mind."

Merriam-Webster Dictionary – "The act or power of forming a mental image of something not present to the senses or never before wholly perceived in reality."

TeachThought.com – "The ability to form mental images, phonological passages, analogies, or narratives of something that is not perceived through our senses."

Wikipedia – "Imagination is the ability to produce and simulate novel objects, sensations, and ideas in the mind without any immediate input of the senses. It is also described as the forming of experiences in one's mind, which can be re-creations of past experiences such as vivid memories with imagined changes, or they can be completely invented and possibly fantastic scenes."

These definitions to me sound relatively positive.

Romanticism, the late 18th and 19th century reaction against the Enlightenment, was an artistic and philosophical movement that redefined the fundamental ways in which people in Western cultures thought about themselves and about their world. The Romantics tended to define Imagination as our ultimate "shaping" or creative power, the approximate human equivalent of the creative powers of nature or even deity. It is dynamic, an active, rather than passive power, with many functions. Imagination is the primary faculty for creating all art and I would add, for shaping our world.

Watering Our Field: Imagination in Astrology

Writers and philosophers influenced by Romanticism include Byron, Shelley, Mary Shelley, Jane Austin, Blake, Wordsworth, Coleridge, Keats, Emily Bronte, Herder, Hegel, Novalis, Goethe, Fichte, Schelling, Hawthorne, Emerson, Margaret Fuller, Washington Irving, Thoreau, Melville, Emily Dickinson, Whitman, Longfellow, Poe, Nietzsche, and in the 20th century; Jung, Eliade, Campbell, Hillman, Thomas Moore, Patrick Harpur, and others.

According to Rick Tarnas in his book, *The Passion of the Western Mind*, "Indeed, for many Romantics, imagination was in some sense the whole of existence, the true ground of being, the medium of all realities, It both pervaded consciousness and constituted the world."

Consider what Tarnas is saying here, Imagination can be described "as the medium of all realities," as That out of which the universe is always and everywhere emerging, we might imagine these relations as Imagination :: Originating Mystery :: Source :: Matrix :: Pleroma :: Pre-cosmic Night :: Cosmic Womb :: Whole :: Dao :: Buddhist Emptiness :: Boundless Void :: Great Mother :: World Soul :: Collective Unconscious :: Larger Self :: Cosmos :: the Invisible and other descriptive efforts. I suggest we can construe these abstractions as the ungraspable Interiority of the World attempting to articulate itself in numerous creative revelations of the Sacred.

In one sense then, Imagination is the matrix out of which emerges what Daoists call, the "ten thousand things," the phenomenal world, the Visible. To put it more astrologically, it could mean Pisces as the womb out of which Aries is born; the first distinction, the first separation, the first cry of "I am."

Astrology as imaginal ground; astrology affords us with a story. It is a discipline that provides a framework for imagining a profound intimacy between us and our environment. It pictures an ecological model of humanity envisioning people as interdependent and inseparable expressions of a living cosmos, like eddies in a stream. Astrology, as a marvelous outflowing of Imagination, locates humanity within a cosmological context reminding us of our place in the universe. Astrology is a language that uses myth, metaphor, symbol, narrative, and image as its medium for conveying its fantasies of cosmic intimacy.

Joseph Campbell writing in *Thou Art That* asserts, "The mysterious procession of the night sky... with the soundless movement of the planetary lights through fixed stars, had provided the fundamental revelation... of a cosmic order. The human imagination reacted from its core, and a vast concept took form: the universe as a living being...within whose womb all the worlds... had their existence."

Ponder the role Imagination plays in our work. Consider the fundamental image in astrology; the natal chart reflects a condensation of a moment and place containing at least several factors; signs, houses, planets, and aspects.

The chart we are after requires time and location. Bear in mind, the place of birth is only discernible if we resort to the imagined coordinates of latitude and longitude, the conceptual net that we cast over a shifting and dynamic reality. There are no actual grid lines on the landscape that exist, they are imaginary constructs that allow us to orient to location – here and not there. It is a method for organizing and navigating the environment. It's a very useful strategy for constraining the wiggliness of reality in the same manner that we use a net to capture and hold a fish. Coordinates allow us to orient ourselves within a larger context.

Time may be considered the measure of change and clockworks give us a sense of control within an endlessly transforming reality. The clock and the grid allow us for example to meet for lunch on a certain corner at noon. Grids on the map and minutes on the clock are social fictions, conventionally agreed upon navigational tools that we employ with great success.

Where else is Imagination prominent? The sidereal zodiac images the stars splashed across the heavens becoming constellations in a wondrous act of Imagination. There is a Ram, there's a Bull, over there is a Lion, and there's a Centaur.

When we examine the tropical zodiac, we find it too is imaginal and not actual. It is a fantasy describing an ever-spiraling cyclic process; the shifting, seasonal, angular relationship between earth and Sun divided into 12 phases. You cannot point to it or hold it in your hand; it's an imaginal construct, a fiction.

The houses are space/time abstractions convened as twelve contexts imaged as areas of life based on the turning earth. These too are fantasies and have all the concreteness of an inch or an hour.

The houses based upon rotational motion and the tropical zodiac based upon orbital revolution are essentially systems of measurement like geographic coordinates that help us make sense of the twisting, squirming processes of nature. We often tend to confuse methods of measurements with reality itself so that these abstract imaginings become reified as actual things in our lives.

The planets in the solar system, though having physical reality, by which I mean we can land a spaceship on one, have been imagined as divinities, psychological functions, kinds of action, moods, behaviors, etc. Many astrologers refer to them as planetary archetypes and yet for Jung who popularized the term, archetypes, understood them as hypothetical entities (meaning they do not actually exist), irrepresentable in themselves and only exist as archetypal images after the fact of a manifestation. In other words, the astrological planets, so rich in mythology are fantasies, personified energetic processes of a universe in which we are one of its many expressions.

We come to aspects. By using a specific system of measuring from an agreed upon location, aspects describe the measure of relations (not things) between two or more bodies in space in constant motion to which we have assigned meaning. These aspects come into being temporarily then dissolve just as easily in their ever-circling dance - nothing concrete here.

Then we have nodes, midpoints, retrogradation, declinations, progressions, Arabic parts, vertexes, antiscia points, trans-Neptunian planets, Black Moon Lilith, sensitive points, and on and on that too are imaginal expressions. It turns out then that astrology is not so much filled with facts as it is with fantasies.

I do not dismiss these as being merely made up, but rather, Imagination as our most valuable human capacity. It is simply that we live in fictive realities, our lives are narratives and fantasies. We are immersed in a realm of fictions. In *Opus Posthumous*, the poet Wallace Stevens wrote, "The final belief is to believe in a fiction, which you know to be a fiction, there being nothing else. The exquisite truth is to know that it is a fiction and that you believe in it willingly."

Whether we are speaking of astrology, theology, philosophy, mathematics, economics, politics, psychology, people, or places, they are filled with our fantasies. Many of you are having fantasies about me right now or about other people that shape the way we choose to feel about and interact with one another, whether we like or dislike someone, whether we are drawn toward or repelled by someone.

I believe it was the child developmental psychologist, Piaget who suggested that perceptions depend on the world view of a person and our world view is the result of arranging perceptions into existing imagery via Imagination. So, the position I am establishing here contrasts with the astrologers who adhere to the Platonist notion of ideal forms implying that "essence precedes existence" which posits archetypes existing as actual entities prior to the phenomenal world. The Platonic archetypes are regarded as the really "Real" and are perfect or ideal forms of which the things of the world are only imperfect approximations. This view privileges a dualism of essence before existence that separates concrete living from some ideal, perfect dimension which originates us.

If we consider the essence/existence polarity as mutually dependent (arising together) then cosmos and humanity shape and reflect one another. Without Imagination there are no "ten thousand things" and without "the ten thousand things" there is no imagining. The imaginal and the concrete are like two sides of a coin. Seeing is not believing, seeing is imagining. Imagination sits as the invisible root beneath the visible tree of astrology.

I think it is accepted that Pisces has much to do with Imagination. It is imaged as two fish tied together swimming in opposite directions similar to the yin/yang symbol: an image of the unsummed totality of existence. It is unconditionally receiving, exquisitely sensitive to pressure, seeking the lowest level, boundless, formless, flowing, vague, deep, enfolding, merging, diluting, dissolving, and yielding. Water tends to form into a spherical shape when unobstructed, an image of wholeness, inclusivity, and totality. I'm reminded of a popular medieval definition of God, "an infinite sphere whose center is everywhere and whose circumference is nowhere."

Pisces as the ending phase of any cycle of activity is the boundless ocean into which old forms dissolve and out of which new forms arise. It is a phase of closing accounts, a consolidation, a cleanup (coming to terms with the past) and seed preparation (for the next phase). In *The Zodiac: A Life Epitome*, early 20th century

British astrologer Walter Sampson described Pisces as "the final decaying processes by which things are resolved back into their primal elements, disintegrated, scattered, their identity completely vanishing."

And according to Isabel Hickey in *Astrology: A Cosmic Science*, Pisces is a "cleaning up of the odds and ends that have not been cleared in the other eleven signs." It is the "dustbin of the zodiac."

Psychologically, Pisces is a metaphor for Imagination; for image-making. It's the human need for Ultimacy, for transcendence, for self-dissolution, unitive consciousness, a longing for union, for something beyond or within. It may reflect irrational, arational, or suprarational states. It is the preeminent symbol of what is Unconscious, out of awareness, behind us, out of view, invisible like the back side of our head.

As the closing phase of zodiacal process, it is the cosmic compost into which everything returns and out of which everything emerges. It is the pre-cosmic chaos, necessary for new creation. In it we feel the pull of oceanic tides, are lured by the seductive song of sirens promising ecstasy, feel a desire to return to the bliss of the womb, we experience nostalgia for paradise, a yearning for homecoming. Expressively, humanity has had imaginings of a Golden Age or Garden of Eden in some distant past and of a future paradisal afterlife. Imagistically, it seems, coming or going, we find fantasies of paradise at our beginning and our ending (Pisces).

Houses provide specific contexts within which a life is lived. Often within the 12th context, we find the leftovers, the ill-fitted, the nameless, dispossessed, disenfranchised, disempowered, disabled, disheartened, dislocated, the incarcerated, the visionaries, the dreamers, the psychedelic adventurers, wilderness explorers, mystics, and mentally ill citizens inhabiting (whether chronically or temporarily) settings like long term care facilities, prisons, hospitals, rehab centers, psychiatric units, social service agencies, homeless shelters, disaster relief locations, refugee camps, retirement communities, retreat centers, communes, convents, monasteries, spas, vacation spots, the wilderness, utopian communities, etc. all in the hopes of returning to the social order to again be contributing members of the community at best, or to live in isolation from the social order in the margins, on the fringes, or off the grid.

The 12th house is the arena of life that is closeted, out of the limelight, offstage, behind the green curtain, the larger embrace out of which the Ascendant emerges. Planets in this house are waiting in the wings anticipating their entrance or perhaps more often than not are its denizens; directors, stage managers, designers, lighting crews, roadies, home health aides, hospital staff, correctional personnel, restaurant dishwashers are all working behind the scenes, the unseen angels who help make the project a success by their working in the 12th.

I've mentioned the environmental contexts of the 12th, what about its internal contexts? This is where we imagine places called the Unconscious, the Otherworld, the afterlife, the *Mundus Imaginalis*. It is the place of fairy queens and sirens, trolls, unicorns and gnomes, angels and demons, a place of dreams, nightmares, monsters and grotesqueries, of great inspirations, bliss, ecstasy, and unclaimed baggage.

What we term planetary principles have a threaded connection to Imagination. Think of the signs as containers of meaning, the planets imagined as rulers or agents are a coalescence of the meaning of their respective signs. It's as if the sign was the field and the planet, its focus.

Neptune as the agent for Pisces naturally has the responsibility to symbolically act on Pisces' behalf. Neptune has been called the planet of Imagination exemplifying our capacity for imagining, for compassion, for empathy, for dissolution, for idealism, for delusion, for deception, for glamour, for enchantment, for union and others. Obviously, Neptune touching any planet in the chart may mirror a softening, dissolving, or refining quality in that planet's storying of a life.

We've looked at defining Imagination, how its presence undergirds our very act of astrology, and where Imagination is expressed in the chart.

Now before our client enters the consultation room, we have done some chart prep and erected a scaffolding of possibilities about this person; what to anticipate in their self- presentation, perhaps imagine a sense of their relational style, the manner in which they assert themselves, what their major interests might be, imagining how their relationship with parents and or siblings might look, we're able to spin fantasies of all kinds about this person from their chart material. We've cobbled bits and pieces of a narrative together.

The task now is to invite the client to voice their story and for us to be present, listening closely to their unspooling story, quietly gathering the threads of their tale and weaving it into a coherent narrative that can be explored through the metaphorical power of the astrological symbols. If we interrupt in the telling of their tale with a need to inject some astrological nugget, it may freeze the imaginal process at play between us, and the energy and vitality may dissipate. We should carry our biases with awareness and attentively trail their story along as they disclose it to us.

In the poem "The Speed of Darkness," Muriel Rukeyser asserts, "The universe is made of stories, not atoms." Stories are wild creatures, letting them loose; we follow after them, never knowing where we will end up. It is the nature of story – to inspire, uplift,

Watering Our Field: Imagination in Astrology

sadden, inform, frighten, teach, reassure, surprise, heal, provide structure, connection, and meaning that deepens us into life.

When working with clients keep the imaginal ground present through story, narrative, symbol, opening a path to a different kind of practice. For example, rather than starting by being chart-centered, consider being client-centered, open by saying, "Our session today is an excursion of discovery. I'd like to temporarily put aside (or bracket) any thoughts about your chart or astrology and we'll begin by sharing some of your story with me and see where it leads." The kinds of fantasies the client lives by are introduced in this beginning.

This gives us an opportunity to reshape our image of the person, to hear how they narrate their lives, to get a sense of where to begin in the chart, find out what brings them here today, what they're hoping for, how will they know if they find it? Let them speak about their life; current and past situations, their joys and sorrows, their successes, and failures, and whatever else is pertinent. It might take 20-30 minutes before the chart becomes the focus in this relationship.

Since Imagination is associated with Pisces, we should not overlook the watery element when working with clients. It will be helpful to attend to both the client's and our own shifting tides as the session proceeds, the ebb and flow of the feelings that surface and recede, the emotions expressed, perhaps as a storm of anger, a flood of tears, a fog of confusion, or a waveless calm. Water encourages empathy and compassion where the client can feel heard and accepted.

Imagination is fundamental to human be-ing. As Tarnas noted above, it can be imagined as the "whole of existence" and the "medium of all realities." It therefore shapes our understanding and practice of astrology, how we imagine astrology's purpose,

221

and how we perceive those who come to us as clients. Astrology is rooted in Imagination and watered by the fantasies and images we carry. Bringing Imagination to our field, I believe can enrich our practice. Being aware of just how much we rely on imagining, valuing that process, using it more overtly in a session, following where it goes and seeing what discoveries appear in the session can be an emotionally moving experience.

My own bias in working with clients is my imagining that we are all journeying round, back to the place out of which we emerged. The quiet whisper of Home, regarded as that place of origin, of safety, of comfort, of completeness, of destination, may be calling us. A rewarding session might include the client feeling a restoration of lost parts of themselves, be both frustrating and inspiring moving them inward with curiosity and openness, be a healing moment. A skilled consultation may deftly entice the client into deepening life, creating room on the couch for the things disdained and disowned, neither fixing nor mending but accepting that how the person experiences their life is enough.

One definition of healing is a coming to terms with the actuality of a situation. This is not just passive resignation but rather engages in us reflective action; being curious rather than reactive, holding the tension of conflict, practicing patience in the face of uncertainty, maintaining a compassionate and non-judgmental attitude.

The consultation began where it ends, two people in the presence of Imagination sharing their humanity. The client if fortunate will leave with more questions than answers, imagining more *materia prima* for their own alchemical work. Perhaps T. S. Eliot's words (lines 239-42) from "Little Gidding" are relevant to our efforts.

"We shall not cease from exploration
And the end of all **our** exploring

> Will be to arrive where we started
> And know the place for the first time."

We tend to live life through a series of stumbles and gains, questioning and learning, despairing then celebrating, imagining perhaps a larger, guiding mystery of which we are a part.

It's not that our lives have been written in the stars as much as they've been scribbled on the waters of Imagination, the wild rushing cosmic river that surges, swells, and tumbles, that eddies us out to form for a brief time before we are unformed and returned to this great flowing creativity. In the end, the planets circle round, the seasons change, Spring comes, grass grows, the air is redolent with fragrance, and we are overwhelmed with beauty and grace.

15

Emerson and the Transcendentalist Legacy

American Transcendentalism was an intellectual movement situated in New England that flowered during the second third of the 19th century. This loosely-knit tapestry of ideas impacted the fields of American religion, philosophy, education, literature, poetry, and social policy essentially by reimagining the manner in which humanity is conceivably related to God and Nature. It has its roots in Neo-Platonic thought, the philosophy of Kant, German Idealism (Fichte, Schelling, and Hegel), the German Romantics like Goethe, Schiller, and Novalis, English Romanticism (Coleridge, Wordsworth, Byron, Shelley, and Blake) and Hinduism. Its appearance can be viewed as a reaction against Calvinistic Puritanism and Lockean empiricism, and its growth in American soil produced its own unique identity and culturally reshaped the American landscape as no other ideological movement has done in our history. I believe that this movement has left a legacy for the practice of natal astrology in our time.

The seminal figure of this movement was American born, Ralph Waldo Emerson, essayist, poet, lecturer, and minister, considered one of the giants in the history of American intellectual life. Even to this day he has been referred to as "the architect of American intellectual culture." Other significant figures associated with Transcendentalism are Henry David Thoreau, Margaret Fuller, George Ripley, Bronson Alcott, Theodore Parker, Elizabeth Peabody, and Orestes Brownson. Biographical and historical information in this chapter come from an Emerson biography titled *Emerson: A Mind on Fire* by Robert Richardson Other sources are *Emerson, Thoreau, and the Transcendentalist* by Ashton Nichols and Lawrence Buell's, *The American Transcendentalists*.

I would like to begin with an examination of Emerson's chart to gather some sense of who this man was since he is considered the movement's single most defining figure. I am using the birth data from AstroDatabank which is given a Rodden rating of AA having come apparently from Emerson's father's diary.

In establishing the legend for Emerson's chart, (using 2 points for the Sun, 2 for the Moon and 2 for the ruler of the Ascendant, 1 point for each of the rest), we find a predominance of 10 planets in

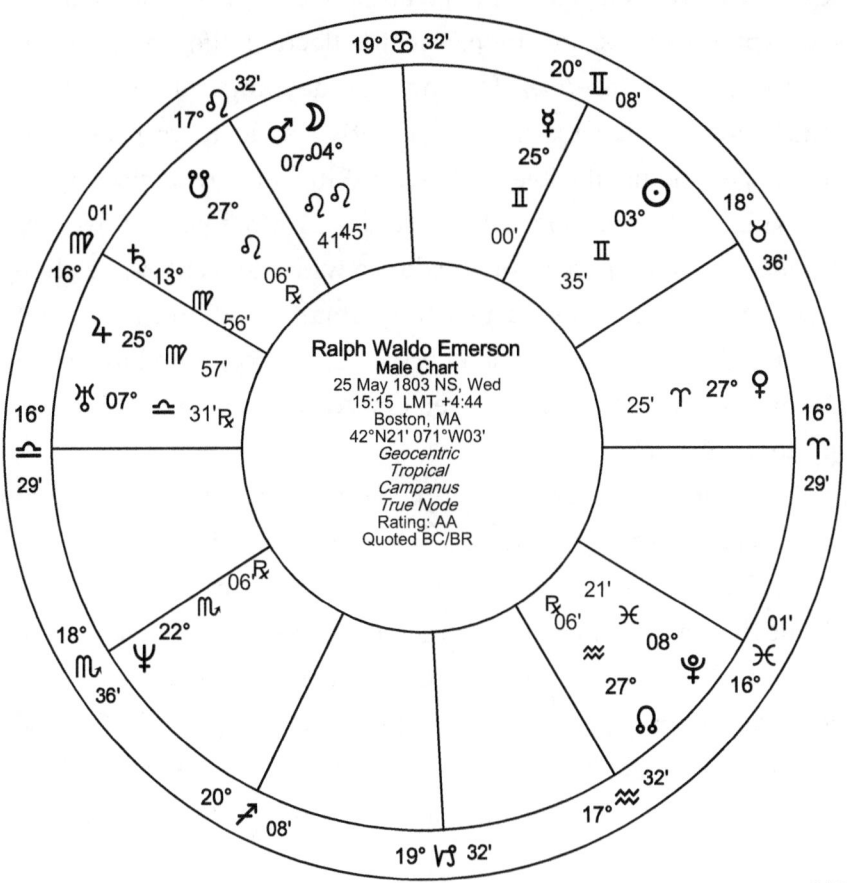

individual signs, 9 planets in yang signs, 5 in fire, 4 in air for a fire/water mix, 6 in mutable signs, and 6 each in personal and interpersonal signs. Pluto in Pisces in the 5th house is the singleton planet in a transpersonal sign. Some interesting things that jump out are that Neptune/Scorpio/2nd and Pluto/Pisces/5th are in mutual reception in the lower half of the chart and both are apex planets in two separate yods, the rest of the planets are in the upper half of the chart and are all disposited by Mercury in Gemini in the 9th house.

My first imaginings about Emerson would be someone who perhaps championed individuality, focusing on interests of a personal nature (individual signs), who might be oriented around adventure, freedom, directness (yang), with a knack for creativity, self-expressiveness, intuition, the intellectual life, learning and communicating (fire/air). Having a wide range of interests, he might possess a versatile and adaptive style to problems and challenges, being flexible in his thinking and responses to life (mutability). In his biography, *Emerson: A Mind on Fire*, we find, "Emerson lived for ideas, but he did so with the reckless, headlong ardor of a lover. He associated the human mind and its capacity for thought with activity and energy....He concentrated instead on the individual's sources of power, on access to the central fires that ignite the mind."

Looking at his dispositorships we find that the longest chain in the chart leading to Mercury/Gemini/9th begins with the lead planet Uranus in Libra (also in trine to the Sun) then stimulates Venus that in turn, tickles Mars, then activates the Sun which leads at last to Mercury. We might imagine this as when his need for engendering progress, liberation, and awakening (Uranus) ascends (his interest in abolition, women's rights, the abuse of the Native Americans, and a more egalitarian economic system), it triggers his need for aesthetic concerns, fairness, and balance in the treatment of others (Venus) that motivate him to take direct action (Mars) in line with his centrality of solar identity and purpose (to learn and communicate), leading him in the direction of thinking, writing, and lecturing (Mercury) on these topics.

Neptune in Scorpio in the 2nd is in mutual reception with Pluto in Pisces in the 5th and may create a self-contained system so that when Emerson was addressing issues of personal resources (gaining his own income from lecturing and writing about religious, mystical, and topics of compassionate concern for others) and sought more equitable distribution of wealth, this might trigger an obsessiveness and self-expressiveness about these topics that furthered his income-producing creative activities. Additionally with Pluto in the 5th house, he may have had intense desires for romantic engagement or toward having children. The loss of his first wife after 17 months of marriage and his first child around the age of five were deeply transformative to him and certainly impacted upon his sense of security and comfort (back to Neptune in the 2nd). According to his biographer, Emerson wrote quite movingly about these losses, transforming these deaths (Pluto) into a higher, more refined and poetic (Neptune) sense of tragedy.

One of the aspect configurations that intrigues me is the Mercury/Gemini/9th in closing square to Jupiter in Virgo/12th, the closing quincunx to Neptune/Scorpio/2nd and the sextile to Venus/Aries/7th. It seems somehow appropriate that the man considered "one of the greatest thinkers America has produced" and known as "the intellectual father and emotional godfather of Transcendentalism in America" (though he preferred the term 'Idealism') has an ongoing dialogue between Mercury (teaching/writing), Jupiter (philosophy) and Neptune (idealism) in his chart.

Let us look more closely at these elements. Mercury in Gemini is right at home suggesting that Mercury is easily supported in fulfilling its function of thinking, cognition, and gathering and dispersing information by its own sign, Gemini whose very need is the need for learning, communicating, and data exchange with the immediate environment. Mercury then functions in the very modality most suited to accomplish its ends. When this is located in the 9th house having to do with matters of meaning seeking, ideology, and ethical values the suggestion is that the world of everyday fact gathering is the place where these ideologies, philosophical beliefs, and morals can be discerned. We hear this echoed in Emerson's words from one of his most famous essays, "The American Scholar." He writes,

"I ask not for the great, the remote, the romantic; what is doing in Italy, in Arabia; what is Greek art, or Provencal minstrelsy; I embrace the common, I explore and sit at the feet of the familiar, the low. Give me insight into to-day, and you may have the antique and future worlds."

Emerson is saying that he is not interested in faraway places or times to discover the eternal verities; he can learn all he needs to know in observing the world of the mundane which surrounds him in its immediacy.

> "[S]how me the sublime presence of the highest spiritual cause lurking, as always it does lurk, in these suburbs and extremities of nature; let me see every trifle bristling with the polarity that ranges it instantly on an eternal law,"

and again,

"This writing is bloodwarm. Man is surprised to find that things near are not less beautiful and wondrous than things remote. The near explains the far. The drop is a small ocean."

It is easy to see the reflection of Mercury/Gemini/9th in these words. Emerson lived all his adult life in Concord, MA., traveling only for lecture tours and to recover from loss.

In "The American Scholar," Emerson is attempting to give definition to and establish an identity for the American scholar. The time is here for a man to become a "university of knowledges." He states,

"We have listened too long to the courtly muses of Europe. The spirit of the American freeman is already suspected of being timid, imitative, tame…. We will walk on our own feet; we will work with our own hands; we will speak our own minds."

Emerson hoped that the ideal of the scholar would be one that all citizens would rally behind and embrace.

Some of the above also resonates quite well with Jupiter in Virgo in the 12th house. Jupiter in Virgo suggests a great Jupiterian interest in the small matters in life. God may be found in the details. This brings an image of the knowledge seeker combing through the minutiae of life, looking through the microscope to discover divinity. Emerson fancied himself as both naturalist and scientist and felt no natural conflict between these arenas of inquiry and religion. The Transcendentalist movement essentially founded by Emerson "embodies the desire to reconcile science and rationality with religion." With Jupiter/Virgo in the 12th house we can add the dimension that offers Emerson a matrix of faith that the world is immanently divine (Jupiter/12th) and he has the analytical tools

(Virgo) to thoroughly investigate the Divine Laws inherent in Nature. These ideas are well reflected in his essays "Pantheism," "The Over-Soul," and "Spiritual Laws."

Neptune in Scorpio in the 2nd house images a kind of invisibility and dissolutiveness as regards 2nd house matters. Neptune may work in a hidden manner to erode or dissolve the person's sense of safety, security, and comfort especially with regard to material resources. We do find that although Emerson was born into a family of moderate means, his father died when Emerson was eight years old and left the family in precarious financial circumstances. His mother had to sell his father's library and take in borders to help the family's struggle. The story is also told of young Emerson having to share the family's single overcoat with his brother with whom he would take turns wearing it to keep warm in the cold in the face of taunting by other children more fortunate. Emerson "felt his poverty keenly and later remarked that his life would have been quite different had he had money." These experiences engendered a sensitivity to the less fortunate in life and helped form the belief that what is mine is yours and what is yours is mine suggesting the permeable boundaries found with Neptune in the house it is tenanted. Emerson charged at one time that, "It is the vulgarity of this country [...] to believe that naked wealth, unrelieved by any use or design, is merit."

The aspects associated with Mercury, Jupiter, and Neptune will help to enhance our understanding of this American icon. Mercury in closing square to Jupiter suggests a dynamic growth inducing relationship between Emerson's desire to think and learn about the world and his need to seek the truth of matters and broaden his framework of understanding the nature of things. The aspect resonates with the house placement of Mercury and with much of what has been said already. The aspect can denote the big thinker concerned with issues of religion and philosophy. The expected exaggerative and tall tales qualities of Jupiter are likely muted somewhat by its situation in Virgo lending a bit of thoroughness and applicability to his thinking. There is the tendency to express ideas in writing or lecturing in an enthusiastic and inspiring style.

Mercury in closing quincunx to Neptune suggests the possibility of crisis and the need for transformation in the relationship between these two planetary functions. Mercury in Gemini would like to communicate the facts; Neptune reflects the need for transcendence and the urge toward dissolution of forms and facts. One of the interesting facets of this planetary alliance is that in school Emerson was not much of a student, mediocre at best and not intended for great things, and especially at Harvard his biographer notes that an eye inflammation resulting in vision problems (Mercury/Neptune) halted his schooling for about half a year.

As a writer, Emerson was not known for his large body of systematic writings but rather his wide ranging interests about which he often had something profound to say. The Mercury/Neptune pairing suggests a creative imagination prone to reverie, fantasy, imagery, inattentiveness, distractibility and daydreaming that could be imagined as having been a problem for him in his early schooling that eventually would become a bit more channeled in his thinking and in his application to poetry. His poetry was highly regarded and he was well respected as a poet with poems like "Threnody" about the loss of his son, "The Concord Hymn," written upon completion of a local monument, and "Brahma" expressing his understanding of Hinduism. The planetary pairing also suggests a certain skill in shaping metaphor and rhetoric, and reflects a pervasive romantic idealism. In his first major published essay titled, "Nature," the topic of vision comes into focus as it didn't during his years at Harvard, now expressing a somewhat more integrated functioning of the Mercury/Neptune dynamic. He writes, "I become a transparent eye-ball; I am nothing; I see all; the currents of the Universal Being circulate through me; I am part or particle of God." And again in the same essay, a return to the theme of inspired vision, "So shall we come to look at the world with new eyes."

Jupiter in sextile to Neptune colludes to mirror a style of philosophizing that was broad and inclusive, entertaining unifying, synthesizing, with imaginative views of religion, philosophy, and social policy. He was, perhaps, at times too abstract and ill fitted for common understanding. A recent president of the Emerson Society noted of Emerson's style that, "People went away tremendously uplifted - and had no idea what they just heard," suggesting that even though Emerson was quite capable of promoting these broad ideas in a warm and entrancing fashion, they may have been too abstract for the listening audience. In a noted example, a local washerwoman who heard Emerson address an audience said although she did not understand what he was saying, she liked "to go up and see him stand up there and look as though he thought everyone else is as good as he is." This seems to image the sense of commonality that Emerson was able to get across to his audience.

Mercury sextile Venus engenders a love of language, an ease of communication, eloquence in speech, maybe a melodious voice but also with Venus in Aries for all one knows a tendency to leave others behind if they were not able to keep up with him. They conceivably had to pull their own intellectual weight. Emerson was not without his detractors and for example, had been accused at times of not having much to say about the concept of evil. He noted that if he were sent to hell that he would "make a heaven there." He even had nice things to say about weeds, "What is a weed? A plant whose virtues have not been discovered." Surely making nice was part of how Emerson moved through the world.

I would not want to overlook the fact that Neptune is the apex planet of a yod suggesting a certain amount of stress on the Neptunian function of the search for ultimate beauty and love. If Neptune was over functioning in Emerson's young life we might find a tendency to be out of touch with the mundane realities of living, perchance a child living in his own world, a home life deprived of material goods, vision (literally and figuratively) that was out of focus, a Utopian dreamer. It is interesting to note that although Emerson wrote much on how things could be better in society and on the brotherhood of humanity he never actually participated in the Transcendentalist experiments in communal living at Brook Farm and Fruitlands. Social transformation for Emerson (and Thoreau) was a consequence of individual transformation.

I believe that I would be remiss if I did not mention his solar aspects of Sun/8th square Pluto/5th and Sun trine Uranus which also informs Emerson's life. The Sun/Pluto square has been associated with the need to construct a false self in response to the fear of having the self (Sun) stripped away or endangered (Pluto). He struggled much with his identity prior to his Saturn return and had initially resigned himself to the family story of four generations of ministers. He went to Harvard Divinity School specifically to fulfill that expectation. The aspect further reflects that his father was taken out of the picture by death early in young Emerson's life when Emerson was eight. The family was plunged into impoverished conditions and in some sense the light may have gone out of his life at that time. I might suggest that he did not reclaim that light until after the death of his first wife and the resignation of his pastorate after only three years as a minister at age 29 around his Saturn return and a year after his wife died. Death was no stranger to Emerson being born into a family that had lost a child three years before he was born, then the loss of a brother when Emerson was four, then the loss of his father, the loss of another sister and two more brothers, his first wife; all before he was 33, then six years later, the death of his first child, which devastated him. Emerson was known to affect black clothing as an adult, did not tolerate loud laughter, and did not allow death as a subject of jest in his presence. I can imagine this echoing the early wounding of losing so many.

He looked for intellectual mentoring and support elsewhere after his father died and found it in his father's younger sister Mary Moody Emerson symbolized by the planets in the 12th (Father's sibling – derived houses). She was described as the family matriarch after Emerson's father's passing and was known according to Buell for her "unsystematic brilliance, her spiritual intensity, her biting wit, and her eccentric force" (Uranus), her interest in religion and philosophy (Jupiter), and the conservative perspective (Saturn) she retained throughout her life with regard to these subjects. She had been compared to Emerson in possessing a "headlong free associative style of thought and expression." She was seen as having a tremendous impact upon his intellectual development and character and urged him toward the clergy. With his Uranus in the 12th, his aunt can be seen as bringing all that of which Emerson was unaware of in his life (including the unconscious and grand social issues) into his awareness, prodding him to waken, progressively challenging his thinking throughout their 40-year letter writing relationship.

After his realization that the clergy was not for him, he did some supply preaching over the years but he never joined any other organized denomination for the rest of his life. He was known to be rather iconoclastic, considered the "first philosopher of American individualism," and one of his most famous essays, "Self Reliance," wrote, "Whoso would be a man must be a nonconformist" (Sun/Uranus). Frank Schulman in his article states, "To be self-reliant, in Emersonian terms, was to listen to and heed the still small voice of God within. Therefore, self-reliance also meant to him self-mastery, especially of the passions and temper." Do we hear the presence of Pluto in the 5th here? The ideas Emerson espoused were generally considered to be according to Nichols "anticlerical, anti-organizational, anti-orthodox, and perhaps even antisocial." For Emerson the world needed to be understood in terms of spirit rather than matter, individuals rather than collectives, not unusual for a man with so much fire/air and individual signs.

He expressed in his essays and lectures a very holistic perspective (Sun/Uranus) recognizing the need and necessity of contraries in life. I suspect he was quite the observer of and witness to life and probably knew what it meant for everything to have a place and a right to exist, even the negative phenomena. He also had a Pluto/Saturn opposition in his chart mirroring the need to demolish the status quo, tear down the idols of the standing order, and transform the culture in which he lived.

There is the suggestion that with so few earth planets, and the earth signs Capricorn on the IC but its ruler conjunct the 12th, Virgo on the 12th house cusp, and Taurus on the 8th house cusp, his earth function may have been inferior and in need of coming to awareness. His two earth planets are attached to the 12th house and may have been hard to freely access. He once "tried working in his yard and garden on the theory that manual labor should be a part of the scholar's life, but it left him too tired to do his other work. He concluded, "The writer shall not dig." Certainly his work was optimistic, hopeful, promising awakening, seeking emancipation for all the downtrodden, disenfranchised, and dispossessed. His ideas were often considered dangerous by the powers that be. He railed against slavery, the Indian Removal Act, economic inequality and for women's rights. He is embraced by poets, romantics, and religionists and disparaged by those in power. John Quincy Adams called Emerson's thinking, "wild and visionary phantasies." This attitude was not just for their spiritual heresy but because "their implications were politically radical and dangerous to society," according to Nichols. Transcendentalism itself was viewed by some conservative alarmists as a danger because it inverted the structures of power in society placing the locus of authority in the individual rather than it remaining in the institutions of society.

Whereas Emerson could be seen to be too abstract in his thinking, his friend and follower, Thoreau, was seen as an individual who lived what he preached. His gospel was one of "simplify, simplify, simplify," strip away all the inessentials, a philosophy one might expect from a man with Sun and Jupiter trine Pluto. With the Sun trine Pluto the notion of individualism is intensely charged.

Transcendentalism came on the scene in 1836 with the publication of Emerson's foundational essay, "Nature," and the first meeting of what was known as the Transcendentalist Club (8 September 1836) in Cambridge, MA, a discussion group that existed for several years. During this period, Uranus was in Pisces and Neptune in Aquarius with Uranus trine Saturn, and forming a quincunx with Mercury/Venus/ and Jupiter. Emerson's name became a household word in a little over a decade. And within two more decades Transcendentalism disrupted the way America did religion, philosophy, education, and social policy and left quite a substantial footprint in the American landscape.

Transcendentalism with its emphasis on social progress, free education for all citizens, liberal theology, innovative, new forms in literature and poetry, freedom of inquiry, and the uniqueness of the individual now containing a spark of the Divine, radiates the presence of Uranus. The remaining figures mentioned at the beginning of the article, of whom I have only date and place of birth are interesting in terms of Uranus' pervasiveness. This cabal of dissenters, reformers, and eccentrics brought Uranus into prominence in America. Thoreau had Uranus in Sagittarius in a very wide conjunction with Jupiter and quincunx the Moon, Mercury, Mars, squaring Saturn, and opposing Venus. Fuller, the editor of the Transcendentalist publication *The Dial* had Jupiter opposing Uranus; Alcott, the 'philosopher of conversation' and utopian educator, Jupiter/Mercury squaring Uranus; Brownson, the social radical, had Jupiter conjunct Uranus; Elizabeth Peabody, the educational reformer, Mercury trine Uranus; Parker, the firebrand preacher, Mars square Uranus and an extremely wide Jupiter/Uranus quincunx; and the utopian dreamer, George Ripley, founder of the communal living experiment, Brook Farm, had Sun/Uranus in tight conjunction with the Moon in Sagittarius square Jupiter, in addition to Jupiter in close sextile to Neptune.

So, how is Transcendentalism to be defined and what is its legacy for contemporary astrology? After researching the subject it seems that it is generally agreed that Transcendentalism is not a well systematized body of thought but a loose confederation of ideas that can be characterized as follows. Human nature is not sinful nor depraved (What need for a redeemer?). There is a spark of divinity within each and every person (What need for a mediator between humanity and God?). The idea of an inner self that could communicate with the Divine came into prominence. Since one can experience a direct inner intuition and experience of the Divine, the senses (empiricism) can be transcended and knowledge of Truth, Beauty, and Goodness can be gained via intuitive revelation. Every individual in their particular relationship to their inner divinity can discover their own authority and need not the mediation of scriptures and clergy. The soul of the person and the soul of nature were united in what Emerson termed the Over-Soul. In Emerson's most famous and foundational essay titled "Nature" he begins:

> "The foregoing generations beheld God and nature face to face; we, through their eyes. Why should we not also enjoy an original relation to the universe? Why should not we have a poetry and philosophy of insight and not of tradition, and a religion by revelation to us, and not the history of theirs?"

This and what followed in the essay provoked a crack in the culture's cosmic egg and a new world was brought into being with the individual having a unique and special place in the economy of society.

Let us consider the traditional structures of power in conservative 19th century America. Adults had authority over children, teachers had power over students, clergy had power over the congregation, and institutions held power over individuals. With the rise of Transcendentalism the structures of power were reversed. Children were no long viewed as little adults, a *tabula rasa* waiting to be filled, but rather full of divinity and wisdom yet to be developed. In education, children were to be unfolded in their true nature, not molded into society's needs. In religion, the individual was capable of receiving his or her own empowering revelation of the Divine, what need for clergy, papacy, or Scripture? Social institutions could err (slavery was legal, for example). The individual had a divine obligation to question and challenge the institutions of power, to follow the rhythms of a different drummer if needed as Thoreau pointed out.

Emerson and the Transcendentalist Legacy

How does this Transcendentalist vision of humanity and its relation to the Divine and to nature apply to our practice of astrology? If astrologers are styling their readings in the manner of telling the client how he is or what is in store for him, the astrologer is usurping the power of the client, crippling imagination, and using the client's circumstance in the service of the institution of astrology. For example, if my client has Sun in Gemini and I tell them that they are the kind of person who enjoys communicating with others and interested in life-long learning or they have Mars square Uranus and that makes them impulsive, reckless, craving excitement, and accident prone, I immediately shatter the possibilities for releasing startling new insights for the client by blockading the imaginative flow between client and astrologer. This kind of descriptive and predictive reading empowers the astrological tradition and the status of the astrologer while at the same time, disempowering the client.

If we reverse the power structure as in Transcendentalist perspective, we can shape our consultation by saying, "The Sun is in Gemini in your chart. One of the ways of understanding the Sun is that it has to do with our need for validation and approval. If it's located in Gemini, one way to read this is that the Sun is able to meet its need for feeling approved and recognized by approaching life with an attitude of curiosity, engaging it as an immense opportunity for learning, and even examining whether there is an overarching value to communication for you. Does this resonate at all with your own experience?"

When we do this, we open the door for the client to explore the validity of the statement and how else Sun in Gemini might it be understood? We initiate a dialogue with the client that fosters imaginative possibilities within the planetary configuration and allow it to reveal its meaning for the client. The astrologer shares his fantasies of what things could mean and the client in return allows his inner life to unfold in the context of the session. Typically, one is not able to address all the features of the chart in this kind of session if imagination is in full flowering. The client should be able to bring a specific issue or two to the session that they would like to explore from an astrological perspective.

The focus then is not on the authoritative performance of the astrologer but on the dialoging process between astrologer and client. It is a client-centered, not chart-centered encounter. My job during the session is to foster an environment conducive to allowing the inner wisdom of the client to be drawn out and unleashed. This is what the process of education is about for the Transcendentalists; in Latin, *e* (out of) *ducere* (to lead), education is to draw out that which is within. For the Transcendentalists, the mind was not a passive mirror reflecting the external world of the senses (hearing it all from the astrologer) but rather an active co-creator in the process of engaging life (imagining the possibilities inherent in the chart).

The legacy of Transcendentalism for the practice of astrology requires us to rethink our stance toward what it is we do with clients. Do we trust in the process of our encounter with the client, having faith that what is important for the client at this moment will emerge in the context of the session through an exploration of the symbolism? When we promote specific interpretations we are boxing in the chart, placing limits on how the chart will speak to us. Giving the client the tools to interpret his or her chart with our guidance through dialoguing honors the uniqueness of the client and respects the dignity of the person who sits before us. It is a challenge issued over 150 years ago, are we yet able to meet it?

16

Moving Astrology Toward the Sciences

In my fifty years of involvement with astrology there have been divided points of view as to whether astrology should be located in the sciences where it could attempt to gain greater cultural respectability or is it more appropriately situated in the humanities (some astrologers say both)? I think arguments can be made for both perspectives but this article wishes to raise some of the difficulties that could ensue if our beloved discipline were to become culturally accepted and established as a helping profession in the sciences.

I believe that there are few people who would deny the immense push for STEM (Science, Technology, Engineering, Math) education in our institutions of higher learning. We simply don't hear any promotion of the humanities in education. History, religion, moral philosophy, civics, geography, literature, drama, theater, dance, and other arts have simply fallen by the wayside relegated as less important to our society.

As I have been a member of the mental health professions for nearly four decades and have watched them become more empirically oriented and evidenced based in order to gain greater legitimacy and acceptability as helping professions, there have been numerous developments that have troubled me. The professions I am referencing are psychology, counseling, marital and family therapy, and social work. These professions require laws, rules and regulations governing their practice. I write here only about regulated helping professions in the United States. Other nations could have different structural bureaucracies, but the laws tend to run along similar lines.

I'm also writing specifically about what is generally known as natal astrology. Presently, astrology is a kind of Wild West frontier practice, not much regulatory oversight, few agreed upon definitions, and a smorgasbord of methods and techniques. To professionalize these would likely need to be standardized in some fashion.

The first concern I have is with regulatory licensing boards that would be needed in our emerging profession. Having licensing boards protects the consumers of astrology. One area involves an agreed upon definition of astrology along with its scope of practice, i.e., what is it and what do astrologers do. Then there are standards of care (what consumers can normally expect from astrologers practicing the profession). Astrology practices will need to be reliable, effective, and cause no harm. Astrologers would have to demonstrate competence. This would be accomplished through empirically validated and evidence based interventions used by astrologers in their work with clients. In order to develop these, we will need peer-reviewed replicable research that follows standardized models of inquiry.

The licensing board will require a code of ethics, ways to have ethical violations reported, investigated and the power to implement penalties (suspension, supervision, or surrendering of license to practice).

We will also need standardized educational and training models for astrologers who then will have to pass state licensing exams. And of course, new astrologers will need periods of supervision by astrologers who have been grandfathered in and who are skilled in the methods the new astrologers wish to use. Newly minted astrologers and their licensed supervisors will both be liable for the work the new astrologer performs. If an unsatisfied consumer chooses to submit a complaint or worse; sue the astrologer for negligence or malpractice, the supervisee and supervisor would wisely have liability insurance in place in order to reduce personal costs should the client litigate successfully.

Another concern is dual relationship; the idea of clients who are also students of the astrologer raises this issue, as would testimonials (using clients to be promoters of your practice), friendships, romances, etc. with past or present clients. These would be ethical violations.

Then there is the problem of detailed documentation and record keeping that is similar to the other helping professions and requires great care and thoroughness should ethical or legal issues arise. Investigators would need full access to what transpired between client and astrologer in the session.

Astrologers could not claim they were doing astrological 'counseling' or 'psychological' astrology as those descriptors are proprietary and allowed legal use only by those licensed in the professions of counseling or psychology. There would be additional and different rules, regulations, and standards for those astrologers practicing different kinds of astrology such as horary, financial, electional, mundane, etc. requiring additional credentials. I doubt medical astrology would even be allowed unless the astrologer was also an MD, DO, Nurse Practitioner, or Chiropractic Physician in the U.S.

Astrology has made a valiant effort to landscape its own turf over the years and admirably so. Organizations like the International Society for Astrological Research, the National Council for Geocosmic Research, the Organization for Professional Astrology, the Association for Astrological Networking, the Association for Young Astrologers, the American Federation of Astrologers, and the Astrological Association of Great Britain have all worked hard to raise the standards of the practice of astrology through training, education, legal and ethical codes, research, certification, national and international conferences.

The existence of educational bodies like Kepler College, the International Academy of Astrology, Academy of AstroPsychology, the London School of Astrology, the Centre for Psychological Astrology, the Canadian Association for Astrological Education, and the marvelous programs at the University of Wales Trinity Saint David are an amazing testimony to the desire of the astrological community to establish a well-trained and educated body of members. Additionally, there are other international programs that have worked to professionalize the practice of astrology in their own countries.

Let me close with a personal anecdote, I worked for three decades in prison mental health where I taught astrology to inmates for twenty years and used astrology as an adjunct to the counseling process. Though my colleagues were aware of my work, we did keep it under the administrative radar and I was never bothered or hassled by anyone. It was after all education, inmates were learning and liked it and if there is one primary thing you want in a prison, it is well behaved, calm residents who cause no trouble.

After I retired, I worked with a small portion of the general public using my home office and seeing occasional astrology clients there. My business cards and brochures said Therapeutic Astrology with my credentials from ISAR next to my name, my nationally board certified clinical mental health counselor specialty status, and the designated letters of my title as a licensed professional clinical counselor. I made it clear in my brochures that I was not offering counseling but dialoguing and consultation. The state licensing board heard about this and immediately sent a cease and desist letter my way. My response to them was that I was not doing counseling because at the very least, counseling requires an assessment, diagnosis, and treatment, none of which I was doing. The board accepted this (as far as I know) but required me to remove my counseling credentials from my marketing literature since if I wasn't doing counseling there was no reason to include the designation. Actually, a valid point I thought, so I removed the credentials from my brochures and cards and that was the end of the matter. Had I persisted I would have most likely lost my counseling license and privileges. This brief entanglement with my licensing board was sufficient for me.

I trust it is evident how complicated and entangled it would be for astrology to attempt to align itself with the dominant cultural paradigms. Of course, if astrology wants to find a category for itself other than a culturally sanctioned helping profession, it might absolve itself of many of these legal necessities. Rather than astrology seeking to align itself with the sciences maybe it could be planted in the humanities, remain in the cultural margins and call itself astrology consultations, spiritual advising, performance art, life review sessions, life timing dialogues, or some such thing. I think that should we wish to move forward toward the established and acceptable helping professions in our society, we will inevitably face these hurdles that will very much narrow the freedoms that we currently enjoy in our practices of astrology.

17

Elemental Spirituality

"There is one spectacle grander than the sea,
That is the sky;
There is one spectacle grander than the sky,
That is the interior of the soul."

Victor Hugo

"Who can distinguish darkness from the soul?"

W. B. Yeats

It is easy to imagine ourselves as having been thrown into this world, utterly vulnerable and fundamentally alone, estranged from our Creator. We find ourselves in a world that is essentially commodity, reserved for our use and stewardship, an object filled with objects possessing no soul or consciousness and separate from humanity. We are the Creator's children, the crown of creation. Life is a temporary situation; our true home is elsewhere, somewhere out there where we will, at some point, ascend to spend eternity.

But just for a moment, imagine matters differently, that each of us is born out of a living Cosmos, carrying a defining image, a calling, a destiny, a genius which has its own interests and claims upon us. It is something both us and Other. Perhaps it is something that takes an interest in our doings, keeps us from harm's way, and cares about us. It is neither god nor goddess, angel nor demon, but an exquisite unnamable beauty residing at the core of our existence. What if this fantasy were the true condition? What if this story was the way of the world?

Elemental Spirituality

What if our lives are not journeys in a linear fashion from birth to death or quests moving upward on a spiritual path seeking self-realization and union with the Divine? What if our lives are more like trees, rooted in one spot with an ever widening circle of small awakenings and an ever deepening awareness of the roots of our being? What if?

I think when we look at the writings within spiritual astrology and humanistic/transpersonal astrology we find parallels to classic Eastern and Western spirituality. Reading through some of the modern writers in spiritual astrology like Hickey, Oken, and Loftus, we find language that points us toward the Divine, flying up toward Spirit, ascending, lifting away from sensuous, embodied experience to a plane, dimension, or reality that is our true goal. Hickey writes in *Astrology: A Cosmic Science*, "Once you transcend the earth plane, you must read by inner perception and understanding. The study of psychological astrology prepares the student for higher planes of greater glory and power." In *A Spiritual Approach to Astrology*, Loftus asks, "Why aren't we still resting on a cloud watching the animals' adapting to the ever-changing environmental conditions?" She is suggesting that our true place is far above our animal nature and clearly leads us to the idea that we are living in a fallen condition. The saying, 'as above, so below' so common in astrology, suggests a causal emphasis from on high. There appears to be a belief that there is a purposive evolution toward Spirit which is generally depicted as somehow away from and above our daily experience.

Though somewhat more camouflaged, we find a similar orientation in contemporary humanistic/transpersonal astrology in its search for peak experiences and self-realization, where we discover levity and bliss, illumination by the light, as to see with clarity into the nature of matters from a higher, expanded consciousness, and where we experience a joyful heart. This sojourn is characteristically an ego-driven strategy where we extend personal desire and effort to meet the challenges of this strenuous ascent to actualize our potential for wholeness and evolve a greater consciousness of the Light. There is a focus upon growth, improvement, taking action, and going somewhere. Even our culture tells us that we grow up, not out, over, across, or down.

The dominant understanding within the humanistic/transpersonal approach is that astrology can be used as a tool for personal growth and beyond. This is boldly evident in the writings of Rudhyar, Meyer, Arroyo, and Cunningham. I think it can also be stated that the line is sometimes blurred between spiritual goals and psychological goals, especially evident in the excellent works of Rudhyar, Bogart, and Landwehr so that one suspects that a humanistic/transpersonal astrology is actually a modern form of spiritual path or practice. The humanistic/transpersonal approach has faith that we can change through dedicated, self-directed effort in the direction of higher states of consciousness that are typically associated with manifestations of Spirit.

The point that I wish to establish here is that whether we are discussing spiritual astrology, humanistic/transpersonal astrology, or classic spirituality, we read the language and imagery of expansiveness and ascension.

In the history of spirituality and the literature of spiritual and humanistic/transpersonal astrology, I believe verticality has privilege; "up" has greater positive value than "down." There is a predominance of images of ascension, a symbol which has traditionally reflected transcending the human condition. The Divine is up there, on the mountaintop, in the sky, above the clouds, away from the dirt and grit of human living. We clamber up the mountainside, climb the ladder, seek the Higher Power, arc toward the peak experience, take flight, and ascend to the heavens to encounter this loftiness of Spirit. Elevation, exaltation, and ascension, all reflect the qualities of Spirit. This tradition within spirituality and humanistic/transpersonal astrology manifests itself through prominent fire and air imagery; vital, quick, active, high, electrifying, stirring, radiant, confident, detached, rarefied, distant, with talk of numinous sparks, divine light, burning bushes, and god-filled whirlwinds.

Even in our dying, which classically moves us toward the underworld, it is not uncommon to hear stories of near death experiences in which the person is ascending, moving up toward the light.

In the James Hillman's book, *Puer Papers*, excerpts from a letter by the Dalai Lama clearly express that,

"The relation of height to spirituality is not merely metaphorical. It is physical reality. The most spiritual people on the planet live in the highest places... I call the high and light aspects of my being spirit.... Spirit is a land of high white peaks and glittering jewel-like lakes and flowers. Life is sparse and sounds travel great distances."

I might also add that the panoramic view from the heights is about as close to 'all seeing' that we will get to experience. Visionary, prophetic, and superior qualities are nuanced in such images. Many religions have holy Mountains such as Mt. Olympus, Mt. Fuji, Mt. Sinai, and the Mount of Olives, which all have sacred connotations. These geographic areas have long been considered as the abodes of the gods or places where hierophanies have occurred in various traditions. Believers engage imagery reflecting the climb upward toward communing and union with the Divine.

Now there is nothing inherently wrong with this upward gazing perspective, but matters become problematic when this direction becomes the exclusive metaphor in our lives. When our astrology and spirituality are wrapped in so much fire and air we may be in jeopardy of becoming lopsided with an overemphasis on yang energies. Coincident with this is the repression of the yin which may visit us with a vengeance uninvited; addictions, depressions, senseless explosions of violence, eating disorders and body dysmorphias.

If we assume as many do that spirituality is closely associated with Pisces and its agent, Neptune, we notice that Pisces in its archetypal relations to the fire and air signs is semi-sextile, square, and quincunx to them. In contrast, the sextile, trine, and opposition reflect the natural relationship of Pisces to the water and earth signs. Neptune, as a symbol of spirituality then, in challenging aspect to the rulers of the fire and air signs, Sun, Mars, Jupiter, Mercury, Venus, and Uranus, risks the danger of being a bit too spirited, too heroic, inflated, superficial, syrupy, detached from life, and filled with hubris. These features are not uncommon occurrences in people traveling spiritual paths, especially early on, or those who isolate themselves from the larger community in favor of a community of like-minded believers.

Let us avert our eyes from the heavens now, drifting into the valley and begin downshifting metaphors.

In an article in the *Harvard Divinity Bulletin* (Winter, Vol.34, #1), author Jalaja Bonheim is quoted,

> "Make no mistake: those who tell us we can have whatever we want, be whoever we want to be, and have full control over our lives are merely playing into our desire to avoid the discomfort of feeling our vulnerability. True wholeness has nothing to do with getting what we want. Paradoxically, we achieve true wholeness only by embracing our fragility and

sometimes our brokenness.... Life did not intend for us to be inviolable, but to be used for fodder for its workings. We are meant to be chewed up and digested and transformed into the blood and sinews of the world."

Notice that the imagery here is fully embodied, away from the head and lower in the gut.

In the 6th chapter of the Chinese classic, the Dao De Jing we read…

> "The Valley Spirit never ceases or expires,
> She is called the Mother of the Abyss,
> Her Gateway is the Root and Origin of all that is.
> Enduring without end, limitless and unborn,
> Inexhaustible,
> Draw upon Her,
> She will not be drained,
> Her support is without fail."

I wish to offer for consideration the possibility of an underground stream of spirituality that has been poorly articulated and frequently overlooked. This approach, like water, moves downward toward the lowlands, the lonesome valley, the shaded glade, the dark wood, the shadowed path, the secret cave, the vale of tears. This is a perspective viewed through water and earth imagery that our spiritual traditions have often ignored. It carries more languid, meandering, sinking, and brooding images in its display. In contrast to the spirited yang experience, there is a more pronounced soulful yin quality to the shape of this perspective. Neptune in its natural relationship to the sovereigns of earth and water; Moon, Mercury, Venus, Saturn, and Pluto reflect a harmony of purpose. There is a willingness to descend to the dark abyss. The relations suggest a more soulful spirituality reflecting attachment, humility, sensuousness, patience, realism, depth, and embodied life.

Often this path begins at a point of personal failure or catastrophe, when we no longer measure up to the fire and air values so infused in culture and we have quit the challenge of the spiritual climb. It has been characterized as a dark night of the soul in Christian mysticism and the night sea journey in myth. It is at this juncture in our lives when our resources are exhausted and we can't go on that we are embraced by gravity and like the proverbial dung that rolls downhill, we begin an unwanted descent. This downward spin has less a feel of being ego driven and more a sense of being out of our control; it accompanies a feeling of resistance or surrender to something larger than our selves. In this plunge away from our well ordered, well lit, and well controlled lives we are opened to the world, made vulnerable, wounded, and inferior. No longer rising and floating, but rather, falling and sinking deeper into the solitude of our being and the flowing of life.

These moments mark occasions for affirming and embracing the realities that everything changes and fades, that suffering is an integral facet of existence, and that our expectations for love, success, and fairness will not all be fulfilled.

The poet and novelist, D. H. Lawrence in his poem, "Phoenix" wrote,

> *"Are you willing to be sponged out, erased, cancelled, made nothing?*
> *Are you willing to be made nothing?*
> *dipped into oblivion?*
> *If not you will never really change.*
> *The Phoenix renews her youth*
> *only when she is burnt, burnt alive, burnt down*

to hot and flocculent ash.
Then the small stirring of a new bub in the nest
with strands of down like floating ash
shows that she is renewing her youth like the eagle,
immortal bird."

This ominous, Scorpionic verse suggests that real change is only possible if one is willing to say yes to life, to let go and face the world without props. To be emptied, to burn out, to suffer betrayals, to experience failure, to drown in sorrow, to have our hearts shattered, all of these are invitations to engage life more fully. Existence is both joyous and tragic and it is in these dark moments when we find ourselves walking in the valley of the shadow of Death that an opening presents itself.

Harvard professor Kim Patton stated in her Harvard Divinity School address (Harvard Divinity Bulletin, Vol. 34, #1) that "the broken heart is not a regrettable symptom of derailment, but rather is the starting point of anything that matters." These affairs are the pivot points around which our lives may change direction.

The poet John Keats in a letter to his brother asserted,

"Call the world if you please, "the vale of Soul-Making." Then you will find out the use of the world…. I say soul-making. Soul as distinguished from an Intelligence. There may be intelligences or sparks of divinity in millions but they are not Souls till they acquire identities, till each one is personally itself….Do you not see how necessary a World of pain and troubles is to school an Intelligence and make it a Soul. A place where the heart must feel and suffer in a thousand diverse ways!"

When we are blown off course, knocked off our pedestals, derailed from our well-worn and rutted track, these are the moments in which we are initiated into living, when hearts are broken, and soul is forged deep in the furnace of our suffering.

Many of us spend a lifetime seeking a fiery and airy enlightenment that will express a peaceful and harmonious balance in our lives. But life is too precious and fragile to exhaust on this task when occasions for endarkenment occur almost daily; the onset of illness, the breakup of a marriage, the loss of a parent, the growing and departing of children, sudden financial misfortunes, or the death of a dream.

In the tradition of alchemy, there is the darkening or blackening process that is the starting point for real spiritual transformation. That process often begins through the yin of living, in despair, melancholy, sadness, disappointment, dejection, emptiness, or mourning.

Yet these are the very experiences that our culture tends to disdain and wants to be rid of as quickly as possible through either medication or therapy, or both. In her book, *All Sickness is Homesickness*, Dianne Connelly writes,

> "The symptom sits in the person's history. It is a request for support; not support for simply getting rid of, or fixing it; but support for bearing it, for suffering it as an experience of life, support for seeing the wisdom and embraceability of the symptom. It may even be said that a symptom, no matter how awesome or terrible, is life requesting to be embraced in all its manifestations."

But we are uncomfortable with this personal darkness, psychologically or otherwise, not only in reference to our inner landscapes but to the outer ones as well. We try to save daylight and avoid the dark by manipulating our clocks. We light up our cities, our homes, keeping night lights and security lights on to keep the darkness at bay. We do similar things with silence, an increasingly rare commodity, keeping the television or radio on even when we are not watching or listening. Even during the lull in the action at sporting events, music is played or chatter is produced to keep silence from seeping into our experience. We also do this with solitude often eyeing those who wish to be alone as being somewhat off track and in need of more socialization.

This reluctance to engage darkness, silence, and emptiness are symptoms of a diminished cultural soul and an arid spirituality, a spirituality that wishes to detach itself from the earth and water of life in the valley where everything is included. It wishes to separate itself from all the messiness, weepiness, and coarseness that are so much a part of living. This is a spirituality that classically attempts to transcend the human condition through renouncing bodily desires via fasting, denying sleep, abstaining from sex, meditating incessantly, and avoiding sensuous experience. It is an austere, ascetic life.

But if we are asked anything by Divine Life, it is not to be something other than human but to be fully human. The real juiciness of life, the lustiness and earthiness reside in the lushness of the valley. This is where we live a sensuous, bodied life, where we attach to and cherish the things of the world. The idea of detachment in spirituality should not be construed as an airy withdrawing from the world but rather recognizing that it all goes away and being able to radically accept this. In so doing, we can love the world fiercely in all its ephemeral radiance. This leads to a more soulful perspective, a spirituality of the vale, a spirituality that rather than lifting us above the human condition as with fire and air, drives us ever more deeply into our humanness and plants us firmly in the bosom of an earthly life.

Spiritualities of air (height) and water (depth) echo the cultural polarity of brain above heart, mind superior to emotion, thinking over feeling. There is a valuation that again pulls us upward toward the brain where we become heady, intellectual, spirited, and lightheaded. Thinking is a rational enterprise, trustworthy, and viewed as superior to feelings. The feeling world alas, is marked as irrational, inferior, and untrustworthy.

But I believe that it is in the move downward, toward the heart when it is heavy and weighed down with matters that are grave that soul is shaped. This requires an openness and vulnerability to life. The poet Rilke writes in "Sonnets to Orpheus" of the flower possessing an infinite muscle of reception in its capacity to be fully open to the world and describes the fragile magnificence of the rose (and life) that even in its blooming it has already begun to fade. In the end, Rilke laments that "we violent ones remain a little longer. Ah, but when in which of all our lives shall we at last be open and receivers."

With Spirit we try to realize the pinnacle of our spiritual questing, to finish the journey and reach the solitary summit, but soul is a different matter, there is no summary statement to be made, no finality. Perhaps there is no traveling to a destination, no journey, but rather a simple awakening to place, to the root and origin of our becoming. Soul remains in motion, spiraling, spinning in mystery, animating the world, luring us to open fully in faith to the richness of life. Perhaps we can sense that a world without soul, (*anima* Latin for soul) is an inanimate world, lifeless and sterile. When the world is ensouled however, it is animated, living, vital, connected, a place in which we feel at home.

Elemental Spirituality

Let me end with something from The Velveteen Rabbit by Margery Williams.

"What is Real?" asked the Rabbit one day, when they were lying side by side near the nursery fender, before Nana came to tidy the room. "Does it mean having things that buzz inside you and a stick out handle?"

"Real isn't how you are made," said the Skin Horse. "It's a thing that happens to you. When a child loves you for a long, long time, not just to play with, but REALLY loves you, then you become Real."

"Does it hurt?' asked the Rabbit.

"Sometimes," said the Skin Horse, for he was always truthful. "When you are Real you don't mind being hurt."

"Does it happen all at once, like being wound up," he asked, "or bit by bit?"

"It doesn't happen all at once," said the Skin Horse. "You become. It takes a long time. That's why it doesn't happen often to people who break easily, or have sharp edges, or who have to be carefully kept. Generally, by the time you are Real, most of your hair has been loved off, and your eyes drop out and you get loose in the joints and very shabby. But these things don't matter at all, because once you are Real you can't be ugly, except to people who don't understand."

Can we hear the echo of Keats' soul-making here? Can we not feel the presence of the Moon, Venus, Saturn, and Pluto? Not only will we not be ugly, but we will not be a partial, unused, shallow, superficial person. We will have lived a life of use and relatedness, of attachment and loss, a life that matters, a life of fullness and depth.

In closing, when the yang of fire and air dominate our cultural imagination, we shape a world that becomes a place for the heroic ego to storm the heavens and march to the gates of Hell. There is nothing to stop us in our desires to improve, to progress, to increase our technology and control of the world. Fire and air however lose their sense of proportion, desiring that which promises new, bigger, and better. Our fantasies of being a materialistic (earthy) culture are a defense against a true love of the material. As a culture in which fire/air dominate we are idealistic abstractionists, not materialists. We are a consumer society in love with the idea of material. How else can one explain fast food promoted via wonderfully sensuous and gustatory imagery yet leaving much to be desired in the actual eating? How do we account for plastic that has the appearance of real wood, micro polyesters that mimic silk and faux stone masquerading as real rock?

Our spirituality is inflated with hubris, becoming proud of our humility. Our astrology blusters with words of inspiration and claims of knowing what the cosmos wants with promises to share it with our clients. But we ignore the invisibles of repressed and forgotten water and earth at great peril. Inspiration and intellection without grounding in memory is mania, a trajectory toward burnout, a rendezvous with conflagration, a path toward nuclear extinction.

A true materialist loves the material world, and is a disciple of earth and water, cherishing the things of the world, repairing not despairing, recognizing the sacredness of a living cosmos. In this sense then, it seems prudent to affirm a more soulful spirituality, one that walks in the vale, allowing us to see the necessity of tears and sorrow, to embrace the loam of mortality, and to esteem the treasures of darkness. When our spirituality no longer promises paradise but plants us firmly in the present, and our astrology no longer predicts the future but immerses us fully in the moment, then our lives, in tune now with the rhythms of soil and sea, may truly blossom.

18

Letter to a Young Astrologer

"Perhaps the truth depends on a walk around the lake."
                                                    WALLACE STEVENS

Dear friend,

You, who possess youth and vigor, who have yet more road ahead than behind, please allow my words to ring out from an aging wilderness. Let me speak of the crossroads that astrology and astrologers now face.

Quite simply and to the point, astrology's importance to society is dependent upon the values that society upholds as worthy and legitimate. To the extent that astrology can align itself with the particular complex of values that permeates the fabric of American culture will determine what value astrology has to society. And this will be the bane of astrology.

Please bear with me as I step outside the bounds of our still sacred art in order to establish my position. My contention as an American, is that America is a monoculture and I would like to spend some wordy currency gathering purchase for what is meant by this term. My argument will meander around the idea that despite the rise of postmodern thinking the values that American society holds dear can all be located under the rubric of William Blake's metaphor, 'single vision;' that peculiar point of view that accepts one truth only.

Years ago, Rudhyar mentioned that the Sun is also a star in a book of the same name. This can be understood not only as a reminder but as a call beckoning us to a new larger understanding of an astrology that will have a deeper value to society than it presently holds. Rudhyar's phrase implies that the Sun on one hand is the monarch of the solar system, an image that has shaped our cultural imagination and is reflective of a solar civilization (spirit, masculine, patriarchal). The dominance of solar imagery was already widespread in the early 4th century at the beginning of the Christian Roman Empire through the presence of Mithraism (a solar cult). The solar culture we have inherited with its One God and his single begotten Son unconsciously filters our view, coloring even the secular arenas of culture. Languishing in the background, as Rudhyar noted, is the very real recognition of the Sun as one of many member stars in the galactic community of the Milky Way.

The Western emphasis on the rights of the individual generally outweighing the rights of community effortlessly induces us to more easily esteem the Sun in its role as the sole sovereign. Its participation in the galactic body politic too closely mimics the communitarian perspective. And if there is one thing many in the West historically disdain, it's anything that resembles communism (politics), communes (social collectives), and the compassionate notion of commutations (law). These knee-jerk reactions to the Many should be a clue for us about our cultural fear of a polytheistic metaphysic to which we will return later.

If there is a single metaphysical hook upon which [Euro-America] hangs, it is the idea of One, of singleness, of mono. Perhaps the fundamental belief in our culture is the image of the One God. Our culture has been so deeply influenced by monotheism that to suggest more than one deity is heresy even now.

Within the framework of this cultural monotheism, we find a monogenism; the dogma of humanity's descent from a single set of parents; Adam and Eve. Whether this narrative is literally true is beside the point, the power of this myth has infused Western culture. This thinking even permeates the sciences with the universe flaring forth in a singular and one time only event. Additionally, we have the belief that there is a line of common descent for all life from a single-celled creature millions of years ago; evolution's monogenesis. This singleness of vision also reflects the manner in which humans should bond. Monogamy has been established as the preferred mode of long term relating though in these early years of the 21st century, serial monogamy has become increasingly acceptable but never polygamy. These ideas seem so unquestioningly natural and sensible that we rarely look at the underlying fantasy of the One out of which they arise.

In the arena of psychology, consider the normal way that we imagine ourselves, we are monocentric. We conceive of a single self at the center of our being. At the very least, a monarchial ego that tells the body where to go and what to do, lording over it like master to slave. Theologically, we believe a single divine immortal soul in each of us, behind the scenes, incarnating at birth and passing beyond at the time of death. In both narratives, there is a singleness of being. Truth is to be found in the reality of the One, not in the illusion of the Many.

In a different cultural arena, I believe it was Joseph Campbell who noted that one could tell something about what a people believed and valued through their architecture. During the medieval and Renaissance eras the great monolith of a civilization was the cathedral, the tallest and largest lone structure in a town or city aspiring to the heavens. Of course, in the last century there has been the decline of formal religion and the new God sits in the tall towers of the corporation. Skyscrapers, an apt name, occasionally in competition to be the tallest one of many, now monopolize the skyline dwarfing any cathedral. And as sacred testament to this corporate idolatry, to the divinity of the Almighty Dollar, one of the most popular parlor pastimes in the 20th century that now has a global edition, is the game, Monopoly.

In astrology, the Sun has been associated with singleness of purpose. We direct our will toward the pursuit of knowledge seeking a single Truth. Using reasoning and logic as its primary tools, scientific inquiry into the world is oriented around 'either/or' thinking, either this statement is true or it is not. There is a singleness of truth not a multiplicity of truths. The scientific method tends to have this monocular vision which of course limits what it sees and evaluates to those matters to which its method can be appropriately applied. It is through reasoning and logic that areas of knowledge become legitimate and valued by society. To the extent that astrology can shape itself to this cultural paradigm, organize itself around chains of solid reasoning, successfully posit and test astrological hypotheses, find singularities of meaning in its practice and application is the degree to which astrology will have legitimate value to society. Read caution here.

There is a difficulty with this; it leaves us with a single narrative about human experience, a monotonous monologue that drones on and on drowning out the still small voices of that "mobile army of metaphors" that Nietzsche called truth.

A scientific astrology, and by this I mean an astrology that produces results, that has practical application and reliable methods, is an astrology of Virgo. It seeks only to find the best technique to work a chart, the straightest route from chart to person, and the most efficient procedure to analyze and detail the truth, in other words, an astrology that has utilitarian value and provides concrete answers. Americans love this.

This is not the kind of astrology that I find most valuable, however. This is the kind of astrology that can easily play on the fears, uncertainties, and greed of consumers. Of course, this is the kind of astrology that the public will clamor after, the kind that will give them answers and help them avoid troubles. You can make a good living massaging the anxieties of clientele. Give the public what it wants and you'll make a fortune.

My vision is to let astrology move toward greater affiliation with the arts and humanities and less with the sciences. The arts, however, typically have little value to society; witness the reduction in funding that comes with cuts in education. How many art and music courses are required in the schools? The arts seem always the first to go. It is rare that the sciences experience such reductions. There is a notion that for America to remain number One (at least in our own eyes) we must throw our financial weight into educating our children, not to be well rounded citizens, but rather competitors in the field of advancing technologies for global development.

The arts educate us to a world of beauty and present a multitude of approaches to experiencing the world. Please do not underestimate the power and need for beauty in our lives, my young friend. If we had the choice wouldn't almost all live in a beautiful place? In our relationships, wouldn't each of us, given the opportunity to, partner with a person in whom we saw great beauty of some nature? Does not the attractive presentation of food enhance the appreciation of the meal? Are we not more likely to extend care to a beautiful garden than to a littered back lot in urban decay? Beauty is a powerful motivating force and art can be a means for the discovery of it. Art educates the aesthetic sense within us. Art is truly redemptive and redeems truth by prisming it into a multitude of guises. Art splits the One white Light of Being into the Many, it shifts our thinking from a monocentric point of view to a polycentric spectrum of perspectives. For instance, if I seek to have my portrait painted by a surrealist, an impressionist, a pop artist, a caricaturist, and a medievalist, I will get several different images of how I am as a person, each containing an insight that can only be drawn out from that particular expression. Even a photographer, who works with a medium most would say provides the truest representation of its subject, is only able to capture a single facet of my soul and not a larger sense of my being. If I hear a piece of music performed by an orchestra, a rock band, and a solo artist, these present a widely nuanced set of listening experiences that can deepen my appreciation of this particular piece, in other words, I become more conscious of what was only potential.

One image or performance is not truer than another, each is valid and each potentially enriches me. The planets in the chart suggest a community of selves, a polycentrism of being, each planet having its own style of consciousness, its own attitudes, its own feeling state, and behaviors. Sometimes we filter the world through Mars or Jupiter and at other times Venus or Saturn, all have legitimacy and value.

Astrology as art has a different function not a lesser one than a scientific astrology conjoined to the ruling cultural paradigm. With astrology in its role as the redeemer of a polycentric perspective, it is important to support astrological diversity in order to maintain a healthy and beautiful astrological ecosystem. Though I am a therapeutic astrologer with little interest in traditional astrology, prediction, harmonics, fixed stars, past lives, etc., let those whose burning passion is for these aspects of astrology flourish. Our diversity is that which displays the beauty within astrology. What great outpourings of Imagination all these approaches and methods display. Let astrology be a richly effulgent field of Imagination because it is Imagination that gives the world soulfulness; depth, value, relatedness, and meaning.

As astrologers, let us employ more organic and artistic metaphors and less mechanical/technological ones in our use of language. Mechanical metaphors often speak in the language of push/pull, of force and cause and effect. When we use language about planets influencing us or transits affecting us we fracture our intimate connection to the world and estrange ourselves from the cosmos. We also suffer an internal fragmentation when we pit the outer planets of our being against the Sun of our identity as if these distant gods were something other than the deepest dynamics of we who express them. The chart does not cause our being; it reflects our being as a mirror reflects our appearance. We need to contemplate the power of this statement and not just give it lip service. The difficulty with technological metaphors is that they reinforce a cleft way of being. In the West, we have an image of God as a potter in his making of humanity from clay. This God has a Son who is a carpenter, another maker of things. This infuses our own sense of origins as having been made from the outside in and placed in the world much like a model maker inserts a figure into a diorama.

A more Daoist and organic image is one of humanity having been grown as a natural and spontaneous expression of the world from the inside out, an emergent property if you will of the larger environment. If the rhythms and cycles of the natural world so closely resonate with our own, how could our birth be anything but a particular intimate flowering of the world blossoming forth in a perfect moment? Organic metaphors do what astrology does best; provide a framework for imagining a profound intimacy between ourselves and our world. It connects us to the world and discloses that each and every person is a particular kind of outflowing of the near cosmos. We come out of this world, we don't come into it. It is not a mere fancy to say that we are made of starstuff. Each and every atom of our being was forged in the deep furnace within the heart of a star.

These two images, techno and organic, make all the difference in our astrology and in our orientation to the environment; what need do we have to care for the environment if our true home is not this world but an eternal heaven or some other plane of existence? Our relationship to the environment will have all the earmarks of that of a renter to their apartment. And since we tend to culturally mistreat the environment, viewing it as a place of resources and commodities for our collective use, then the apartment is more like low income housing and the beauty of the world disappears into the great maw of consuming indifference.

Our astrology suffers when it becomes a method for slipping through life as easily and trouble free as possible. Your clients will ask great things of you; what shall I do, oh astrologer? Who shall I marry? Will I recover from this illness? Where shall I live? When shall I begin? Please do not disdain their questions my young friend; they reflect a worrisome and anxious attitude. Compassion and understanding are the proper responses and with a gentle nudging toward exploring who is the god behind the mask of these questions. Help your clients to take ownership of their lives even when life appears out of their control. In affirming and owning all our planets, consciousness deepens and soul is made. Let your clients leave the consultation with a renewed hope that their inner pantheon conspires for their benefit, departing not with the answers but with the curiosity and the courage to face the questions life demands of them. Assist your clients to discover the beauty and the harmony (even when it's dissonant) that is their life.

I have a vision of astrology that has the feel of Uranus in Pisces, a vision that keeps astrology wild, somewhat mysterious, and on the borders of respectability. True to its Uranian affiliation, astrology is a "Trickster" discipline. The mythological Trickster is the tension between the innovative and the customary, operating on the outskirts of convention, freeing the goods of heaven for the benefit of humanity. Their true value to society is in their outsider status. Their movement epitomizes the topsy-turvy shaking of the foundations of both culture and client. Tricksters express the prophetic voice in the wilderness calling the people back to a deeper vision of what it means to be human. Tricksters are culture-creators bestowing a boon upon humanity like Prometheus' gift of fire.

Let us not bring too much Saturn into this archaic tradition by over regulating, obsessive professionalizing, conditionally accepting only those who have been officially sanctioned, and organized to such a degree that astrology becomes conventional, rigid, and top heavy, eventually collapsing under the weight of its own self-importance. In wanting to organize, regulate, establish codes and protocols we risk losing the principle of wildness on which, according to Thoreau, depends the preservation of the world. It may be misguided to align astrology too closely to the dominant paradigm (that of scientific inquiry) thereby rupturing the crucial dance of tension between the principles of Saturn and Uranus.

In my view, astrology's value to society is in its capacity to inhabit and remain in the margins of culture, to stand on the outside so as to not lose its multiple perspectives. It is astrology's duty as merry prankster, as court jester, to dance around the throne of the King keeping him from inflation and *hubris*, pointing out his foibles, loosening him with laughter so that he doesn't take himself too seriously. Astrology is an intrusion upon the status quo and not a feature of it, as many astrologers would like. It's a kind of judo, throwing our habitual style of doing things (whether culture or client) off balance so that defenses are momentarily weakened and change can occur. It is to help clients break through to a deeper consciousness that brings them closer to the ground of their being and to provoke in culture, the revelation of its place as an integral organ of the larger planetary environment. What Jungians have said about Trickster can be equally applied to astrology that wherever and "whenever he [Trickster] appears and in spite of his unimpressive exterior, he brings the possibility of transforming the meaningless into the meaningful."

Yes, we will continue to be looked at with suspicion and with some disdain. We will remain the butt of jokes but also, and here's the key, there will be those with the secret hope that maybe astrologers do know something of sacred importance, and they will invite us in.

Therefore my friend, stand upright, speak clearly, walk proudly, head raised, we traffic in the oddest of wisdoms. May our guiding motto be *caveat emptor*! Let us be dangerous agents of change.

Very sincerely, I remain
In the service of dark skies,
Brad Kochunas

Acknowledgments

Every book is a collaboration of many hearts, minds, and hands. I owe Margaret Cahill of The Wessex Astrologer a debt of gratitude for having interest and finding value in my writing. I am also indebted to Kirk Little and Gary Phillipson for bringing Margaret to my attention. Kudos to astrologer Crystal Eves for reading, correcting, and commenting on an early draft of this work. My thinking about astrology has been enriched by astrologers Dane Rudhyar, Greg Bogart, Andrea Conlon, Joe Landwehr, Glenn Perry, Stephen Arroyo, Brian Clark, Clare Martin, Howard Sasportas and Liz Greene.

It's very hard to break open one's cosmic egg to view the many absurdities that keep the dominant cultural paradigm intact and so I am beholden to the Grateful Dead, The Band, Firesign Theatre, Monty Python, Kurt Vonnegut, Alan Watts, D. T. Suzuki, Mircea Eliade, Franz Kafka, Albert Camus, and Salvador Dali for cracking that paradigm and widening the fissure so many years back.

With the help of the work of Patrick Curry, David Abram, Thomas Berry, Vine Deloria, Jr., V. F. Cordova, Robin Wall Kimmerer, Greg Cajete, Freya Mathews, Christian De Quincey, Theodore Roszak, David Fideler, James Hillman, Thomas Moore, Robert Romanyshyn, and Patrick Harpur, with special mention going to Mary Oliver and Nancy Wood, their collective writings have moved me away from the transcendent sky and grounded me in the immanent, present, relational, contextual, interiority of the world. This led to the shaping of my worldview in which astrology fits as an eco-imaginal discipline.

Last, little happens without mentors and friends who support one's efforts; the late Jim Barron, Dave Helm, James Kelly, Booth Hemingway, Terry Wieand, Jerry Miller, and Willis Greiner.

And much gratitude to Connie Jenkins.

About the Author

Brad Kochunas is a retired clinical mental health counselor and therapeutic astrologer. He spent three decades working in prison mental health where he used astrology as an adjunct to the counseling process and taught an astrology class there for 20 years. He developed and coordinated the meditation program for ten years in addition to conducting classes on spirituality and mental health, grief education, and yoga.

His interest in astrology began as an undergrad majoring in comparative religions, his graduate degree in history of religions focused on astrology as a sacred tradition. His post-master's education was in counseling, gestalt training, and the Academy of AstroPsycholgy developed by Glenn Perry, Ph. D.

He has been an adjunct college instructor, staff trainer, lecturer, and award-winning writer. His articles have appeared in *Counseling and Values, The Mountain Astrologer,* the ISAR *International Astrologer,* the NCGR *Geocosmic Journal,* the *Career Astrologer,* and the *Astrological Journal.* He has been a popular speaker at numerous conferences in North America and is the author of *The Astrological Imagination: Where Psyche and Cosmos Meet.*

He welcomes constructive comments and can be reached at kochunas@outlook.com.

www.ingramcontent.com/pod-product-compliance
Lightning Source LLC
Chambersburg PA
CBHW062005220426
43662CB00010B/1237